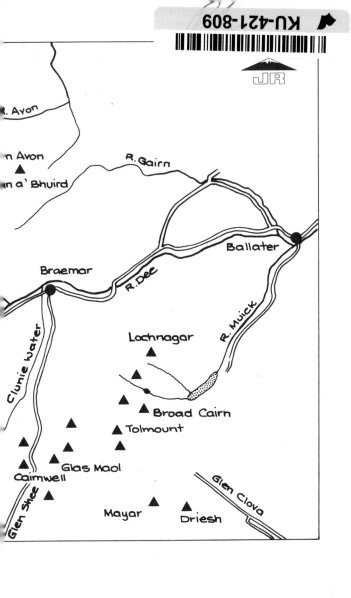

JR

R. Avon

n Avon

n a' Bhuird

R. Gairn

Braemar

Ballater

R. Dee

R. Muick

Clunie Water

Lochnagar

Broad Cairn

Tolmount

Cairnwell

Glas Maol

Glen Shee

Mayar

Driesh

Glen Clova

Rory.

HAPPY BIRTHDAY

This is a subtle hint!!

Frank & Tor.

The Cairngorms

Rock and Ice Climbs

Volume 1

Including
Cairn Gorm, Ben Macdui and Braeriach

Allen Fyffe
Andrew Nisbet

Series Editor: Roger Everett

SCOTTISH MOUNTAINEERING CLUB
CLIMBERS' GUIDE

Published in Great Britain by the Scottish Mountaineering Trust, 1995
Copyright © The Scottish Mountaineering Club

First edition 1961
Second edition 1973
Third edition 1985
Reprinted 1990
Fourth edition 1995

British Library Cataloguing in Publication Data

A catalogue record for this book is available from
the British Library

Maps drawn by Jim Renny
Diagrams drawn by Kev Howett
Production by Scottish Mountaineering Trust (Publications) Ltd
Typeset by Westec, North Connel
Colour Separations by Arneg, Glasgow
Printed by GNP Booth, Clydebank
        and St Edmundsbury Press, Bury St Edmunds
Bound by Hunter and Foulis, Edinburgh

Distributed by Cordee, 3a DeMontfort Street, Leicester, LE1 7HD

Contents

vi

List of Illustrations

List of Diagrams and Maps

The Climber and the Mountain Environment

With increasing numbers of walkers and climbers going to the Scottish hills, it is important that all of us who do so should recognise our responsibilities to the mountain environment in which we find our pleasure and recreation, to our fellow climbers, and to those who live and work on the land.

The Scottish Mountaineering Club and Trust, who jointly produce this and other guidebooks, wish to point out to all who avail themselves of the information in these books that it is in everyone's interest that good relations are maintained between visitors and landowners, particularly when there might be conflicts of interest, for example during the stalking season. The description of a climbing, walking or skiing route in any of these books does not imply that a right of way exists, and it is the responsibility of all climbers to ascertain the position before setting out. In cases of doubt it is best to enquire locally.

During stalking and shooting seasons in particular, much harm can be done in deer forests and on grouse moors by people walking through them. Normally the deer stalking season is from 1st July to 20th October, when stag shooting ends. Hinds may continue to be culled until 15th February. The grouse shooting season is from 12th August until 10th December. These activities are important for the economy of many Highland estates. During these seasons, therefore, consideration should be given to consulting the local landowner, factor or keeper before taking to the hills.

Climbers and hill walkers are recommended to consult the book HEADING FOR THE SCOTTISH HILLS, published by the Scottish Mountaineering Trust on behalf of the Mountaineering Council of Scotland and the Scottish Landowners Federation, which gives the names and addresses of factors and keepers who may be contacted for information regarding access to the hills.

It is important to avoid disturbance to sheep, particularly during the lambing season between March and May. Dogs should not be taken onto the hills at this time, and at all times should be kept under close control.

Always try to follow a path or track through cultivated land and forests, and avoid causing damage to fences, dykes and gates by climbing over them carelessly. Do not leave litter anywhere, but take it down from the hill in your rucksack.

The number of walkers and climbers on the hills is leading to increased, and in some cases very unsightly erosion of footpaths and hillsides. Some of the revenue from the sale of this and other SMC guidebooks is used by the Trust to assist financially the work being carried out to repair and maintain hill paths in Scotland. However, it is important for all of us to recognise our responsibility to minimise the erosive effect of our passage over the hills so that the enjoyment of future climbers shall not be spoiled by landscape damage caused by ourselves.

As a general rule, where a path exists walkers should follow it and even where it is wet and muddy should avoid walking along its edges, the effect of which is to extend erosion sideways. Do not take short-cuts at the corners of zigzag paths. Remember that the worst effects of erosion are likely to be caused during or soon after prolonged wet weather when the ground is soft and waterlogged. A route on stony or rocky hillside is likely to cause less erosion than on a grassy one at such times.

Although the use of bicycles can often be very helpful for reaching remote crags and hills, the erosion damage that can be caused by them when used 'off road' on soft footpaths and open hillsides is such that their use on such terrain must cause concern. It is the editorial policy of the Scottish Mountaineering Club that the use of bicycles in hill country may be recommended on hard tracks such as forest roads or private roads following rights of way, but it is not recommended on footpaths or open hillsides where the environmental damage that they cause may be considerable. Readers are asked to bear these points in mind, particularly in conditions when the ground is wet and soft after rain.

The proliferation of cairns on hills detracts from the feeling of wildness, and may be confusing rather than helpful as regards route-finding. The indiscriminate building of cairns on the hills is therefore to be discouraged.

Climbers are reminded that they should not drive along private estate roads without permission, and when parking their cars should avoid blocking access to private roads and land, and should avoid causing any hazard to other road users.

Finally, the Scottish Mountaineering Club and the Scottish Mountaineering Trust can accept no liability for damage to property nor for personal injury resulting from the use of any route described in their publications.

Acknowledgements

A great many people have contributed to this guidebook over a number of years. First we must thank the authors of previous SMC guides; Mac Smith, Bill March, Dougie Dinwoodie and Greg Strange, whose work provided the backbone for this edition. Thanks also to Donald Bennet and Roger Everett, Publications Manager and Editor of Climbing Guidebooks respectively. Kev Howett produced the outstanding diagrams and Jim Renny the maps.

Many thanks to those who submitted slides for consideration, it is unfortunate that we could only include a small selection of the excellent contributions. A large number of people contributed with suggestions, corrections and information, while others read texts, checked proofs, graded routes and generally provided encouragement, not least by climbing with the authors. Their names are listed alphabetically. We apologise for any inadvertently missed out.

Rab Anderson, Rob Archbold, John Ashbridge, Steve Blagbrough, Jim Blyth, Colin Bruce, Martin Burrows-Smith, Rick Campbell, Andy Cunningham, Brian Davison, Ian Dillon, Sam Dring, Dougie Dinwoodie, Graeme Ettle, Brian Findlay, Chris Forrest, Andrew Fraser, Bruce Goodlad, Donald Green, Jas Hepburn, Alec Keith, Alan Kerr, Doug Lang, Gary Latter, John Lyall, James Maclaurin, Richard Mansfield, Alastair Matthewson, Wilson Moir, Neil Morrison, Kathy Murphy, Grahame Nicoll, Iain Peter, Jonathon Preston, Tom Prentice, George Reid, Niall Ritchie, Ged Reilly, Doug Rennie, Simon Richardson, Alastair Robertson, Alf Robertson, Alastair Ross, Mark Ryle, Malcolm Sclater, Colin Stewart, Peter Stewart, Greg Strange, Walter Taylor, Andy Tibbs, Roger Wild and Blyth Wright.

Introduction

This, the latest of the SMC Rock and Ice guides to the Cairngorms, sees the area divided into northern and southern sections. One volume for the whole region would now be too large. Any division of the Cairngorms is not totally satisfactory as they are best considered as a single climbing area. However, the present arrangement produces two guides which are of manageable size and fairly logical in that most of the area described in this volume is best approached from Strathspey, and most of the area of Volume 2 is reached from Deeside.

This guide now contains all routes, although some may only be noted. Routes which have been climbed in summer and winter are given descriptions for both seasons. Modern summer grades have been used, with individual pitch grades for routes of VS and above if available. Modern winter grades are also given, using the 'dual system' for routes of grade IV and above.

Cairngorm rock is, to quote Mac Smith the writer of the first climbing guide to the area, 'honest granite'. It is generally sound and much of it is of an overlapping slab structure. This often gives superb climbing, particularly in the upper grades, where guile, footwork and friction may be the keys to success. Protection is average overall, certainly not as poor as once was thought, and with a rack of modern gear most of the climbs can be made safe enough. Vegetation, particularly lichen, can be a problem on some of the less popular climbs, but this is not unique to the Cairngorms.

In winter the climbing can be as much on rock and frozen turf as on snow and ice, particularly away from the gullies. Good neve is less common here than in the west as the area receives fewer freeze-thaw cycles. However, this may give more consistent conditions for longer periods. The approaches to the corries range from very short to long and arduous, and fitness, mountaineering ability and experience all play a part in success and safety.

It will be obvious that we have relied on the work of previous guidebook authors such as Bill March, and the information on new routes published annually in the SMC Journal. The foundation, however, remains Mac Smith's two-volume masterpiece of 1961 which turned the Cairngorms into a major climbing ground and established many of its traditions and legends.

Geology

The area covered in this guide and its companion Volume 2 consists of two roughly circular granite masses, that of Lochnagar and Creag an Dubh Loch in the south and the main Cairngorm massif in the north. These large granite plutons were formed about 500 million years ago during the Caledonian orogeny, when they formed the roots of a vast mountain chain. These were, with wind, weather and time, worn down to below sea-level and covered with sediment. About 50 million years ago they rose again to form a great flat plain which was eroded to reveal the old mountain roots which, because of their resistant nature, were left higher than the surrounding area.

The present day appearance of the Cairngorms is one of a high plateau with gently rolling slopes. This shape was produced by a period of tropical and sub-tropical weathering during the Tertiary period. It was then modified by the action of ice during the Quaternary period. These ice sheets and glaciers were selective in their erosion and left us pre-glacial features such as the rounded hills and tors, but also gouged out great troughs such as the Lairig Ghru and Loch Avon, and the many corries that cut into these mountains. It is these features of glacial erosion which provide the climbing in the Cairngorms.

The rock itself is a remarkably homogenous granite, although that in the Lochnagar region differs somewhat from that in the central Cairngorm area. It is generally fairly coarse-grained and pinkish in colour when freshly exposed, but it weathers to grey. The three joint systems are regular and approximately at right angles to each other. Because of the uniform nature of the rock there has been little to encourage preferential weathering, giving many cliffs their massive appearance. The majority of gullies are the lines of small vertical faults or crush lines, and many of them are of poor and shattered rock. Typical of Cairngorm granite is its 'woolsack' appearance, due to its vertical joints and sheeting, a type of joint which roughly parallels the surface and becomes thicker with depth, probably due to pressure release as the deeply buried rock was revealed by erosion. These rounded blocks are seen in many cliffs but are most notable in No.4 Buttress of Coire an Lochain.

The rock may also be cut by pegmatite or aplite veins. The former consist of large crystals and the latter are veins of fine grained rock. Several routes use these veins, which sometimes weather to give a ladder of tiny square holds. Occasionally, cavities in these veins contain crystals of quartz, which may be tinted to give it a smoky yellow to dark brown colour, the semi-precious Cairngorm stones that lured the first explorers onto these cliffs. Gas pockets or druses, which may contain crystals, can also be found in places.

History

NORTHERN CAIRNGORMS

The first climbing ground to be opened up in the Cairngorms was Gleann Einich, being accessible from the railway line. After an ascent of Pinnacle Ridge by Harold Raeburn in March 1902, the SMC held an Easter meet here and climbed several routes. Although of poor quality, they remained popular until the early fifties. The only good rock in the jungle of vegetation was provided by Roberts' Ridge, climbed in 1938 by J.H.B.Bell and party, including E.E.Roberts on his 64th birthday.

Apart from early exploration by Raeburn, including Pygmy Ridge (1904) and Raeburn's Buttress (1907), Coire an t-Sneachda and Coire an Lochain remained virtually untouched until the thirties, and the Loch Avon basin until the fifties. The exception was Clach Dhian Chimney, which repulsed at least three attempts, one involving a fatality, until its ascent by W.S.Thomson in 1947.

The two northern corries are best known in winter, and the early exploration took place in winter as well as summer. E.M.Davidson and A.Henderson were the most active, with winter ascents of Aladdin's Couloir and The Vent, and a descent of The Couloir (1935). Development was slow in the forties (Savage Slit in 1945) and early fifties (Left Branch of Y Gully, 1952) until Tom Patey climbed many of today's best known winter routes in 1958 and 1959, including his route on Aladdin's Buttress, Fiacaill Couloir, Central Crack Route and Western Route, all solo.

Exploration of the Loch Avon basin by the Aberdeen group, usually approaching from Braemar, began slowly in the early fifties with I.M.Brooker's ascent of Deep Cut Chimney (1952) and Hell's Lum (1952) and Ken Grassick and H.Bates' ascent of the loose main face of Carn Etchachan in 1952-53. The first winter route, Scorpion (1952), with its now notorious 'sting in the tail', was climbed in epic style by the powerful team of Ken Grassick, Graeme Nicol, Tom Patey and Mike Taylor, and was one of the earliest Grade V routes. In the mid fifties, Tom Patey climbed six routes on the Upper Tier of Carn Etchachan and several more routes appeared on Stag Rocks, Mac Smith being the most active.

In 1957 and 1958, Ronnie Sellars and G.Annand visited Hell's Lum Crag (Brimstone Grooves, Hellfire Corner and Devil's Delight) as well as climbing The Citadel, the first route on the main bastion of Shelter Stone Crag and a major breakthrough. Big routes were done in the winter too, with Route Major and Sticil Face in 1957. The Coire Cas ski road was opened in July 1960. Now that the easiest approach had switched to Aviemore, the area became popular with visitors from all parts of Scotland. Summer activity continued steadily into the sixties; two of the plums, The Clean Sweep (1961) and The Needle (1962) were picked up by Robin Smith. The Needle was the first Extreme in the Cairngorms and set a standard which could not be matched by the Aberdonians, whose greatest feats were always in winter (Sticil Face being no less an achievement). These incursions by Edinburgh climbers set up Loch Avon as a more cosmopolitan climbing area, but the Aberdonians continued to dominate elsewhere. Shelter Stone Crag remained at the forefront of rock climbing difficulty in the late sixties, surpassing even Creag an Dubh-loch which was also under intense development. Rab Carrington's The Pin and Ken Spence's Steeple (both 1968) were followed up by Haystack (Carrington and Ian Nicolson, 1971), the hardest route in the Cairngorms for a considerable time. Also at this time, during preparation of a new guide to the area by Bill March, locally-based climbers were very active. Glenmore Lodge instructors such as Bill March and John Cunningham, and Aviemore cobbler George Shields, led this group and between 1968 and 1971 they climbed over 30 new routes in the area and established Stac an Fharaidh as a fine slab climbing cliff.

In winter, the Northern Corries were by now fairly well developed, but the Loch Avon basin was comparatively neglected. Activity resumed in the late sixties, with March particularly busy, picking off some of the more obvious lines such as Raeburn's Buttress. At this time, John Cunningham was developing his front-pointing technique using ice daggers on steeper ice. This culminated in The Chancer, a fine icicle climb on Hell's Lum Crag. Later that winter, Chouinard visited the area and introduced his curved picks. Cunningham and March immediately took these up and went on to produce some fine routes such as Salamander and Devil's Delight.

On the rock climbing front, rising standards during the seventies saw a movement away from the obvious faults onto the intervening faces. Fyffe and partners climbed many HVS routes on Stag Rocks and Cairn Etchachan, and increasing attention was paid to Hell's Lum where Fyffe with Bob Barton climbed several slightly harder routes into the early 1980s. By now, Edinburgh climbers, particularly Hamilton and Cuthbertson, along with Pete Whillance, who were pushing up standards around Scotland, moved onto the big faces of Creag an Dubh-loch and the Shelter Stone Crag. Dinwoodie's ascent of Cupid's Bow in 1978, on sight without chalk but using a little aid, had shown the limit of traditional techniques and this was proven by two epic failures on what became Run of the Arrow. There was much heart-searching over ethics. Whillance's ascent of this route in 1982 took pride of place, but other fine hard lines such as The Harp were also climbed. Repeats of these modern hard routes were rare at first, with 'the big three' on the Main Bastion drawing the crowds, but now they see regular ascents. However, Run of the Arrow, which has recently lost Dinwoodie's hammered retreat nuts, part of the protection and an island of comparative safety in a sea of slabs, has become somewhat less appealing. However, Hell's Lum, although slow to dry in places, has seen many repeats of the recent routes with generally favourable comments. Other small crags have frequent ascents of a limited number of classic routes, Magic Crack in Coire an t-Sneachda being an obvious example.

The blank sections of Shelter Stone's Central Slabs have remained the obvious challenge, ignored by most as too serious. However, Rick Campbell has not been discouraged and in 1989 he freed Thor. Next on his list was Aphrodite, the Cairngorm's first and probably hardest E7. Climbed on sight, Campbell ran out of rope above the hardest climbing, and with no belay had to improvise and finish off the climb the next day. He then went on to add Realm of the Senses and L'Elisir d'Amore, both involving desperate and serious slab climbing to complete his trilogy of E7 routes. Climbing these last two routes in one push all the way up the Central Slabs is surely a challenge for the slab climbers of the next generation!

Winter climbing in the 1980s and 1990s has belatedly followed the rock climbing pattern. Increasing standards and new techniques such as torquing, followed by their application to the harder natural lines (usually snowed-up rock climbs such as Fallout Corner) was initially met with reluctance but has now gained general acceptance. New climbs have often become shorter and the quality of the climbing has become as important as continuity of line. As a result, a huge number of winter routes of increasing technical difficulty have appeared, many in the very accessible Northern Corries; 'mixed climbing', often an option when ice conditions are poor, has grown enormously in popularity in the 1990s. Coire an Lochain in particular has developed a concentration of routes of the highest technical standard (8), partly because the blocky nature of the rock here encourages very hard yet well protected climbing. It is likely that the new two-tier and open-ended grading system will encourage more to progress to the harder routes, very few of which have been repeated.

Most notable in the mid 1980s was MacLean and Nisbet's ascent of their Needle Winter Variations, at that time a last great problem. This required two weeks of effort before the two-day ascent. A repeat is perhaps not too far off as the technical grade of 8 is climbed by several these days; only the commitment of applying the technical difficulty to longer routes and finding the right conditions is required.

At the end of 1985, Andy Cunningham and Nisbet climbed Fallout Corner, setting the pattern of winter ascents of VS to E1 summer routes. This has continued until the present day, with a large number of new lines occupying a group of aficionados of this style of climbing. Rab Anderson meticulously worked his way through the gaps to find a number of new lines, as did Graeme Ettle, John Lyall and Jonathan Preston. In 1986, Cunningham opened development of The Mess of Pottage in Coire an t-Sneachda, an unaccountably neglected buttress and most of the local activists had a piece the action here. Fyffe, usually with Cunningham, adopted the Fiacaill Buttress and produced several hard though devious climbs, but Coire an Lochain remained the favoured crag as it suited this style of climbing. Ettle, Nisbet, Brian Davison and Preston produced the hardest routes, usually involving several earlier failures.

Most icefalls in the area have been climbed, but they remain popular when in condition, Hell's Lum being the best. Carn Etchachan's mixed routes, although very fine, have been slow to gain popularity, probably due to the length of the approach. The more dramatic Shelter Stone Crag has seen an increase in the number of ascents of some of the harder routes, such as Postern and Citadel, the latter providing a much tougher proposition. Sticil Face remains the winter classic in the Loch Avon basin.

One trend seen in this area, but particularly in the Northern Corries, is the marginal conditions in which climbing is taking place. Whether some routes were done in any type of winter conditions is debatable and the ascents of turfy routes when thawing is leading to the destruction of the vegetation. Routes like Belhaven and Invernookie are two of the climbs whose difficulty is increasing as the turf disappears.

CREAGAN A' CHOIRE ETCHACHAN,
COIRE SPUTAN DEARG AND BEINN A' BHUIRD

Summer

These cliffs are in the remote plateau most accessible from Braemar, and although the latter is described in Volume 2 of this guidebook, their histories are closely intertwined. They have never achieved the popularity of the big cliffs of Shelter Stone, Lochnagar or Creag an Dubh-loch, nor do they have the accessibility of the Northern Corries or Loch Avon. Consequently development has been fairly recent and almost exclusively by Aberdonians.

Before 1948, activity was confined to easy snow climbs on Beinn a' Bhuird and to Mitre Ridge, the focus of pre-war attention and at 200m high, the only feature to rival the bigger cliffs. Determined efforts resulted in ascents of the ridge and Cumming-Crofton Route on the same day in July 1933. Only Eagle Ridge could rival these for difficulty in the pre-war period. Two further routes on Mitre Ridge were climbed by the Armed Forces during the War.

Early guides had described the rock of Creagan a' Choire Etchachan as "rather fragmentary" and Sputan "not suited for climbing, the rocks being rounded and devoid of holds". Once the post-war move was made out from the gullies onto the buttresses, these descriptions were quickly proved wrong. Sputan Dearg, with its clean juggy rock and fine, low grade buttresses, was the first to attract attention. After Pinnacle Buttress and the excellent Crystal Ridge were climbed in the summer of 1948, a further eight routes, including most of the main buttresses, followed in 1949. The main activists were Bill Brooker, J. Tewnion and Mac Smith. In the fifties, Brooker, Smith, Tom Patey and others, including the 'Kincorth Club' (Freddy Malcolm, Alec Thom, and Dick Barclay) moved away from Sputan Dearg and began to develop Creagan a' Choire Etchachan and the Beinn a' Bhuird corries. Standards were rising and by 1956 most of the obvious lines up to Mild VS had been climbed. Important climbs were Hourglass Buttress (1953), Squareface (1953) and The Carpet (1955). In September 1955, Patey and John Hay made a move on to the Crimson Slabs, the first attempt on one of the smooth Cairngorm faces. The result was The Dagger, the hardest route in the Cairngorms at that time. Hay returned to the slabs the following year to put up the companion route, Djibangi. These routes opened up great possibilities and became the major test pieces in the area for almost a decade. Also from 1956 were Talisman and another test piece, Amethyst Wall. A temporary lull fell over this area and in 1961 Mac Smith's climbers' guide to the Cairngorms was published.

Such had been the level of activity in the early fifties that further development required a rise in standards. This was to come in the mid-sixties, with the arrival of a new generation. They called themselves 'The Spiders' and included John Bower, Mike Forbes, Brian Lawrie and Mike Rennie. VS routes became commonplace and PAs replaced boots, although Ronnie Kerr's very early first ascent of The Sheath (1961), perhaps the earliest HVS in the Cairngorms, was achieved in boots. Although Beinn a' Bhuird was largely neglected, several fine routes were established on Sputan Dearg, such as Grey Slab and Terminal Wall (1963) and Jim McArney's free finish to Amethyst Wall (1964). Meanwhile, at Creagan a' Choire Etchachan in 1966, Mike Forbes and Mike Rennie made an impressive ascent of the oft-tried Stiletto, the fore-runner of a new rise in technical standards. A few months later they climbed the popular Scabbard.

In the period from 1970 to 1972 there was a new burst of activity before the publication of Greg Strange's guide to the area in 1973. Strange, along with Dougie Dinwoodie, Brian Lawrie and others of the Etchachan Club, tidied up many of the good VS lines. Since 1973, the rock climbing standard has risen relentlessly and the attention of those leading HVS and above, an increasing number, has switched to the bigger, steeper cliffs such as Creag an Dubh Loch or the Shelter Stone Crag. The competitiveness of modern rock climbing has caused accessibility of rock to often overshadow the traditional mountain day. Even so, the classic routes of VS and below have remained popular, while exploration has been sporadic, at least partly because these remote cliffs have limited steep or smooth rock for E-grade routes. Some recent finds of smaller and more obscure buttresses, such as Black Crag, have yielded routes in the modern idiom to those who are prepared to make the effort.

Although it remains a rock climbing backwater, Beinn a' Bhuird saw a burst of activity when the HVS grade was explored in the late 1970s by members of the Etchachan Club (including Greg Strange, Rob Archbold, Norman Keir, Gordon Stephen and Andy Nisbet). The west face of Mitre Ridge became established as a fine modern face with several routes, including Slochd Wall (free, 1979) and The Empty Quarter (1983). Since then, remoteness and limited high quality rock has caused it to revert to a quiet venue. In a similar way, Sputan Dearg has restricted modern style rock and although the middle grade routes are of high quality, they are short and have received little encouraging publicity. Aberdeen-based climbers, particularly Simon Richardson and Greg Strange, have recently climbed a number of new routes.

Creagan a' Choire Etchachan is now by far the most popular of the three, both for classic and new routes (although not since 1986), but it is limited somewhat by the stubborn seeps typical of south-facing Cairngorm slabs. Scalpel (Dinwoodie and Strange, 1977) and Sgian Dubh (Nisbet and Mary Bridges, 1978) were two obvious HVS lines but a number of harder routes were established in the mid 1980s. Henchman (Hamilton and Anderson, 1983) and Talking Drums (MacLean and Nisbet, 1986) are two fine routes on the wall right of the classic Talisman, but most of the activity was concentrated on the Crimson Slabs by the granite slab-loving Aberdeen climbers who squeezed nine more routes. Although *'Classic Rock'* has condemned Talisman to permanent popularity, the fine VS routes of Dagger, Djibangi and Scabbard continue to see many ascents.

Winter

In the fifties, the standards of winter climbing were advancing rapidly, as well as the growing attitude that all rock climbs were potentially winter routes. Many of the buttresses as well as the gully climbs received ascents by the Aberdeen climbers, although the remoteness kept progress at a lower pace than summer. The south-facing Sputan Dearg was rarely visited and many of the best routes on the icy Creagan a' Choire Etchachan were left for the crampon-shod later generations, apart from The Corridor (Freddy Malcolm and Alec Thom, 1954). Garbh Choire of Beinn a' Bhuird gave the best routes such as Mitre Ridge, by Brooker and Patey in 1953 and South-East Gully, by Ronnie Sellars and George Annand in 1959.

Development was slow for a period, but it was revived in the late sixties by the Spiders, now in crampons but still step-cutting. John Bower and Jim McArtney were particularly to the fore, with McArtney on ice (Djibangi, 1965) and Bower on technical winter rock, The Carpet and Hourglass Buttress (1970) were several years ahead of their time. With the advent of front-pointing, ice-climbing was suddenly in vogue and the icy Creagan a' Choire Etchachan became popular. New ice routes included Carmine Groove (1974) and The Dagger (1977). Equally popular was the remote and serious Garbh Choire, with Flume Direct (1974), East Wall Direct (1974) and Crucible Route (1978). Only in the late seventies did technical winter rock re-emerge, one of the first and hardest being Cumming-Crofton Route by Dick Renshaw and

Greg Strange in 1977. This was the year when powder lay deep and unchanged for 3 months and their round trip to the Mitre Ridge and back took over 24 hours. Mitre Ridge itself was repeated in 1974, and twice more in 1977, to become established as a classic winter route.

Winter development of these cliffs has been steady but slow throughout the 1980s into the 1990s. Many of the existing routes up to grade V, and some of the new ones, have been repeated occasionally, with Sputan Dearg the neglected exception. During the poor winters of the early 1980s, the snowy rock theme continued with the development of Grey Man's Crag at Sputan Dearg and the east face of Mitre Ridge. These routes, often accomplished by Nisbet and partners, did not gain universal approval as valid winter climbs, although they were quite snowy by present standards.

Creagan a' Choire Etchachan saw repeats of many of the harder ice routes, although Avalanche Gully and the free ascent of the icicle of Square Cut Gully both waited until 1985. Mixed climbing must always be an option here, as the crag is susceptible to morning sun, and recent routes, many by Richardson and partners in early season, have not usually been icy. However, Andy and Gill Nisbet took advantage of exceptional conditions in December 1992 to climb three icy routes. This icy climbing and the proximity of the Hutchison Hut has maintained the popularity of Creagan a' Choire Etchachan, with Djibangi, once thought rarely in condition, seeing many ascents and the more reliable Red Chimney as a common option.

The CAIRN TOUL and BRAERIACH MASSIF

The Cairn Toul-Braeriach amphitheatre is the most remote of all the great Cairngorm climbing areas. Not only has its development been the slowest but an air of mystery has always been encouraged by its devotees. Strangely enough the first recorded scramble in the Cairngorms was the tracing of the source of the River Dee to the plateau above Garbh Choire Dhaidh in 1810. At the turn of the century, A.W.Russell made several visits to Coire Bhrochain, climbing West Gully (summer) in 1898 and East Gully (winter) in 1901. Until the Second World War, visits were almost always confined to Coire Bhrochain, and ascents were made of Black Pinnacle (1911) and Braeriach Pinnacle (1931). The only significant venture away from Coire Bhrochain was A.H.Hendry's ascent of The Chokestone Gully in 1937, also the first winter route of any difficulty on Braeriach.

There was sudden activity from 1940 to 1942, with the start of exploration of Garbh Choire Mor by the Tewnions and further routes in Coire Bhrochain by W.T.Hendry and others, as well as the first route in Garbh Choire Dhaidh. Activity ceased again until the great age of Cairngorm exploration in the fifties, but here it was less pronounced than in the more accessible areas. Garbh Choire Mor was opened up with four of the main buttresses, including Sphinx Ridge, climbed by Mac Smith and Kenny Winram in 1950 to 1953. The two following years saw the first three routes on the main slabs of Garbh Choire Dhaidh, including The Great Rift. By 1955, most of the obvious lines had been climbed, except for a few steeper buttresses, and with little scope for modern face routes, summer exploration slowed and has never been more than sporadic since. The year 1955, however, saw the start of more regular winter climbing on Braeriach, but ascents were still occasional and confined to the more accessible Coire Bhrochain until 1964.

The winter potential was still enormous and the building of the Garbh Choire bothy in 1967 by the Aberdeen University Lairig Club eased the access problem and helped to soften the hostile reputation. Leading activist Jerry Light battled with giant cornices and put up a series of fine winter routes, including The Great Rift (1965) with Nicol, and Phoenix Gully (1967). A series of April visits by Raymond Simpson, Greg Strange and others established this as the best time to reduce cornice problems and they climbed many of the best remaining lines including the hard Bugaboo Rib (1970). Since the early 1970s, summer climbing visits have become very rare and development has reverted to the sporadic, mainly in winter, but the large volumes of snow here survives most thaws and this has led to some very fine ice climbs. Those on thicker ice in the drainage lines include Vulcan (1975), White Nile (1977), The Culvert (1981) and Ebony Chimney (1982). New route seekers were then forced onto the harder buttresses, usually involving limited turf on thinly iced slabs, with pride of place going to the trio in Garbh Choire Mor; Tower of Babel (1988), Phoenix Edge (1991) and Hot Lips (1993). Most of the obvious lines have now been climbed and the future is hard to predict. One clue is the increased popularity of ski and climb day trips, usually from Glen Feshie. Another is that the most popular route of all is the easier Angel's Ridge. But the chance of seeing another climbing party in the area remains as small as ever.

Notes on the Use of the Guide

Classification of Routes

Summer

For summer rock climbs the following grades have been used: Easy, Moderate, Difficult, Very Difficult, Severe, Hard Severe, Very Severe (VS), Hard Very Severe (HVS), Extremely Severe. The Extremely Severe grade has been subdivided into E1, E2, E3, E4, E5, E6 and E7 in keeping with the rest of Britain.

Technical grades are given for routes of VS and above where known. Much effort has been made to elicit information from active climbers about routes, some of which will have all the relevant pitches graded while others will have only the crux pitch so described. The normal range for technical grades expected on routes of the given overall grade are as follows; VS - 4b, 4c, 5a; HVS - 4c, 5a, 5b; E1 - 5a, 5b, 5c; E2 - 5b, 5c, 6a; E3 - 5c, 6a; E4 - 5c, 6a, 6b; E5 - 6a, 6b. Routes with technical grade at the lower end of the range will be sustained or poorly protected, while those with grades at the upper end of the expected range will most likely have a shorter and generally well protected crux.

Although the British system is thought to be second to none by those familiar with it, it is known to confuse visitors from abroad. For their benefit, it can be assumed that 5a, 5b, 5c and 6a correspond to the American grades of 5.9, 5.10a/b, 5.10c/d and 5.11a/b respectively. Eurocraggers should note that there is little or no fixed protection on these routes and if they are used to cruising bolted French 6c, they may suffer some distress while attempting the corresponding 6a pitches here, with their sometimes spaced and fiddly protection. Grading information is in some cases scanty or even lacking, particularly in some of the older or more obscure routes; climbers should therefore be even more circumspect in their approach to such routes. Further information about any routes is always welcome.

Winter

Winter climbs have been graded using the two-tier system in which the Roman numeral indicates the overall difficulty of the climb and the accompanying Arabic numeral represents the technical difficulty of the hardest sections of climbing. This is built on the old Grades of I to V, which was previously used, but it is only for climbs of Grade IV and above (occasionally grade III) that the two-tier system has been applied. Both parts of the grading system are open-ended.

Grade I - Uncomplicated, average-angled snow climbs normally having no pitches. They may, however, have cornice difficulties or dangerous run-outs.

Grade II - Gullies which contain either individual or minor pitches, or high-angled snow with difficult cornice exits. The easiest buttresses under winter conditions.

Grade III - Gullies which contain ice in quantity. There will normally be at least one substantial pitch and possibly several lesser ones. Sustained buttress climbs, but only technical in short sections.

Grade IV - Steeper and more technical with vertical sections found on ice climbs. Buttress routes will require a good repertoire of techniques.

Grade V - Climbs which are difficult, sustained and serious. If on ice, long sustained ice pitches are to be expected; buttress routes will require a degree of rock climbing ability and the use of axe torquing and hooking and similar winter techniques.

Grade VI - Thin and tenuous ice routes or those with long vertical sections. Buttress routes will include all that has gone before but more of it.

Grade VII - Usually rock routes which are very sustained or technically extreme. Also sustained routes on thin or vertical ice.

Grade VIII - The very hardest buttress routes.

The technical grades which are shown by the Arabic numbers, are based on the technical difficulty of classic winter routes of Grade III, IV and V. This is used as a basis for assessing the technical difficulty of the route, while the Roman numeral gives an indication of the overall seriousness of the climb, in a very similar way to which the E grades and the numerical grades are used in summer. In this way a V,4 is normally a serious ice route, V,5 would be a classic ice route with adequate protection, V,6 would be a classic buttress route and V,7 would indicate a technically difficult but well protected buttress route. Each route is of the same overall difficulty (V) but with differing degrees of seriousness and technical difficulty.

Equipment and Style

It is assumed that a good range of modern nuts and camming devices will be carried for the harder climbs, both in summer and winter. The summer climbs described in this guide are graded assuming the presence and stability of any of the *in situ* pegs that are mentioned. If pegs are essential on new routes, it is hoped that they will be kept to a minimum and left in place; please keep to the Scottish tradition of bold climbs with leader-placed protection. Please make every attempt to find a safe alternative to pegs before resorting to them. Unfortunately pegs are still necessary on some winter routes to make them acceptably safe. This tends to be more often the case on the harder gully climbs than on the better rock of the buttress routes.

Many of the hardest rock climbs that are described in this book will have been cleaned or otherwise inspected prior to the first ascent, but most routes of E2 and many of E3 were climbed on-sight. Although every attempt is made to grade them for an on-sight lead, this should be borne in mind. Many of the difficult winter routes were also initially climbed with prior knowledge; sometimes unintentionally gained by a summer ascent of the route, some through previous failure and sometimes by deliberate inspection prior to a winter ascent. Again, every attempt has been made to grade for an on-sight ascent.

Left and Right

The terms left and right refer to a climber facing the direction being described, i.e. facing the cliff for route descriptions, facing downhill in descent.

Pitch Lengths

Pitch lengths are in metres, rounded to the nearest 5m. The lengths are usually estimates, rather than measurements. 45m ropes are sufficiently long for the Cairngorms, although 50m is popular, especially for the harder winter climbs. Where lengths greater than 50m are given this does not indicate moving together, merely belay where required or desired.

Recommended Routes

No list of recommended routes has been given, instead a star grading system for quality has been used. Stars have been given as a selection guide for occasional visitors and consequently have been allocated somewhat sparingly and spread throughout the grades, although vegetation and poor rock limits the number of stars below VS. Many of the routes without stars are still very good. Higher grade routes tend to be more sustained and on better rock, but somewhat higher standards have therefore been applied. Grade VII and VIII winter routes have not been starred unless they have had sufficient repeat ascents, but most aspirants are unlikely to be influenced by a starring system. Equally, starred routes on different cliffs may vary slightly according to the quality of the cliff, but it is necessary to apply stars as a route selection aid. Winter stars are a problem because quality will vary with conditions, so stars, like the grade, are applied for average conditions which may not exist at the time. Stars have been reduced for rarely-formed ice routes, but one should never be committed to any particular route before inspecting conditions anyway.

*** An outstanding route of the highest quality, combining superb climbing with line, character, situation and other features which make a route great. Could compare with any route in the country.

** As above, but lacking one of the features while having similar quality of climbing.

* Good climbing, but the route may lack line, situation or balance.

First Ascensionists

The year of the first ascent is given in the text. The full date and first ascensionists are listed cliff by cliff in chronological order at the back of the guide. The original aid is also listed, usually with the first free ascent. Details of variations are given under the parent route. Whether the route was ascended in summer or winter conditions is indicated by an S or W at the left end of each line. Winter ascents are listed separately from their corresponding summer route, with different forks of gullies also listed separately. Aid eliminations in winter are noted when known, although these were rarely recorded before the 1970s.

Litter and Vandalism

Litter is a continuing problem at popular camping sites and bothies, despite a slow improvement in recent years. All litter, including spare and unwanted food, should be taken out of the mountains. The justifications for leaving food that is bio-degradable is spurious in these areas, as the breakdown of material in such a cold environment takes years. Likewise, leaving food for birds and animals is misguided as this only attracts scavengers into the area where they prey on the residents. Birds such as the ptarmigan have their eggs taken while hoodie crows become increasingly obvious. If you take it in, take it out again; this includes finger tape and chalk wrappers, litter that climbers cannot blame anyone else for. Another problem is rings of stones used round tents; if you must use them, return the boulders where they came from. In the end, justified complaints by landowners can lead to access problems. Please co-operate by not leaving any traces behind you.

Mountain Rescue

In case of an accident requiring rescue or medical attention, telephone 999 (police). This will usually mean a return to habitation, with the exceptions of the public telephones at Derry Lodge (Map Ref 041 934), the Coire Cas car park (Map Ref 991 059) and at Spittal of Glen Muick (Map Ref 308 850). Give concise information about the location and injuries of the victim and any assistance available at the accident site. Try to leave someone with the casualty. In a party of two with no one nearby, there will be a difficult decision to make. If you decide to go for help, make the casualty warm and comfortable and leave them in a sheltered, well marked place. However, it is often better to stay with the victim.

There is a first-aid box in the corrie of Lochnagar at the usual gearing-up point (Map Ref 251 857) on a small flattening about midway between the Loch and the right side of Central Buttress (cairn). Its contents vary, but there is often a casualty bag and avalanche probes.

Avalanches

Every year avalanches occur in the Cairngorms, sometimes with tragic results. Climbers venturing onto the hills in winter should aquaint themselves with the principles of snow structure and avalanche prediction. There are a number of suitable books on the subject. A knowledge of what to do if involved in an avalanche, either as a victim or an observer, may help to save lives. A knowledge of first aid and artificial resuscitation is an obvious necessity.

Avalanches most often occur following heavy snow fall or during periods of strong thawing conditions, when slopes between 22 and 60 degrees are suspect, with the main danger area being between 30 and 45 degrees. Any danger will last longer in colder conditions when the snow pack takes longer to stabilise. The main danger in the Cairngorms is windslab avalanche, which occurs when snow is re-deposited by the wind. This snow bonds poorly with underlying layers and in these conditions lee slopes are the main danger areas, but pockets of windslab can be found in any sheltered location. Knowledge of the preceding weather, especially wind direction, is of great importance in predicting which slopes and climbs are avalanche prone and this must always be borne in mind.

Climbers and walkers, however, should be able to make their own predictions by studying the pattern of snow deposition from the past and present weather conditions. Being able to dig a snow pit, study the snow profile and assess the relative strengths of the various snow layers and draw sensible conclusions from a profile is an important skill for those venturing on the hills in winter. The sheer test and the Rutchblock test can be very useful tools in assessing avalanche risk, although their application requires some knowledge and experience. A simple indication of severe avalanche risk is when the snow splits easily into slabs with defined boundaries when walked on; these small slabs indicate that much bigger ones may be waiting to peel off. Along with the means to make a realistic risk assessment it is also necessary to understand the principles of movement in avalanche terrain to minimise any risk.

If avalanched, try either to jump free or anchor yourself for as long are possible. If swept down, protect your access to oxygen by 'swimming' to stay on the surface, by keeping your mouth closed and by preserving an air space in front of your face if buried. Wet snow avalanches harden rapidly on settling, so try and break free if possible at this point. If trapped, try to stay calm to reduce oxygen demand.

If a witness to an avalanche, it is VITAL to start a search immediately, given that it is safe to do so. Victims will often be alive at first but their chances lessen quickly if buried. Unless severely injured, some 80% may live if found immediately but this drops rapidly to about 30% after 1 hour and 10% after 3 hours. Mark the burial site if known, the site when last seen and the position of anything else found and search until help arrives. Again, a working knowledge of first aid may save a life, as many victims may have stopped breathing. Remember that IMMEDIATE SEARCHING CAN SAVE LIFES.

Whilst the ability to make your own assessment of risk is vital to anyone venturing into this area, avalanche predictions produced by the Scottish Avalanche Information Service are readily available during the winter. These can be found at police stations, sports shops, tourist information centres and many hotels throughout the area. There is also a display board at the head of Coire Cas car park. This information is also available on local radio and in the local and national press and from the Police SAIS Avalanche Information Service on 01463 713191. For the computer literate to get a report on e-mail, simply mail — avalanches@dcs.gla.ac.uk.

On World Wide Web, access the information by typing in URL. The URL for the avalanche service is http://www.dcs.gla.ac.uk/other/avalanche/

Maps and other sources of information

The maps recommended for use are the following Ordnance Survey 1:50,000 maps. Sheets 35 (Kingussie), 36 (Grantown and Cairngorm) and 43 (Braemar). The 1:25,000 Outdoor Leisure Map entitled the *High Tops of the Cairngorms* is also suitable for the northern section of this guide. The map references of the larger crags and corries in this guide indicate the approximate centre of these features.

The meaning and pronunciation of local place names can be found in *Scottish Hill and Mountain Names* by Peter Drummond, published by the SMT (1991). Much useful information about the hills and the area as a whole can be found in the SMC District Guide *The Cairngorms* by Adam Watson and published by the SMT (1992).

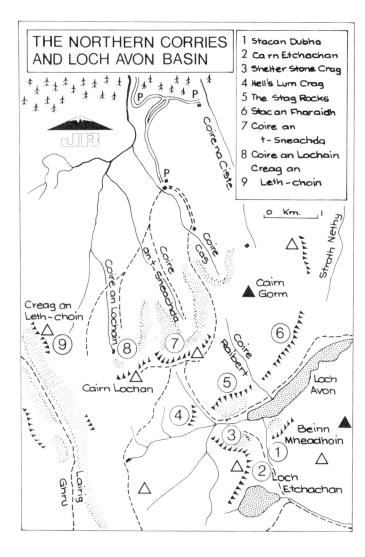

The Northern Corries of Cairn Gorm

The ease of access to the slopes of Cairn Gorm (1245m, Map Ref 006 040), which is provided by the skiing facilities, makes these corries one of the most popular climbing areas in Scotland, especially in winter.

Accommodation

The most convenient centre for accommodation in this area is Aviemore, which is on the main railway and just off the A9 road between Perth and Inverness. Public transport to Aviemore, both by bus and train, is regular and convenient. From the village, further bus services run up to the Coire Cas carpark, which is the most convenient point of access for the Northern Corries. This bus service is more frequent in winter than in summer.

Aviemore and the neighbouring towns and villages in Strathspey provide a wide range of accommodation from hotels and chalets to caravans and hostels. Last minute bookings may be difficult at the height of the tourist and skiing seasons. There are youth hostels at Aviemore and at Loch Morlich, 9km from Aviemore on the road to Cairn Gorm. Camping is not permitted in the Rothiemurchus or Glenmore forests, but there is an official camp site at Loch Morlich.

COIRE AN T-SNEACHDA

(Map Ref 994 033)

Coire an t-Sneachda is the central of the three north-facing corries of Cairn Gorm. It is separated from Coire Cas, the main ski area, by the Fiacaill a' Choire Chais and from Coire an Lochain on its west by the Fiacaill Coire an t-Sneachda (unnamed on the 1:50,000 map). The latter is a hump-backed ridge which steepens after a shallow col to form a narrow rocky ridge leading to the plateau near Cairn Lochan, the westerly top of Cairn Gorm. This can give a pleasant scramble and is usually known as the Fiacaill Ridge.

The corrie itself is deceptive in size as it has a recess which extends westwards. This cannot be seen from the Glenmore area and it contains a large mass of rock buttressing the Fiacaill Ridge. There are four main rock masses in the corrie. High on the left is a rectangular buttress, the Mess of Pottage, which is bounded on its right by Jacob's Ladder, an obvious straight gully. Aladdin's Buttress lies in the centre of the corrie. It has as its lower section a steep dome-shaped rock mass, characterised by some obvious corner lines. Above and to the right, the rock is more broken but shows three prominent ribs jutting up to the skyline. This buttress is bounded on the left by the large dog-leg of Aladdin's Couloir. It is separated from the Mess of Pottage by a wide area of broken ground. Right of Aladdin's Buttress is the more complex Fluted Buttress. This is cut by many gullies, particularly on its left, where Central Gully, the left-most of the Trident Gullies, forms the boundary between these two buttresses. On the right, Fluted Buttress fades out near the lowest point of the skyline where the Goat Track, a convenient if steep ascent route, leads onto the plateau at the head of Coire Domhain. The fourth buttress, Fiacaill Buttress, lies at the head of a westerly recess below the summit of the Fiacaill Ridge.

Because of the broken and vegetated nature of the rock in this corrie, the summer climbing, with some notable exceptions, is generally poor. However, in winter these cliffs give a large number of easier but interesting routes. Some areas of the cliff, such as around the Trident Gullies, are climbable anywhere and a large number of variations are possible. Due to the wealth of good easy and middle grade routes and its ease of access, this is a very popular winter corrie.

Approaches
From Aviemore, follow the ski road to the Coire Cas carpark and contour the Fiacaill a' Choire Chais into the corrie. Then follow the path (on the east of the steam) south-west to the back of the corrie. Alternatively, from the carpark go to the White Lady Shieling, then go diagonally up the corrie on good tracks (not up the line of the ski tow) to cross the Fiacaill a' Choire Chais above the Fiacaill ski tow in the vicinity of the snow fences crossing the ridge. An easy descending traverse then leads into the corrie floor.

THE MESS OF POTTAGE

This small fairly slabby buttress lies high on the left of the corrie. Its left side consists of a dome-shaped mass of rock which has some defined corner and crack lines running up it. The right side is more broken and cut by a couple of diagonal faults and some large areas of easier ground. The right edge of the buttress is defined by the straight regular gully of Jacob's Ladder. The cliff base has an obvious bay right of centre from which a diagonal fault system of corners leads up and left to peter

Smokestack Lightnin', Coire an t-Sneachda (Climber, Andy Cunningham)

out below a roof system near the top of the dome. There is also a horizontal break high up which comes in from the left and makes most of the climbs here easily escapable; this is the line of Topless, Grade II/III. However, the climbing is enjoyable, generally well protected and comes into condition very quickly, only needing a decent covering of snow. On many of the routes it is possible to interchange pitches and to escape fairly easily. It is best early in the season before the build-up is too extensive.

1 The Opening Break 100m III,4   (1990)
A slight, easily abandoned climb near the left edge of the buttress, starting up the main left-facing corner. Climb the cracks leading to the corner, turning the first bulge on the right. Climb the corner to easy ground on the terrace, then go up right. Follow the fault, going left below a steeper wall, and break back right up twin cracks to an easy finish.

2 Honeypot 90m IV,6 *   (1988)
This climb is near the left side and finishes by the obvious square-cut chimney near the left boundary of the upper walls. Start just right of the previous route at a triangular recess. Go diagonally right up the obvious slanting line, then go straight up a gully. Climb the wide but shallow chimney, passing the capping roof on the right wall.
   In summer this route is Very Difficult.

3 Wachacha 90m Hard Severe   (1989)
The obvious crack line in the centre of the left-most section of slabs. Start below an obvious right-facing corner. The pitches can be split.
1. 50m 4b Climb into the corner, swing onto the left edge left where it steepens, then continue up the crack line until easier climbing leads slightly right to below the top wall.
2. 40m 4b Follow a crack and shallow left-facing corner (8m right of the Honeypot chimney), then go through the upper roof system at an obvious crack. Alternatively, trend left to below the upper roof, then come back right to join the pitch at the top of the shallow corner. Drier than the corner line.
Winter: VI,7   (1990)
Loosely constructed round the summer route. Climb a crack left of the summer start and about 6 metres right of Honeypot. Move right and climb a gully to below the top wall. Follow the variation going left then back right below the roof to finish. Alternatively climb direct if there is no ice (harder).

The Couloir, Coire an Lochain

4 Trunk Line 105m VS   (1993)
A direct line of cracks up the centre of the buttress. Start 5 metres left
of the diagonal fault of No Blue Skies.
1. 35m 5a Climb a crack line up a green 'elephant's trunk'. Continue
until a traverse leads right into the diagonal fault (No Blue Skies winter
traverse reversed). Climb the wall above (crux) and follow the crack
past the right end of a roof to a belay on the left.
2. 20m 4b Follow the crack above until a diagonal line leads right
across the top of a slab to a belay on The Melting Pot.
3. 50m 4b Move onto the wall and follow the cracks up the pillar to a
ledge below the final groove of The Message. Follow cracks up the wall
right of the groove to reach the top.

5 No Blue Skies 110m VS   (1994)
Based on the winter line. Start at the diagonal line and follow it into the
horizontal cave. Continue up the crack and corner to easier ground
and a squat pillar. Above, gain a fine flake crack and from near its top,
traverse right to a niche at the top left end to the big roof. An exciting
swing out left reaches good holds and a finish up right (4c).
Winter: VI,7 **   (1990)
An interesting route with a deceptive first pitch. Start where an obvious
diagonal line leads left to a shallow horizontal cave. Climb the diagonal
corner to near the apex, traverse left, then go up the left side of the
apex to exit onto a ledge by the horizontal cave. Continue up the crack
and corner to easier ground and belay by a squat pillar. Climb broken
ground, then gain a fine flake crack (below and left of the big roof) and
follow it to its end. Traverse left along it to a crack, Wachacha, and finish
up this.

6 The Melting Pot 90m V,6 *   (1987)
This route follows the diagonal fault in its middle section, then takes
the continuation crack which passes the right end of the roof system.
The start is made left of the main diagonal fault. Start midway between
the starts of No Blue Skies and The Message. Climb slabs leftwards
into a short obvious right-facing groove with a high vertical left wall. Exit
from the groove over a bulge and traverse left round an arete onto
broken ground leading to the main diagonal fault. Take the obvious line
leading left to the top right corner of a large bay. Climb the overhanging
groove above, then continue up a crack line passing a roof to the top.

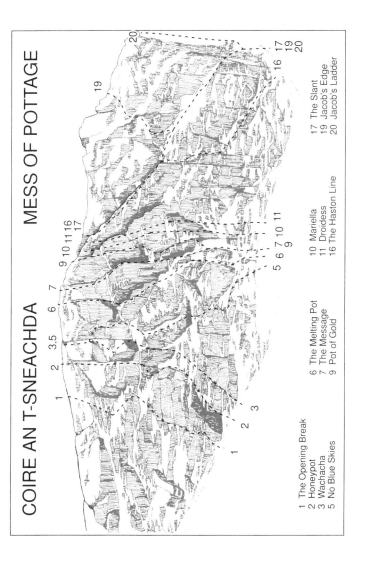

COIRE AN T-SNEACHDA   MESS OF POTTAGE

1 The Opening Break
2 Honeypot
3 Wachacha
5 No Blue Skies

6 The Melting Pot
7 The Message
9 Pot of Gold

10 Mariella
11 Droides
16 The Haston Line

17 The Slant
19 Jacob's Edge
20 Jacob's Ladder

7 The Message 90m IV,6 ** (1986)
A natural system of grooves gives three fairly consistent pitches. It starts up the diagonal fault, then takes the deepest groove running straight up the cliff. Start at the top of the main bay right of the lowest rocks. Climb a blocky chimney and two short corners trending left to the foot of the main deep groove. Climb this, break left, then go up the fault to the foot of a square right-facing corner. Climb the corner to a bulge at the top, swing left onto the edge and finish up cracked slabs.

8 The Hybrid 100m IV,4 *
This eponymous route takes the diagonal fault all the way, that is the start of the Message, then the middle of The Melting Pot. Below the final corner of The Melting Pot climb up and right onto a ledge and finish as for The Message or further right.

9 Pot of Gold 90m Severe (1990)
This pleasant climb, on the buttress right of the deep groove of The Message, is open to variation but keeps to the cleanest rocks. Start just right of the diagonal fault. Climb easy slabs, then a blocky chimney on The Message. A short traverse right leads onto the buttress. Work up right, then go back left over blocks until near The Message. Climb up right to a large ledge, then move left up the centre of the wall above by shallow corners and flakes and finish up a shallow chimney.
Winter: V,6 * (1988)
Good climbing following the summer route.

10 Mariella 80m VS (1989)
Scramble up easy slabs to belay just right of the blocky chimney of The Message.
1. 45m 4b Climb the red groove above, swing left past the roof and continue up the crack line.
2. 35m Move left and climb walls and slabs to the top.
Winter: VI,7 (1991)
Follow the summer route.

11 Droidless 85m VI,6 * (1990)
The parallel crack line 3 metres right of Mariella give a good sustained lower section. Start just on the left of Mariella.
1. 30m Gain the main fault by a slanting corner just on its left, then follow it over the bulge to a ledge below parallel cracks.
2. 20m Continue up the cracks with a difficult start to an easing in angle in a bay below an obvious right-facing corner.
3. 35m Climb the corner then easier ground.

12 The Firefighter 80m IV,6   (1990)
The line just to the right of Droidless, starting 3 metres right of that route.
1. 30m Climb thin cracks to join Droidless for 5m, traverse right under the obvious roofs to pull into a tapering slot, then move up to a ledge.
2. 20m Continue up the obvious chimney to a bay on Mariella.
3. 30m Exit out the right wall up easy grooves to the plateau.

13 The Messenger 80m IV,6   (1991)
Start at the obvious left-facing corner, right of the previous routes.
1. 30m Climb the corner, passing an obvious roof with difficulty.
2. 30m Trend right into and climb an open fault, then take a steep right-facing corner.
3. 20m Easy climbing leads to the top.

14 The Three Decrees 45m V,5   (1994)
An alternative ice start to the previous route. Start down and just right of the bay, 4 metres right of The Messenger. Climb a crack up the wall to gain and follow the thinly iced left-facing corner to the right of The Messenger. Finish as for that route.

   To the right the buttress becomes more broken. The lower slabs are cut by two diagonal faults which lead to a large snowfield shaped like an inverted triangle. A variety of pitches have been done on both the lower and upper rocks which are left for the adventurous to discover for themselves.

15 Yukon Jack 90m IV,5   (1993)
Gain the obvious right-facing corner *via* a crack. Above, climb its continuation, crossing The Haston Line and finish up a chimney in the upper rocks in the same line.

16 The Haston Line III,4   (1965)
The lower slanting fault starting from the corner of the buttress has an awkward corner before a direct ascent can be made to a choice of finishes in the region of the upper snowfield.

17 The Slant I
Start a pitch up Jacob's Ladder at a big bay where a diagonal fault goes left. Follow this and continue diagonally to the easy big upper snowfield.

18 Hidden Chimney II/III *
Start as for The Slant and follow it to reach a wide chimney defining the right side of the steeper upper buttress. Climb this over a chokestone and so to the top. A harder start, Grade III, is possible up the right-facing corner just left of Jacob's Ladder.

19 Jacob's Edge I/II *
Follow The Slant until it is possible to break back right to snow slopes overlooking Jacob's Ladder. It is slightly harder to go to the base of Hidden Chimney and trend back right through a steeper wall.

20 Jacob's Ladder 105m I *   (1939)
The gully bounding the right side of the buttress is generally straight-forward but there can be steeper sections when there is a poor build-up. The cornice can be large.

Between Jacob's Ladder and Aladdin's Couloir lies an area of broken ground with a steeper rock band just below the plateau edge. Several lines of Grade I to Grade II can be worked out here, the best of them being **Forty Thieves** (Grade I), the rib and wide slot on the left of Aladdin's Couloir.

21 Aladdin's Couloir 180m I   (1935)
The obvious large dog-leg gully; an easy ice pitch may form at the narrows before the bend. Above, the gully widens and leads to a col above the pinnacle of Aladdin's Seat. The gully is then wide to the top and the cornice fairly easily out-flanked.

ALADDIN'S BUTTRESS

This is the obvious buttress in the centre of the corrie right of Aladdin's Couloir. Its lower section is a steep dome-shaped mass of rock at the top left of which is a 10m pinnacle, Aladdin's Seat. Above and right of the lower buttress and separated from it by a diagonal break of easier ground are several triangular rock buttresses. The right-hand and best defined is Pygmy Ridge; the ground below this is easy-angled and much of it banks out in winter. The lower rocks of Aladdin's Buttress give some of the most interesting climbing in the corrie. The two main features to aid route location are the big left-facing corner of Doctor's Choice in the centre of the buttress and the wide chimney of Patey's Route near the right side. Routes on this part of the cliff finish on easy ground just below the level of Aladdin's Seat, where the plateau can be gained *via* the top of Aladdin's Couloir or Aladdin's Mirror or these routes used to return to the corrie floor. There is also an abseil descent from some large blocks down the line of Ali Baba. Aladdin's Mirror or the rib on its right are descents on the right side of the buttress.

22 Babes in the Wood 30m E2 5b *   (1986)
A good little pitch up the obvious diagonal crack in the smooth wall which rises from Aladdin's Couloir just before the bend. Gain the diagonal crack *via* cracks and a deep groove at its right end, then follow it left and finish straight up.

23 Ali Baba 30m VS 4c   (1986)
This is the open right-facing corner which deepens with height and is right of Babes in the Wood. Start in a recess right of the corner and go up it until level with it, then go left and follow the corner, going left and back right at the top.

24 Nightline 30m VII,7   (1990)
A direct line up the first cracked groove right of Ali Baba. Climb the crack with increasing difficulty past a V-groove to a ledge, above which a hard cracked bulge gives access to easy ground.

25 Original Summer Route 100m IV,6 *   (1936)
A line on the left of the buttress overlooking the Couloir. Start about 5m up on the right from the foot of the narrow rib on the left of the buttress. Climb a shallow corner to a flake and continue to the obvious break. A harder start takes the shallow groove from the bottom of the toe. Go diagonally up the easy ramp above, then leftwards in an exposed position until a line of corners leads up to the crest of the buttress.
   In summer this is Very Difficult and fairly vegetated.

26 The Lamp 100m IV,5   (1988)
An interesting climb up the linked diagonal breaks just right of Original Summer Route. Start at the top of the bay right of the narrow rib. Climb an open groove over a wedged block and continue to its top. Follow an obvious inclined ledge right to its end in the central bay. Go diagonally right to below breaks leading back left. Follow these by a choice of lines to gain and finish up the buttress crest.
Direct Variation: V,6
After reaching the central bay, go out left towards the crest. When stopped by smooth slabs, return right to thread the overhangs above to reach easy ground.

In summer, **The Lamp Direct** (Severe) approximates to this variation. It is reached *via* the first part of Original Summer Route.

27 The Third Wish 60m V,7   (1993)
Start 5 metres right of The Lamp.
1. 30m Climb through steep scrappy ground (crux) to grooves which lead to the diagonal ramp of The Lamp.
2. 30m Follow The Lamp up right to where it is possible to see its top pitch. Step left into an obvious crack which leads to easy ground.

28 The Prodigal Principal 100m V,5   (1985)
More of an ice route than others here, it takes a line left of Doctor's Choice climbing the obvious chimney left of the top corner of that route. Start left of Doctor's Choice and climb slabs and ramps before moving left into a large snow bay; junction with Doctor's Choice. The exact line depends on the ice build-up; sometimes a steeper but shorter ice line leads directly into the snow bay. Climb a short crack at the back of the bay, then follow easy ground to a narrow chimney immediately left of the big corner of Doctor's Choice. Climb this to the top.

29 The Paramedic 80m VII,7   (1991)
A direct line heading for the grooves between the final corner of Doctor's Choice and Doctor Janis.
1. 25m Follow a crack system 5 metres left of the start of Doctor's Choice to a belay on the left rib of the cave (on ice).
2. 25m Continue up the bulge behind the belay to the base of Doctor's Choice corner.
3. 30m Move into the slim groove on the right wall and climb it to below a roof. A wild swing right avoids a perched block and permits entry into the upper groove and thence to the top; one axe rest.

30 Doctor's Choice 105m IV,4 **   (1972)
An interesting climb taking the prominent large left-facing corner in the centre of the buttress. Start below the corner and climb up to a cave below an overhang. From the foot of the cave, go diagonally left to a snow bay, exit from this on the right and return on easy ground to below the main corner. Climb this to the top (harder if not iced up).

31 Doctor Janis 130m VS   (1990)
The slanting corner right of the main corner of Doctor's Choice is slightly vegetated but has good rock. Start on the right side of the bay below Doctor's Choice.

COIRE AN T-SNEACHDA

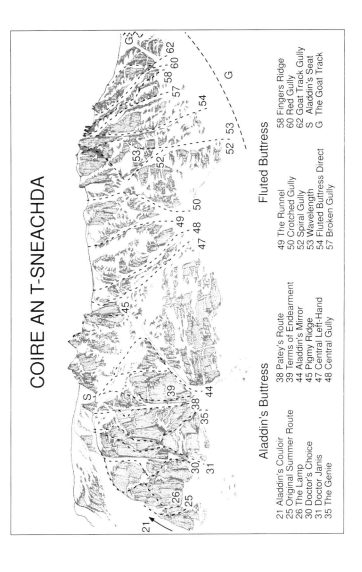

Aladdin's Buttress

21 Aladdin's Couloir
25 Original Summer Route
26 The Lamp
30 Doctor's Choice
31 Doctor Janis
35 The Genie

38 Patey's Route
39 Terms of Endearment
44 Aladdin's Mirror
45 Pigmy Ridge
47 Central Left-Hand
48 Central Gully

Fluted Buttress

49 The Runnel
50 Crotched Gully
52 Spiral Gully
53 Wavelength
54 Fluted Buttress Direct
57 Broken Gully

58 Fingers Ridge
60 Red Gully
62 Goat Track Gully
S Aladdin's Seat
G The Goat Track

1. 45m 4a Climb the main groove until it is blocked by an overhang.
2. 40m 4b Pass the overhang by the slabs on the left, then go straight up to the subsidiary hanging groove which leads into the upper corner.
3. 45m 4c Climb the upper corner.
Winter: V,7 *   (1987)
Follow the main groove slanting up right to near the steep wall. Go left to a snow bay, then move right to gain an awkward narrow ramp which leads left to the main upper corners.

32 Edgewood 120m E2   (1990)
This route is based on the slabs right of Doctor Janis. Start at the foot of the wall which forms the right side of the Doctor's Choice alcove, below and right of the start of the previous route.
1. 45m 4a Climb the arete and slabs to a big ledge on the right.
2. 25m 5b Climb a flake crack and a thin crack, then make a thin exit onto slabs which lead to a belay below The Genie's main corner.
3. 50m 5b Go up the corner for 2m, then go diagonally left across the undercut slab (crux) to the arete. Cross Doctor Janis and continue left to the next arete or climb the roofed recess.

33 The Magic Crack 105m HVS ***   (1981)
An excellent route with a unique finger crack. Start at a deep left-facing corner by a huge beak of rock.
1. 35m 4c Climb the corner and the broad blunt rib above to a platform and large spike belay.
2. 25m 5a Climb the rib a short way, then take the thin clean crack on the right. This leads into corners which run up to below the deep corner of The Genie.
3. 45m 5a Move right and climb the superb finger crack. Cross an overlap and climb the cracked wall above to easier ground.

34 White Magic VII,7 **   (1985)
A unique and excellent route based on The Magic Crack. Follow The Genie to the foot of the main corner, then a short traverse leads to The Magic Crack. Climb this to the overlap, where a traverse right leads to the big ledge above the corner of Damnation. Finish right up a squeeze chimney.

35 The Genie 110m V,6 **   (1982)
A fine climb taking the central of the three main corners. Start at the
foot of Patey's Route and gain a ramp line and the following open
corners which curve up to the foot of the main corner. Climb this to the
top.
   This route is VS in summer.

36 Damnation 90m HVS   (1969)
The rightmost corner gives a good pitch. Start a short way up from the
lowest rocks.
1. 45m Climb up easy cracked slabs and corners to belay at a huge
spike by a pale-coloured corner.
2. 45m 5a Climb the corner and the main one to its top and finish up
the cracked wall on the left.
Winter: VI,5   (1985)
Follow the summer route (ice is needed in the corner). Finish straight
up, including the squeeze chimney of White Magic.

37 Salvation 100m VS   (1989)
This route is on the cracked slabs right of Damnation. Start at the foot
of Patey's Route and climb a short way up a slabby ramp going left.
Just left of the chimney is a prow split by a thin crack.
1. 35m 4b Climb the thin crack, then a short wall and slabs to a broad
ramp.
2. 40m 4c Break through the overlap above at some flakes and climb
cracks up the slab.
3. 25m 4b Move up right to a block, then follow the continuation crack
to the top.
Winter: V,7   (1989)
Take the first pitch just left of the summer line, leaving the ramp *via* a
short chimney groove, then pass left of the short wall. The overlap can
be climbed as for the summer route or about 3 metres right of the flakes.

38 Patey's Route 120m IV,5 *   (1959)
This follows the obvious wide chimney line on the right side of the
buttress and is basically an ice route. There are two main pitches. The
first has a difficult bulge where it narrows, and the upper pitch has a
chokestone which is usually climbed by going out left, then making a
long move back right above the bulge. It can also be climbed by
continuing leftwards.

39 Terms of Endearment 100m III   (1981)
A route on the buttress edge overlooking the chimney of Patey's Route.
Start just inside the initial chimney of that route and traverse a ledge
right onto the crest, then follow the line of least resistance to the top. A
direct start up the wide crack is much harder and a start on the right is
also possible.
  Hard Severe 4b in summer, with the direct start.

40 The Flying Doctors 160m VI,7   (1991)
A left to right girdle, starting 30m up Aladdin's Couloir and taking the
obvious line including part of The Lamp to the foot of the main corner
of Doctor's Choice. Descend a shallow chimney below this until a flake
on the right can be gained. From its top, traverse to the foot of the main
corner of The Genie. Climb this for 7m, break right to the stance on
White Magic, then go under the overlap to the top of the main corner
of Damnation. Traverse right into Patey's Route, descend a short way,
then climb a groove on the crest of Terms of Endearment to finish.

41 Brief Encounter 35m IV,4   (1991)
Start 7 metres left of Honour among Thieves at a crack line. Climb this,
initially on ice, then on turf to the top of the following route.

42 Kuryakin's Corner 35m VI,7   (1992)
Start 5 metres left of Honour among Thieves at a corner with two
right-leaning roofs. Climb the corner, gain the arete just below where
the corner merges with the slab and finish up the slab. When fully iced,
the grade drops to V,5.

43 Honour among Thieves 35m V,4   (1986)
The clean-cut left-facing corner immediately left of Aladdin's Mirror
Direct Start sometimes gives a good ice pitch, but generally it is thin
and poorly protected.

44 Aladdin's Mirror 180m I *   (1946)
An exposed snow route taking the easy ground right of the lower part
of the buttress. Climb the diagonal snow shelf on the right-hand side
to reach open slopes. Trend back left under the upper rocks to reach
Aladdin's Seat and finish up Aladdin's Couloir.

Direct Start: 25m IV,4
A very popular and reliable pitch up the steep ice on the right of the buttress up from the start of Aladdin's Mirror. Variable in length and difficulty, an easy chimney leads to the main route. Other ice lines further right can also be climbed.

Above the easy ground are the steep upper rocks which appear as a set of triangular buttresses separated by gullies and grooves. These give a variety of routes and provide finishes to routes lower down if so desired. The diagonal gully going right to Pygmy Ridge is Grade I, and the chimney line from its start going straight up gives a good Grade III pitch. Other harder finishes up the buttresses are possible.

45 Pygmy Ridge 90m Moderate **   (1904)
The right-hand rock mass gives an excellent little climb, starting from the lowest rocks and following the well defined rib, at one point crossing a horizontal arete.
Winter: IV,5 *
The ridge gives an enjoyable buttress route. It can be approached from above or below and used as a good finish to lower routes.

46 Saturation Point 65m IV,5   (1994)
A fault on the right flank of Pygmy Ridge. Start 5 metres right of Pygmy Ridge and climb the right side of the fault to a ledge (25m). Gain a bigger ledge above and from its right side climb a slabby wall to more broken ground and Pygmy's horizontal crest.

47 Central Left-hand 135m I
Climb the broad easy rib below Pygmy Ridge, overlooking Central Gully, by a choice of lines then finish up the well defined funnel-shaped gully immediately right of Pygmy Ridge. There may be a good but avoidable ice pitch in the upper section.

Between Aladdin's Mirror and Central Left-hand, below Pygmy Ridge, is a slabby area which can give a selection of starts up ice smears or more rocky pitches, all of which end on easy ground.

FLUTED BUTTRESS

The cliff west of Aladdin's Buttress to the lowest point of the corrie rim is Fluted Buttress. A recessed section on the left is split by the Trident Gullies, which spring from the same prominent snow bay which extends high up into the cliffs. Central Gully, which slants left and is the left-hand of the three, forms the boundary between Aladdin's and Fluted Buttresses. The Runnel is the prominent direct line, while the rightmost of the Trident Gullies is Crotched Gully, which uses the wide fault in the upper cliffs. Right of this the rocks are less broken and are cut high up by the right-slanting upper section of Spiral Gully. This lies above a fairly unbroken section of cliff which from below appears as a tapering wedge of rock bounded by Broken Gully on the right. After Broken Gully is Fingers Ridge, with its distinctive pinnacles high up near the plateau. Right again are Red Gully and Goat Track Gully, before the buttress fades out into the easier ground of the Goat Track.

The area of the Trident Gullies is quite low-angled. The rib between Central Gully and The Runnel is Grade I/II and that between The Runnel and Crotched Gully is Grade II/III by the chimney line. Further right, at the highest part of the cliff, the buttress has a slabby lower section which can bank out. If this is not the case, Spiral Gully and routes in the area of Fluted Buttress Direct may have an extra easy pitch to start.

48 Central Gully 135m I (1940)
The leftmost of the Trident Gullies slants left and separates Aladdin's and Fluted Buttresses. It is straightforward with no pitches and an easily outflanked cornice.

49 The Runnel 135m II * (1946)
The central and best defined of the three gullies, rising from the top of the snow bay, gives straightforward climbing to near the top where there is a fine icy chimney leading to the upper slopes. Grooves either side of the chimney can also be climbed.

50 Crotched Gully 135m I/II (1946)
The widest, right-hand gully from the snow bay steepens near its head. From the top, go right to gain the wide upper gully. An alternative is to gain the snow rib on the right of the snow bay and follow this direct into the upper fault, which may have a large cornice.

51 Vortex 60m IV,5 (1992)
The rib between the top sections of Crotched and Spiral Gullies. Follow the shallow groove line up the rib and turn the capping roof on the left or on the right (easier, IV,4). An easy crest leads to the top.

52 Spiral Gully 150m II * (1959)

The upper section of this climb takes the diagonal gully which runs right to finish near the highest part of the cliff. A variety of starts can be found between the rib just right of Crotched Gully and the big twin grooves below the upper fault; the twin grooves are probably best. The upper fault ends at a small col just below the plateau and the cornice is usually easily turned.

Variations:

The grooves in the wall above the diagonal fault offer a variety of finishes. The wide fault directly above the bend is Grade III. The first groove right of this, finishing up a wall and arete is V,7 and the next groove right is IV,5.

53 Wavelength 130m III,4 (1985)

An interesting and varied route which takes the left branch of the fault of Fluted Buttress Direct. Climb Spiral Gully to the level of the twin grooves, then slant up right, sometimes on ice, to gain a diagonal chimney which leads right into the main fault above where it splits. Go up this fault. A steeper corner then leads to the rib overlooking Spiral Gully (the corner can be avoided on the left). Follow the rib to finish. A better final pitch is to cross Spiral Gully and climb the groove directly opposite.

54 Fluted Buttress Direct 135m IV,5 ** (1978)

A good climb which follows the narrow but defined chimney-groove system on the left of the most continuous section of slabby rocks. Move up to then climb the chimney to where it forks and increases in size. Continue up the right fork to the crest of the buttress and climb this to the col between Spiral and Broken Gullies and hence the top.

Piccolo (70m, V,6) climbs the groove on the right of the chimney of Fluted Buttress Direct. It starts up shorts walls, gains the groove by a left traverse across a slab and finishes by crossing Sax Appeal and climbing the edge above.

55 Sax Appeal 50m V,4 (1988)

This poorly protected route takes the obvious shallow corner line right of Fluted Buttress Direct, which curves in to join that route above its fork.

56 Cruising 140m V,5   (1980)
A line up the right side of the steeper rocks. Start above the lower slabs
at a left-facing corner. Climb the corner and continuation fault to a niche
in a steeper section. Climb this and follow the fault rightwards, almost
into Broken Gully, then take a crack line leading back left onto the crest
to join and finish up Fluted Buttress Direct.

Broken Pillar (110m, Difficult) takes a fairly direct line (approximating that of Cruising) up the ill-defined pillar just left of Broken Gully.

57 Broken Gully 130m III   (1967)
The fault between the highest part of the buttress and Fingers Ridge.
The upper section of the gully is large and funnel-shaped. Start in the
first bay right of the lowest rocks. Climb the gully, slanting slightly right
until a traverse can be made onto the top of a slabby pillar, then into
the main gully (this is not very obvious, but it is at the top of a fairly long
pitch). Follow the upper gully to finish up the right or the left of the upper
funnel.
Variation: III,4
The left-hand start takes a smaller gully left of the ordinary start and
leads directly into the upper fault. This can be harder but may also
contain ice in quantity. Very occasionally an icefall flows directly from
the upper gully, giving 8m of near vertical ice.

Broken Fingers (III,4) starts up Broken Gully but continues up the
fault all the way to reach easy ground on the left of Fingers Ridge.

58 Fingers Ridge 140m Difficult   (1954)
The slabby rib which culminates in several obvious pinnacles. Start at
the foot of Red Gully. Go up and left over slabs and ledges to a bay
near the left edge of the buttress. Go left and climb a rib overlooking
Broken Gully, then take a short wall *via* a flake to gain a large
right-facing open groove left of some slabs. Climb this groove to a
narrow ridge, follow this past the fingers to a col, then a short wall leads
to the top. Care must be taken with loose rock on the narrower portion
of the ridge.
Winter: IV,4 **   (1969)
A good Winter route following the summer line.

59 Fingers Ridge Direct 110m VS   (1984)
Pleasant though escapable climbing. Start in the middle of the ridge.
1. 35m 4b Climb directly up pink slabs, cross an awkward bulge and

belay in the open groove.

2. 20m 4b Work up and right by cracks to a stance by Red Gully.

3. 30m 4c Climb the diagonal crack in the fine slab to ledges.

4. 25m Go up the next diagonal crack to join the normal route.

Winter: VI,7   (1990)

Based on the summer route and giving some thin slab climbing. Start as for Fingers Ridge.

1. 30m After about 10m go up an open groove, then traverse thinly right and move up to a ledge next to Red Gully.

2. 10m Climb a turfy crack to the summer stance by Red Gully.

3. 30m Thin climbing just right of the diagonal crack leads to a ledge, then go left and up to ledges.

4. 25m As for the summer line, climb the diagonal crack to join the normal route and continue up the crest.

60 Red Gully 120m II/III **

This good climb, one of the best at its grade in the corrie, follows the fault right of Fingers Ridge. The lower narrow chimney often contains ice in quantity and leads into the easier funnel-shaped upper gully.

61 Western Rib 120m II/III   (1972)

Climb the rib on the right of Red Gully. It may be that the main rib needs to be gained above the toadstool-shaped pinnacle from Goat Track Gully.

62 Goat Track Gully 120m II *

The gully on the extreme right of the buttress, starting just right of Red Gully, cuts up right below a prominent left wall and has one short pitch which is usually taken on the right (can be hard for the grade). Above, the line is more open and less defined.

FIACAILL BUTTRESS

This is the fine mass of rock high up in the western sector of the corrie buttressing the Fiacaill Coire an t-Sneachda. It is split in two by the large diagonal gully of Fiacaill Couloir, but this is hidden from most angles. Left of the gully the face is wedge-shaped and the upper section, above a ledge which cuts the face from the left, is scored by several right-slanting ramps. The face above the gully has more large scale vertical features.

The winter climbing here can sometimes be better than elsewhere in the corrie because of its sheltered position with regards to the prevailing south-west winds.

A small buttress high and left of the main mass contains **White Dwarf** (40m, V,6). This climbs the obvious left-slanting crack then a series of hanging thin grooves.

1 Escapologist 55m VI,7 (1992)

This route climbs to the midway ledge. Start 8 metres left of the main left-slanting groove of Houdini.

1. 30m Slant up left before moving right over a slab to an obvious ledge. Climb up left to a large block.

2. 25m Jump from the top of the block to reach turf and continue up a corner and easier continuation to the terrace.

2 Houdini 160m VI,7 ** (1990)

A fine climb which works its way up the front face of the buttress. Start in the middle of the lower tier and climb the main left-slanting groove to its top, then trend left to the midway ledge. Climb the open right-slanting groove to a ledge with big flakes below a steep wall and traverse delicately right until ramps lead upwards. Go up a short way, step left and climb to the left side of a huge block and belay. Go right, climb a big groove and either thread or pass on the outside of the chokestone. Continue up by some thin climbing to below the upper wall. Climb this diagonally left, starting in a vague niche to gain the top by the step in the wall.

3 The Stirling Bomber 55m V,7 *** (1990)

A great little climb on the lower part of the buttress, taking the obvious right-facing chimney right of centre. Gain the chimney by the crack leading left into it, then follow it to its end on the diagonal fault of Jailbreak. Finish up this to the midway ledge.

4 Fiacaill Buttress Direct 135m HVS (1969/1994)

This route offers good climbing at a consistent grade, although it is a little vegetated. Start at the foot of The Stirling Bomber.

1. 20m 4c Start up towards The Stirling Bomber but go left over a huge flake into the Houdini groove (a right-facing corner with a wide crack), or direct on vegetation.

COIRE AN T-SNEACHDA

FIACAILL BUTTRESS

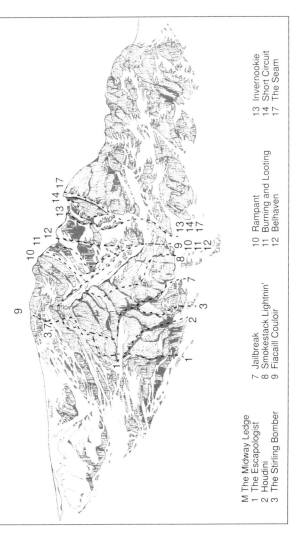

M The Midway Ledge
1 The Escapologist
2 Houdini
3 The Stirling Bomber

7 Jailbreak
8 Smokestack Lightnin'
9 Fiacaill Couloir

10 Rampant
11 Burning and Looting
12 Belhaven

13 Invernookie
14 Short Circuit
17 The Seam

2. 35m 5a Climb the groove then the obvious right-slanting wide crack to the middle terrace. Walk left 10m to the first break left of the roof (Jailbreak).
3. 40m 5a   Pull through the initial bulge, then go up the depression slightly right to a big ramp (Houdini). Climb the ramp and its right edge to a ledge.
4. 20m 4c Continue right to the crest.
5. 20m 4b Finish up left to the step in the headwall (Houdini).

5 Jail House Rock 60m E2   (1994)
Start from the right end of the middle ledge.
1. 15m 5b Climb diagonally right to a big foothold about 3m right of an old peg. Stand precariously on a small slab, make a long reach through the bulge for good holds, then pull through to a small ledge.
2. 15m 5b A big slab now leads right (the original line). Pull out left over an overhanging wall to gain a higher ramp, then follow this rightwards until a move left gains another small ledge.
3. 20m 5a Steep moves up flakes on the left gain another small ramp leading right then left to the final headwall.
4. 10m 5b Climb the overhanging headwall using a dubious flake to a rounded mantelshelf finish.

6 The North-East Cruiser 120m E2   (1990)
A summer route which links the lines of The Stirling Bomber and Houdini.
1. 45m 4c Climb the crack and flake chimney of The Stirling Bomber to the right end of the midway ledge.
2. 25m 5c Go diagonally right along a continuous crack, the lowest of three. Where it becomes blind, descend to a ledge above an overhang, then climb the corner on the right to regain the crack. Pull out right onto a slab and make improbable moves up the overhanging arete on the left to gain a ledge.
3. 25m 5a Keeping on steep ground, go diagonally left using big flakes and cracks (joining Fiacaill Buttress Direct).
4. 25m 4b Continue left to the top of the buttress, breaking through the final steep wall as for Houdini.

7 Jailbreak 120m VII,7   (1986)
The most obvious line on the bottom of the buttress, but with less obvious climbing above. Start about 15 metres from the right edge of Fiacaill Couloir and climb the obvious left-slanting stepped corner to

the midway ledge. Go left about 10 metres and climb up and right until moves left lead to short groove-ramps running right (this is fairly direct and shares some ground with Houdini). At their top, move left to the right side of a huge block. Climb the ramps and corners above to below the vertical top wall. Move right of the obvious chimney (which can be used to give and easier finish). Climb this diagonally left *via* a niche to finish by the step in the top wall (as for Houdini).

8 Smokestack Lightnin' 100m VI,7   (1990)
Good but escapable climbing which zigzags up the right side of the face. Start in a bay just left of Fiacaill Couloir. Climb the bay and go left on the obvious ledge to some large blocks. Continue left into the corner, then trend back up to the right to the next ledge. Traverse left, then go up to the ledge in the deep corner. Gain the hanging flake and go left round onto the front face (1 peg for aid). Go up to a slanting corner which leads to the crest of Fiacaill Buttress and a choice of finishes.
Variation:
The deep corner on pitch 3 is very strenuous (at least one rest).

Fiacaill Buttress (120m, Difficult, III,4) takes the right edge overlooking Fiacaill Couloir, but turns the top wall by going down and left to climb the chimney splitting the top wall. This is the easier finish to Jailbreak.

9 Fiacaill Couloir 150m II/III **   (1958)
This broad diagonal gully cuts deeply through the buttress and ends at a col near its left-hand edge. This gives a fine climb with a choice of lines. Start in the snow bay in the centre of the buttress and follow the gully up and left. Near the top, a chokestone may be difficult if there is a poor build-up. Above the col, go diagonally left to finish.

The next few routes climb the wall overlooking Fiacaill Couloir and start some way up that fault. Starting 8 metres left of Rampant is **Trampled Underfoot** (60m, IV,4) which first climbs steeply on vegetated ledges, then takes a short corner and a ledge into the big ramp up which it finishes.

10 Rampant 75m IV,5   (1979)
This route takes the line of narrow ramps then the big corner in the upper buttress. Start about 2 pitches up Fiacaill Couloir where a big ledge goes right. Climb the ramps up left into a corner, go up this, then

back right at its top. Move right into the big corner and follow this, exiting through a hole onto the ridge.

11 Burning and Looting 75m V,6 *   (1988/1991)
The rib between the corners of Rampant and Belhaven. Start at the beginning of the big ledge leading into Belhaven. From near a huge block on the ledge, go up steeply to a ledge going right, then move into a hanging groove capped by a block. Surmount this into a short slot (strenuous) or turn it on the right, then go up to a ledge (originally Rampant Direct Start). Climb the sharp rib above by cracks and blocks on the right of the crest.

12 Belhaven 75m V,6 **   (1979)
A good climb up the left-facing corner immediately above the start of Fiacaill Couloir. Climb Fiacaill Couloir for a pitch to below the corner. Either climb direct into the corner, good build-up required, or continue up the gully to use the big ledges going right. The main corner gives continuous interest.

13 Invernookie 120m III,4 **   (1969)
An interesting and very popular climb which takes a line of ramps on the wall above and right of Fiacaill Couloir. Start just right of Fiacaill Couloir. Go up and right onto the ramps and follow them to below an overhanging wall. The right corner leads into a chimney-cave from which a right traverse leads to a groove and the ridge.

14 Short Circuit 110m III,4   (1987)
This climb takes the snow ramp above and right of Invernookie. Start as for Invernookie, then go right and up to gain this higher ramp. Go to its end and climb the corner. If there is no ice in the corner, go left round the arete and climb the wide crack to the same snow patch. Climb a short wide crack into the right-hand of two grooves and finish by the crack in the slab on its right.

15 Slaterless 35m IV,6   (1987)
Start on the snow ramp of Short Circuit and climb the crack line right of the corner of that route.

16 Seam-stress 40m IV,6   (1987)
The parallel fault just left of The Seam leads to below a roof which is crossed in an exciting position.

17 The Seam 100m IV,4 ***   (1986)
A very good route which follows the obvious fault immediately left of
the steep triangular wall on the buttress edge. Climb Invernookie for
45m, then move right to the foot of the fault. Climb the chimney fault
direct to the top.

18 Watch Out 50m VS   (1990)
This route takes the cracks up the arete right of The Seam. Scramble
to the foot of the main rocks.
1. 20m Climb to the foot of the cracks.
2. 30m 5a Follow the twin cracks right of The Seam to a roof, swing
onto the right arete and climb an overhanging crack (crux). Move left
onto a slab, then easier climbing leads to the ridge.
Winter: VI,8   (1990)
Climb the summer route.

19 The Hurting 35m E4 6a *   (1991)
Superb sustained climbing up the middle of the triangular wall right of
The Seam. Start at the obvious detached flake. Climb the poorly
protected right-facing groove line for 10m to a ledge and runners.
Continue straight up some hollow flakes, then move right and go up to
the roof (big Friends). Climb the left-hand side of the roof and traverse
right (crux) to a hidden flake crack. Go to the top of this, move left then
diagonally right into a niche to finish easily.

20 Polar Crossing 175m IV,5   (1988)
A traverse across the buttress from left to right, starting at the first ramp
above the midway ledge. Climb the ramp which tapers out, then move
onto the bigger ramp above and climb it to below a steepening.
Descend the open fault (Jailbreak), to gain the big groove (Houdini)
going right onto the crest. Descend Fiacaill Couloir to ledges going
right (Belhaven) and follow the ledges and ramps going right to finish
up The Seam.

COIRE AN LOCHAIN
(Map Ref 985 025)

This compact and well defined corrie lies below Cairn Lochan, the most westerly top of Cairn Gorm. It consists of four main buttresses separated by obvious gullies. These form an arc overlooking the corrie's most outstanding feature, the Great Slab. This is a huge easy-angled slab of pink granite which is visible from a considerable distance. It is also a notoriously avalanche-prone slope, especially in thaw conditions, and particularly in the spring when huge full depth avalanches can occur. It is usually advisable to approach winter routes up the flanks of the Great Slab.

The four buttresses are numbered from left to right. The Vent separates No.1 from No.2 Buttress, while the obvious diagonal fault of The Couloir in the centre of the corrie lies between No.2 and No.3. Between No.3 and No.4 is a large recess tucked in the corner of the corrie and housing the two branches of Y Gully.

Approaches
From the head of the carpark in Coire Cas, contour round the base of the Fiacaill a' Choire Chais and follow the well marked path round to the Allt Coire an t-Sneachda. Cross the burn and follow any of a number of paths which lead roughly south into the corrie.

NO.1 BUTTRESS

This is the buttress on the left side of the corrie. It has a steep right wall rising out of The Vent and a front face which merges into more broken ground on the left. The front and side walls are cut by some large corners and the rock has the blocky appearance that characterises this corrie.

1 Iron Butterfly 150m III   (1969)
Flutters its way up the broken left flank of the buttress. Start in a huge corner or bay about 40 metres left of The Vent. Climb a groove in the corner to a ledge below a prominent flake crack. Move right and move up snow to below a steep wall, then turn this on the left to gain another snowfield. Climb this to the next wall, then go diagonally right to a wide gully which leads to the top.

2 Coronary By-pass 100m V,7 (1994)

This route takes a line right of the upper gully of Iron Butterfly and left of Auricle, but slants left across the lower face to get there. Start 5 metres up from the corner of the buttress.

1. 35m Climb the chimney/corner to easier ground, then slant up left to below the big corner of Auricle.

2. 10m Gain the big ledge on the left and follow it to its end.

3. 10m Climb the open corner (crux).

4. 30m Go up and right by a narrow flake chimney, then move right to climb a deep corner crack. Continue in the same line to a big ledge, passing left of a rock crevasse.

5. 25m Climb the crack in the corner and continue up the slot and corner, or slant right in a rock crevasse to easy ground.

3 Auricle 90m Hard Severe (1969)

A steep climb up the front face of the buttress taking the big right-facing corner. Start below a broken corner crack. Climb the crack and short walls above, bearing left to a good rock ledge below an obvious wide crack in the corner. Climb the corner and continue to a large fin-like flake. From the top of the flake climb an overhanging recess to the top of the buttress which is separated by a crevasse from the main face. Step over this and continue to the plateau.

Winter: VI,7 (1984)

Climb the summer route.

4 Ventriloquist 80m HVS * (1990)

A good route climbing cracks in the wall just right of Auricle. Start 5 metres left of Ventricle.

1. 30m 4c Climb the chimney-crack (as for Auricle), then move right to climb a crack line into a recess and pull out right to below a wide crack 3m right of Auricle's crux groove.

2. 20m 5a Climb the crack (crux), then move up right by two short corners to a ledge.

3. 30m 4b Step up left from the ledge to a line of flakes and traverse right to a thin crack. Climb the crack, making a short detour on the right at the steepest section, cross the crevasse and finish up the deep crack.

Winter: VII,7 (1990)

A strenuous but well protected climb. Follow the summer line in 5 pitches, except climb the thin crack on pitch 3 from its base, 2 metres right of the summer belay.

5 Ventricle 95m HVS   (1968)
This route takes the cracks and grooves on the left wall of The Vent.
Start near the bend in the face.
1. 15m 5a Climb an overhanging crack (crux), move right along a ledge
and climb a wall near the right edge to a small mossy recess.
2. 15m Climb directly above the belay and up the face, heading for an
obvious groove and make an awkward move onto a ledge.
3. 20m Take the right-hand of two shallow grooves to reach the steep
groove and climb this until a traverse can be made to the top of a groove
and a block belay.
4. 45m Climb the wide crack in the groove and the steep wall above
to ledges.
Winter: VII,9   (1984)
A line close to the summer route but only the initial crack and pitch 3
coincided. Two fierce overhanging grooves left of pitch 2 were the crux
(1 peg for aid, 1 rest on pitch 3). Pitch 4 was avoided by traversing right
to finish as for Inventive.

6 Big Daddy 80m VIII,8   (1990)
Climb the first pitch of Daddy Longlegs, sustained. Climb the wide crack
of Ventricle (summer line), then traverse left to finish up Ventriloquist.

7 Daddy Longlegs 70m HVS *   (1968)
Two good pitches but escape is possible at mid-height. Start up the
steep groove on the left wall of The Vent about 15 metres below the
chokestone.
1. 35m 5a Climb the groove, step right into a second groove and follow
this past an overhang to ledges.
2. 10m Scramble up left.
3. 25m 4c Climb two consecutive vertical cracks in the wall right of the
wide corner crack of Ventricle.

8 Inventive 70m IV,5   (1994)
This route takes the largest corner on the left wall of The Vent. Follow
The Vent to below the chokestone and climb a groove leading to the
main left-facing corner. Alternatively, from above the chokestone,
traverse left and go up to the corner. Climb the big corner to the top.

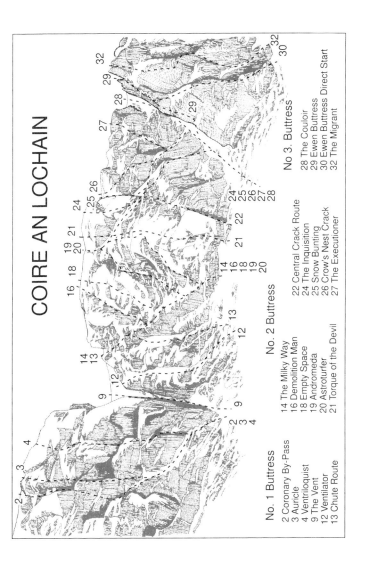

COIRE AN LOCHAIN

No. 1 Buttress

2 Coronary By-Pass
3 Auricle
4 Ventriloquist
9 The Vent
12 Ventilator
13 Chute Route

No. 2 Buttress

14 The Milky Way
16 Demolition Man
18 Empty Space
19 Andromeda
20 Astroturfer
21 Torque of the Devil

22 Central Crack Route
24 The Inquisition
25 Snow Bunting
26 Crow's Nest Crack
27 The Executioner

No 3. Buttress

28 The Couloir
29 Ewen Buttress
30 Ewen Buttress Direct Start
32 The Migrant

9 The Vent 100m II/III *   (1935)
A pleasant but short-lived route up the obvious gully between No.1 and
No.2 Buttress. It is narrow and defined at the bottom, but opens out into
an easy-angled funnel above. The difficulties depend on the build-up
and the amount of ice on the lower chokestone section, which can be
harder in lean conditions.
   In summer it is very wet, mossy and Severe.

NO.2 BUTTRESS

This, the widest buttress, lies between The Vent and The Couloir. Its
left-hand side consists of several vertical ribs which do not extend all
the way to the plateau. The central and right-hand sections are
characterised by steep walls and horizontal breaks and are topped by
a conspicuous square-cut wall. It is noted for its winter rather than its
rock climbs.

10 Vent Rib and Traverse 100m Difficult   (1949)
Climb the rib right of The Vent for a pitch to where it becomes smooth,
traverse right a long way, then go round the corner to a flake. Go behind
a block, then slant across a slab to easy ground which leads to the top.

11 Vent Rib Direct 90m IV,6   (1992)
Climb the rib all the way, taking a vertical groove just right of the crest
up the steep section, or start more easily on the left side by a vegetated
crack (IV,5).

12 Ventilator 100m II   (1970)
The corner on the right of the defined rib. Start at the top of the snow
bay on the right of the rib. Traverse into the corner and climb this to
reach the top of the defined rib, then finish up the top open funnel of
The Vent.

13 Chute Route 70m IV,4   (1968)
A fine ice pitch up the groove at the left corner of the big bay right of
The Vent. Climb the iced groove with a smooth left wall for a pitch and
finish up the top of The Milky Way.

14 The Milky Way 100m II/III *   (1959)
This pleasant route takes the obvious diagonal line on the left of the
more massive section of the buttress. Start at the foot of the wide

shallow fault and slant up left over steps to finish in a bowl near the top of The Vent. An alternative start is to go up the big snow bay on the left of the fault and gain it by a short steep groove at its top.

The next five routes lie left of the central part of the buttress and start at varying distances up the big open fault of Milky Way.

15 Appetite for Destruction 100m V,6   (1995)
This route takes a steep corner tucked into the right side of the upper tower. Climb Milky Way to below the tower, then trend right below it. Work up and left into the main corner to belay below a roof. Continue up the corner, moving right at the thread at its top and finish direct.

16 Demolition Man 120m IV,5   (1986)
Climb Milky Way to below the fall-line coming from the fault on the right of the square-cut upper tower. From the base of the tower a line of stepped ledges runs diagonally right to finish.

17 The Andromeda Strain 110m IV,4   (1985)
This route takes a line on the right of the upper tower. Climb Milky Way for about 40m, then ascend the wall above (crux) and traverse left into the wide fault on the right of the tower. Finish up the fault.

18 Empty Space 110m IV,5   (1992)
The steep wall between Andromeda and the upper tower. Start up Milky Way, then go up a right-facing corner, trending up and diagonally right to a small left-facing corner and so to a block belay. Climb the steep wall behind the belay to easier ground.

19 Andromeda 120m IV,4 *   (1971)
The big corner line which slants up right. Start up Milky Way, then trend right into the main corner where there is a choice of routes. The left and central grooves are IV,4 while the lower faults leading right are easier. These all lead onto the buttress crest. Finish as for Central Crack Route on the left of the conspicuous upper wall.

20 Astroturfer 120m III   (1985)
Start as for the previous routes but take the lowest chimney line leading right onto the crest. Climb the subsequent wall on its right, then climb the front of the buttress to finish by Central Crack Route.

21 Torque of the Devil 115m VI,8   (1988)
This route takes the front of the buttress between Central Crack Route
and Astroturfer. Start below a shallow left-facing corner. Climb to the
base of the corner and climb the crack in its right wall, then the wall on
the right, to a ledge. Move right to climb a short chimney, then traverse
left beneath a steep wall to below a line of weakness. Climb this to a
ledge. Move up to join Astroturfer and finish up this.

22 Central Crack Route 120m IV,5 *   (1958)
A fine climb taking the fault right of the centre of the buttress. Start just
right of the lowest rocks. Climb the slanting right-facing corner crack
with difficulty (crux), then continue up the fault for about 75m. Zigzag
up to below the great square wall and exit on its left. The cornice can
be huge and necessitate a long traverse.
   In summer the route is an unpleasant Moderate.

23 The Crack 20m VI,8   (1992)
The obvious wide crack in the headwall (VS in summer) gives a logical
finish to Torque of the Devil.

24 The Inquisition 80m HVS   (1992)
Surprisingly good for this part of the cliff. Starts at the obvious corner
on the wall some way up The Couloir.
1. 50m 5a Climb the superb smooth corner followed by easy ledges
to below a steep prow just left of the *cul de sac*.
2. 20m 4c Climb the steep crack up the prow, then move left to a ledge.
Go left up the wall to the higher of two platforms.
3. 10m 5a Climb the overhanging crack and flake to the plateau.
Winter: VI,8   (1992)
Follow the summer route, except on pitch 2 follow the cracks on the left
to the platform. A rest was used on the last pitch.

25 Snow Bunting 90m III   (1992)
The easiest line on this part of the face, starting just below the
dead-end left branch.
1. 45m Climb the left branch and move up left to a ledge, as for Crow's
Nest Crack. Belay at the left end of the ledge.
2. 45m Step left and climb the easy-angled snow bay until a wide
stepped crack on the left can be climbed. Move right under a roof, then
go up to easier broken ground leading to the top.

26 Crow's Nest Crack 100m III   (1983)
This is the chimney and corner line starting high up The Couloir, where
it has a vague left branch. Much of the route banks out later in the
season. Traverse left to a wall and continue to an obvious chimney.
Climb this and traverse left above it, climb a wall, then finish right by a
flake and a bulge.
   In summer this is Difficult and often wet.

27 The Executioner 70m VII,7   (1992)
A serious line of weakness to the right of Crow's Nest Crack. Start as
for that route, but move out right to a ledge with a large block. Ascend
the block-capped groove above with care, and gain a wide crack on the
right. Follow series of ledges to the final wall, then climb this by a bold
left-trending line. The first ascent was climbed in virtually snowless
conditions.

28 The Couloir 150m I *   (1935)
Loose and unpleasant in summer, this obvious wide slanting gully is
usually straightforward under snow. The cornice can be large but a way
through can normally found above the small col.

EWEN BUTTRESS (NO.3 BUTTRESS)

A well defined buttress lying between the diagonal of The Couloir and
the Left Branch of Y Gully. Its left flank forms an easier angled rib, Ewen
Buttress, overlooking The Couloir. Then comes a huge overhanging
groove-recess right of which is a steep and more massive frontal face.
Where this turns into the Left Branch of Y Gully are a set of well defined
vertical features, mostly corners.

29 Ewen Buttress 90m III   (1959)
The left edge of the buttress overlooking The Couloir. Start just inside
The Couloir. Climb steep broken ground to a saddle. The face above is
cut by an open gully which may be difficult to gain but above it,
straightforward climbing leads to the top at the same point as The
Couloir.

30 Ewen Buttress, Direct Start 45m IV,5
The obvious fault right of the toe of No.3 Buttress leads steeply up and
left to join the normal route above the first pitch.

31 The Vagrant 95m VS   (1970)
Start below a prominent rib on the left side of the steep frontal face.
1. 40m Climb right then left onto the rib, and follow this moving up right
at the top to below a steep wall.
2. 20m Follow flake cracks on the wall, straight up at first, then trending
left to below twin cracks.
3. 20m Climb a crack to the top ledge, move right round the edge, then
go up to grass ledges.
4. 15m Finish up the apparent pinnacle above.

32 The Migrant 95m VI,7 **   (1986)
An attempt on the huge groove on the left of No.3 Buttress, but very
good nevertheless. Start at the groove 5 metres right of Ewen Buttress
Direct Start. Climb the deceptively steep groove and make a delicate
step right to a belay. Work up right under the overhanging wall and go
through it at the first possible place into the huge groove left of Nocando
Crack. Descend a short way and break out left to a ledge on the left
arete. Follow the ledge left, then go up over a chokestone to the top of
a pinnacle. Move left to gain the rib above and follow it to easier ground.
Go easily right to the finish of Ewen Buttress.
Variation Start:
Climb the shallow groove leading directly to the short overhanging wall
and the huge groove.

33 New Age Traveller 100m VI,7   (1993)
1. 40m Start as for Migrant and continue in the same line immediately
under the steep wall.
2. 15m A short right traverse and a short wall lead to a ramp slanting
left in a very airy position under the headwall.
3. 15m A very well protected right-slanting crack leads to the top of the
wall.
4. 30m Now easily join and finish up Ewen Buttress.

   Nocando Crack (70m, HVS) starts up The Vicar, then climbs the
corner and huge flakes on the right wall of the recess. In winter it is
VII,8 with aid on pitch 3, which goes left of the line of the flake.

Bulgy, No. 4 Buttress, Coire an Lochain (Climber, Tom Prentice)

34 The Vicar 70m E1 ** (1968)

A magnificent top pitch, but the start is usually slimy. It takes the shallow corner and arete on the right of the recess.

1. 35m 5a Climb up a vile overhanging groove, then go up left towards the back of the recess. Under a second overhanging groove, traverse right and mantelshelf onto a ledge with large blocks. Climb a steep crack to a second ledge directly above the first.

2. 35m 5a Climb the shallow corner directly above the belay, sometimes on the wall just to its left. Move out onto the arete after about 20m and follow this to the top.

Winter VIII,8 (1992)

Climb pitch 1 in two pitches, then the second pitch moving left and climbing wall cracks where the crack becomes blind. Move onto the left wall and climb cracks which lead close to Nocando Crack; lasso the chokestone at the top of the flake and move back right, thin, into the summer route and follow it to the top.

35 The Demon 60m E2 (1983)

An intimidating route which climbs the steep section in the middle of the buttress. It starts under the arete of The Vicar and goes diagonally right to join a crack line which comes up from the base of the wall. Start just right of the toe of the arete.

1. 30m 5b Go up for 3m, then step left into a shallow groove and follow it to a roof. Traverse right under the roof, then go up slightly right into a thin crack, at the top of which is a cramped stance.

2. 30m 5a Climb up and right on steep layback flakes to enter the main crack system. Follow this to easy ground.

36 The Overseer Direct 70m V,6 (1983/1992)

A steep interesting line near the right edge of the buttress. Start at the foot of the Left Branch of Y Gully. Traverse left along a ledge (may bank out) and climb two consecutive steep corners to reach slabs. Climb direct to the base of a capped chimney. Pull out left and climb a vertical corner to easier ground.

The original version, which is somewhat easier, trends right after the corners to join Hoarmaster.

Route Major, Carn Etchachan (Climber, Grahame Nicoll)

37 The Hoarmaster 60m V,6 **   (1988)
The fine route which takes the square-cut chimney and crack above.
Start at the edge of the buttress and climb the chimney direct for the
first pitch and the fault above direct on the second.
    In summer this is a typical Cairngorm chimney, Severe.

38 Hooker's Corner 60m V,7   (1988)
This route takes the obvious open corner right of the buttress edge.
From the toe of the buttress, climb easily up just right of the corner.
Step across and climb the corner to its top. Finish as for The Hoarmas-
ter up the chimney fault.

39 Conundrum 50m V,7   (1990)
The bottomless groove system right of Hooker's Corner is very steep
but amenable. Start 5 metres right of the previous route but below the
bulging chimney (The Deviant).
1. 30m Move up left into an overhanging groove. With a high runner,
swing out left onto an obvious small ledge on the left arete. Move up to
a chokestone, then swing left again into a wide crack in the right-facing
corner. Go up this, then move back right and go up to a blocky ledge.
2. 20m Return left to the wide crack and follow it to the top.

40 The Deviant 50m IV,6   (1989)
The fault immediately left of Y Gully Left Branch. Start 5 metres right
of Hooker's Corner and climb a line of chimneys. Continue up until
overhanging walls force a traverse right into the main gully and a finish.

41 Left Branch Y Gully 100m III   (1952)
The wide gully between No.3 Buttress and the steep pillar. Start at the
top left of the large recess in the corner of the corrie. Climb up to a
belay right of the icicle. Surmount this (crux), then follow easier ground
to the top. May not be possible unless the icicle is well formed.

    A steep narrow pillar is the main feature of the recess, which bites
back into the plateau between No.3 and No.4 Buttresses. It rises
between the two branches of Y Gully and is sometimes referred to as
No.3½ Buttress.

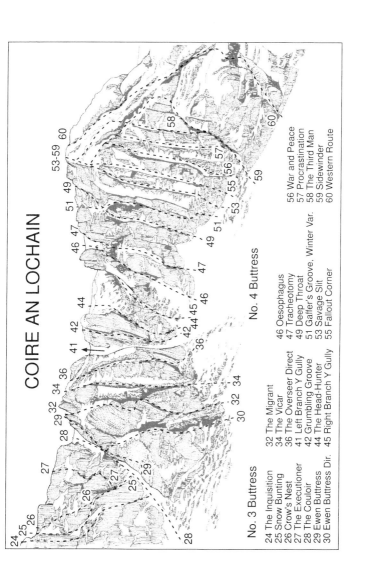

COIRE AN LOCHAIN

No. 3 Buttress

24 The Inquisition
25 Snow Bunting
26 Crow's Nest
27 The Executioner
28 The Couloir
29 Ewen Buttress
30 Ewen Buttress Dir.

32 The Migrant
34 The Vicar
36 The Overseer Direct
41 Left Branch Y Gully
42 Grumbling Groove
44 The Head-Hunter
45 Right Branch Y Gully

No. 4 Buttress

46 Oesophagus
47 Tracheotomy
49 Deep Throat
51 Gaffer's Groove, Winter Var.
53 Savage Slit
55 Fallout Corner

56 War and Peace
57 Procrastination
58 The Third Man
59 Sidewinder
60 Western Route

42 Grumbling Grooves 60m VI,6 *   (1983)
Climb the big groove on the left side of the pillar direct. In summer it is
Severe but loose in places.

43 Never Mind 60m HVS   (1969)
An interesting route up the front of the steep pillar. Start at the lowest
rocks.
1. 10m Scramble up to stance below a groove.
2. 30m 5a Move up and left to climb the left side of the pillar by a crack
in the pink wrinkled wall, which is the right side of a large groove
(Grumbling Groove), until delicate moves lead right into a wide crack
on the front. This leads up and left to a stance on the edge.
3. 20m 5a Go up the wide crack and the continuation corner until a
tension traverse allows a foothold on the lip of the roof on the right to
be gained. Move right, then climb up to the top.

44 The Head-hunter 60m VI,6   (1989)
This is the obvious large groove-ramp line which slants up the right
side of the pillar. Climb the groove to its top and finish by a choice of
lines.

45 Right Branch Y Gully 100m II *   (1934)
On the extreme right of No.4 Buttress, this wide high-angled gully is
generally without pitches, although the cornice can be large and
difficult to negotiate. It can hold a lot of ice in lean conditions.

NO.4 BUTTRESS

This is the largest and most important buttress. From its left side,
starting by the Right Branch of Y Gully, it shows a fine steep wall cut by
a series of compelling vertical lines of which the large central corner
of Savage Slit is unmistakable. On the right side the wall swings round
to form a longer but less steep face looking north. The obvious chimney
of Torquing Heads is a good landmark on this face. After the chimney,
the buttress degenerates into easier ground on the right where several
short Grade II routes can be found in winter.

   Right of the main buttress are several small buttresses and gullies
just below the plateau rim.

46 Oesophagus 70m III *   (1970)
About 10 metres right of the Right Branch is a groove which often holds
ice in quantity. Climb the groove into the upper snow amphitheatre, then
follow this to the top.

In summer this route is Severe; it starts up the initial groove and
finishes up a rotten gully.

47 Tracheotomy 80m VI,7   (1989)
The shallow groove line on the right side of the rib (Oesophagus is the
groove on the left of this rib).
1. 35m Climb the groove up and right to easier ground, which leads to
a large flake on the crest.
2. 45m Step back left into the groove and continue direct to the foot of
the final tower. Move left then back right to climb the crack in the tower
to the crest, and follow this to the top.

48 Puffer 70m Severe   (1969)
This climb takes a pinkish slab 25 metres left of Savage Slit. Start just
left of an overhanging crack in a corner. Climb the left edge of the slab,
move into the centre, then go up to and through an overhang at a gap
and go left to a stance. Climb the open corner above to finish. Wet,
loose and mossy.
Winter: V,6   (1989)
A line approximating to the summer route, but starting up a right-trending corner. This sometimes ices up and may well coincide with the route
Glottal Stop.

49 Deep Throat 70m V,6 **   (1989)
A good route up the wide crack through the stepped overhangs on the
left side of the pillar left of Gaffer's Groove.
1. 30m Climb a wide groove and move up to gain the crack. Follow this
over or round three roofs, then make a delicate traverse across the left
wall below a large roof to belay on a ledge left of a large chokestone.
2. 15m Regain the crack (Puffer goes up left) and follow it to the top of
the pillar.
3. 25m Climb the groove onto the crest and so to the top.

In summer this route is Very Difficult.

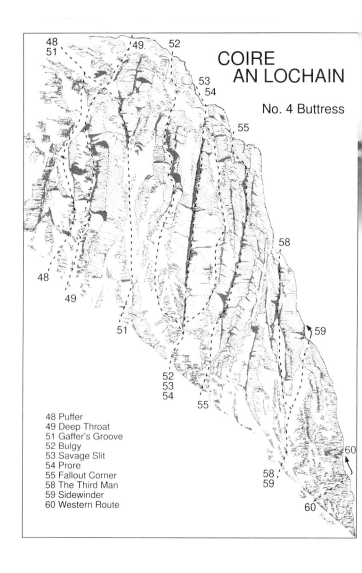

COIRE
AN LOCHAIN

No. 4 Buttress

48 Puffer
49 Deep Throat
51 Gaffer's Groove
52 Bulgy
53 Savage Slit
54 Prore
55 Fallout Corner
58 The Third Man
59 Sidewinder
60 Western Route

50 Aqualung 90m VI,7 (1993)
Another fine continuous line. Start just right of Deep Throat underneath a right-curving diedre.
1. 20m Climb into the curving diedre and follow it to the chimney of Gaffer's Groove.
2. 35m Follow the chimney to a step left to easy ground. Move back right into a steep groove and go up to a large roof.
3. 35m Turn the groove on the right by an awkward wide crack.

51 Gaffer's Groove 60m Severe (1963)
The line of disconnected grooves starting a few metres left of Savage Slit.
1. 20m Move up and traverse left into a large easy groove and climb it to a stance.
2. 15m Traverse left into a groove and climb this to a bulge; a good move leads left into the main groove.
3. 25m Climb the groove to its top, finishing by the more pleasant right wall. Scramble to the top.
Winter: VI,7
Follow the summer route throughout.
Winter variation: V,5 (1975)
This requires a good build-up of ice, but it is a natural winter line. Gain the main groove from below or by traversing from the right above the rectangular roof. Climb the groove and finish up the wide chimney left of the summer route.

52 Bulgy 80m Hard Severe (1968)
Climb the left arete of Savage Slit, and finish up a wide crack through the obvious twin roofs.
Winter: VII,7 (1988)
Follow the summer route, starting with a low traverse in from the foot of Savage Slit.

   When the Wind Blows (VI,7) follows Bulgy to the twin roofs, then works left to finish as for Gaffer's Groove summer route.

53 Savage Slit 70m Severe *** (1945)
This very fine climb up an impeccable line takes the wide crack in the big right-angled corner in the centre of the buttress. Start below the corner.

1. 10m Climb the obvious line to below the corner.
2. 25m Climb the wide crack between the blocky walls.
3. 20m Continue up the crack, or the wall on its right, to the top.
4. 15m Finish up a left-slanting gully and a short wall.
Winter: V,6 **   (1957)
Follow the summer route. It seldom holds ice in quantity because of the impressive depth of the slot. A technical route, which can be climbed both outside, and inside (without a rucksac).

54 Prore 90m VS *   (1969)
This route takes the obvious and spectacular curving arete right of Savage Slit after climbing the first pitch of that route and finishing up its last pitch.
Winter: VIII,8   (1992)
As for the summer route. The crux is moving up the wall near the arete after the initial traverse out right.

55 Fallout Corner 70m VS **   (1964)
An excellent climb up the impressive corner right of Savage Slit. Start below the corner.
1. 10m Go up to below the roof blocking the corner.
2. 30m 4b Cross the roof and climb the corner to its end.
3. 30m Continue in the same line, then scramble to the plateau.
Winter: VI,7 ***   (1985)
A fine, sustained, technical and well protected climb following the summer route.

56 War and Peace 70m HVS   (1968)
This route lies on the steep blocky wall right of Fallout Corner. Start at the leftmost of three corners 10 metres right of the previous route.
1. 20m 4c Climb the left corner to its top, then swing left.
2. 35m 5a Go left below a roof, then climb up above it. Go up under the narrow bulging chimney above, then move up a groove until one can go left under jutting blocks to belay above Fallout Corner.
3. 15m 5a Climb the left-slanting crack just on the right. A pitch of scrambling remains.
Winter: VII,8   (1992)
The initial corner was climbed to a roof at 10m, then thin moves right lead to a block on the arete and a belay below the overhanging wall. Climb the wall (the summer line is the crack to the left). Climb the bulging chimney and groove as for the summer line.

57 Procrastination 70m Severe   (1968)
Pleasantly steep, this route starts up the central and thinnest of three corners; the right-hand one is vegetated.
1. 10m Climb to the start of the corner.
2. 40m Go up the corner and turn a small roof on the right.
3. 20m Move back left and climb the continuation of the groove to a large ledge. Climb the wall above, scramble to above Savage Slit, then continue to the top.
Winter: VI,6   (1979)
Follow the summer line.

58 The Third Man 100m IV,6 *   (1983)
This independent version of what once was Sidewinder Direct offers interesting climbing. Start below the set of three corners as for Sidewinder. Climb the ramp running up right, gain the third corner, then climb it and the subsequent short wall to easier ground. Go up to cross Sidewinder and climb a shallow corner 10 metres right of Sidewinder chimney. Finish up the short wall of Savage Slit.

59 Sidewinder 100m III *   (1983)
This route climbs the buttress by a big zigzag. Start right of the three corners where a ramp leads round onto the frontal face. Climb the ramp line leading up and right onto the north face, then go up a short wall to easier ground. Climb a chimney on the left (the opposite side of Savage Slit) and squeeze through a gap to gain and finish up the top of Savage Slit.

60 Western Route 120m Severe   (1949)
This lies near the edge of the front face. Start near the left corner of the buttress. Climb the diagonal crack slanting right to a platform, then go up to a grassy recess. Climb the corner or the crack on its right. Follow the chimney with a smooth V-wall to easier climbing up the prominent final gully, finishing up flakes on the right wall.
Winter: V,6 **   (1959)
An excellent and sustained climb, following the summer route but taking the crack right of the corner on pitch 2.

61 Occidental Discovery 140m V,7   (1993)
A line up the front face which climbs through and to the left of Western Route. Start below the centre of the face.
1. 30m Take the left-trending easy line which leads to the platform on Western Route.

2. 15m Climb the steep corner for 3m, moving left at a flake, then an overhung niche. Exit from the niche by a fine corner to block belays.

3. 50m Step left and follow a right-trending line of turf to large ledges. Move left into a wide chimney-fault and continue on easier ground to below a steep groove in the final tower.

4. 30m Climb the rightmost and longest groove to belay at the top of Savage Slit.

5. 15m An easy gully leads to the top.

62 Torquing West 115m VII,7   (1992)
This route climbs the front face of the buttress right of Western Route. Start just left of Torquing Heads.

1. 15m Work up and left on ledges to the base of a short right-leaning corner. Climb this strenuously to the ledge above.

2. 15m Climb the steep wall above and right of the corner and pull strenuously into the easier-angled fault above.

3. 40m Continue up the fault, and where it leads into the top chimney of Western Route move right and belay below a steep band.

4. 25m Go right towards Torquing Heads, then climb blocks to a ledge leading precariously back left. Pull over a bulge and climb a short chimney to easier ground.

5. 20m Scramble to the top.

63 Torquing Heads 125m VI,6   (1986)
The prominent chimney-fault on the front face of No.4 Buttress. Climb the fault over a chokestone and a leaning wall (crux) to belay below a wide flake crack. Climb the crack and the bulging chimney above to easy ground and finish up the right of the steep upper buttress.

  Western Slant (120m, IV,4) starts at the right end of the crag and climbs the obvious short chimney visible up on the left. The route continues diagonally left to reach and finish up the gully fault of Western Route.

  No.4 Buttress is girdled by **Transformer** (90m, VS) which starts up Gaffer's Groove and follows the obvious horizontal break right to finish up Western Route.

BYNACK MORE
1090m (Map Ref 042 064)

In Coire Dearg (Map Ref 032 067) on the west flank overlooking Strath Nethy there are some short indefinite buttresses and easy snow climbs, the best being the centrally placed Y-shaped gully.

About 1km south-east of the summit of Bynack More there is a collection of massive granite tors known as the Barns of Bynack. Although impressive in appearance, the climbing is either fairly easy or up some painfully rough cracks. Most of the open faces would appear to be singularly lacking in protection and holds.

MINOR CRAGS AND OUTLYING AREAS

There are short routes to be found on the north-east side of the Chalamain Gap (Map Ref 965 053). These are generally of moderate difficulty on good rock on a series of well defined little buttresses. Much more accessible but of much poorer quality and shorter are the climbs on Cranberry Rocks (Map Ref 001 069), the small outcrop at the outlet of Coire na Ciste just above the car park.

The Loch Avon Basin

Loch Avon (sometimes spelt A'an and always prounounced that way!) lies at 730m in the heart of the northern Cairngorms, entrenched between Cairngorm, Ben Macdui and Beinn Mheadhoin. At its head a superb arc of cliffs cluster round its main feeder streams, the Garbh Uisge, Feith Buidhe and the Allt a' Coire Domhain. Dominating this scene is the spectacular square-topped Shelter Stone Crag, and on its left the sharp and pointed Carn Etchachan. With a height of 280m, these are the biggest cliffs in the area.

The horseshoe extends from the Beinn Mheadhoin — Carn Etchachan col to Coire Raibert. The main easings in this line of cliffs are where the Garbh Uisge and Feith Buidhe cascade from the plateau over a series of glaciated steps, alongside the Allt a' Coire Domhain and by the Allt a' Coire Raibert. These breaks give the normal access routes into the basin.

At its south-western end, Carn Etchachan neighbours Shelter Stone Crag after which is the smaller and more broken Garbh Uisge Crag. At the western and head end of the horseshoe is an area of water-washed and glaciated slabs down which the Garbh Uisge and Feith Buidhe make their way. East of the latter is the flat-faced Hell's Lum Crag which runs round to Coire Domhain. Between these and Allt a' Coire Raibert, Stag Rocks forms the horseshoe's right leg. Still on the north side of the loch, but lying below Cairn Gorm, is a line of glaciated slabs just beneath Stac an Fharaidh. After these, the plateau swings round above The Saddle and into Strath Nethy. On the south side, Beinn Mheadhoin has its own cliff at Stacan Dubha just east of the col by Loch Etchachan. These cliffs look promising from a distance but are less satisfactory on closer acquaintance.

At the foot of Shelter Stone Crag is the Clach Dhian or Shelter Stone, which provides a climbing base under one of the many huge boulders that have sloughed off the crag at some time in the distant past. Also amongst these boulders are several other howffs which, although smaller, may provide more savoury accommodation than the Shelter Stone itself. At the head of the loch and along the banks of the inlet streams are several good camp sites.

Approaches
There are many ways to approach the Shelter Stone and the cliffs of the Loch Avon basin. From the north, the plateau can be gained in a

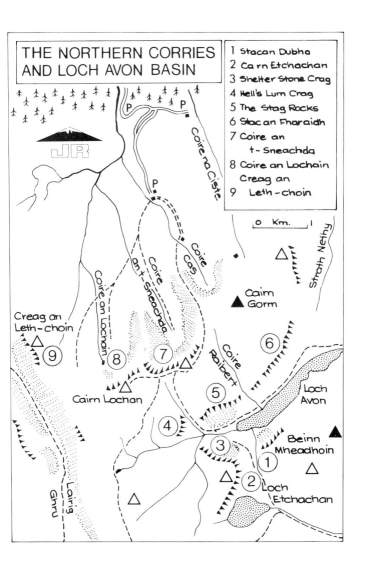

THE NORTHERN CORRIES
AND LOCH AVON BASIN

1 Stacan Dubha
2 Carn Etchachan
3 Shelter Stone Crag
4 Hell's Lum Crag
5 The Stag Rocks
6 Stac an Fharaidh
7 Coire an
   t-Sneachda
8 Coire an Lochain
   Creag an
9 Leth-choin

JR

Coire na Ciste

0 Km. 1

Strath Nethy

Coire Cas

Coire an t-Sneachda

Cairn Gorm

Creag an Leth-choin
⑨

Coire an Lochain
⑧

⑦

Coire Raibert

⑤

⑥

Loch Avon

Cairn Lochan

Hell's Lum
④

Stac an Fharaidh

③

Beinn Mheadhoin
①

②

Loch Etchachan

Lairig Ghru

variety of ways. From the top of the chair lift, go over or round Cairn Gorm. From the Coire Cas carpark, follow the tracks up and into Coire Cas and take the good path up the Fiacaill a' Choire Chais. The Fiacaill a' Choire an t-Sneachda or the Goat Track in Coire an t-Sneachda lead to the head of Coire Domhain. Alternatively, walk into Coire an Lochain, then ascend to the plateau from the corrie or by the ridge on its west. From the plateau, the main descents are down the shoulder overlooking The Saddle at the east end, down Coire Raibert in the centre and down Coire Domhain in the west. Diagonal Gully or the unnamed Y-shaped gully to its west give quick access to Stag Rocks for competent parties.

From the south, a good path leads from Loch Etchachan down by the Allt nan Stacan Dubha which runs north into the head of the loch. A scrambling descent exists on the east bank of the Garbh Uisge and interesting ways up and down can be found on the slabs at the south-west end of the loch.

Accommodation

The most convenient centre for accommodation in this area is Aviemore, which lies on the main railway and just off the A9 between Perth and Inverness. Public transport to Aviemore, both bus and train, is regular and convenient. From the village, further bus services run up to the Coire Cas car park, the most convenient access point for most of this area. This bus service is more regular in the winter, but the ski road is popular with tourists and taxis are readily available in Aviemore. Above the car park, the two stages of the chair lift can be worthwhile for the time and effort they save on certain approaches. The top chair lift is particularly handy, but there can be long queues during peak skiing periods and it does not operate in high winds.

Aviemore and Strathspey provide a wide range of accommodation from hotels and chalets to caravans and hostels, but last minute bookings may be difficult at the height of the tourist and ski seasons. There are youth hostels at Aviemore and Loch Morlich, 9km up the Coire Cas ski road. Camping is not permitted in the Rothiemurchus or Glen More forests, but there is an official site at Loch Morlich. Camping in the mountains is generally unrestricted at most times of the year, although this is affected by stalking and is not recommended in the winter when the weather can be Arctic. There are several bothies in the area which can be used as climbing bases:

Ryvoan (Map Ref 006 114). This bothy is situated on the track between Glen More and Nethy Bridge about 3km from Glen More. A well built stone cottage, it is generally in good order but a bit out of the way for most of the cliffs.

Nethy Bothy (Map Ref 020 105). Situated at the head of Strath Nethy on the track from Glen More over Bynack More, this rather unsavoury corrugated iron shed is well away from the climbing areas.

Fords of Avon Refuge (Map Ref 032 042). A small refuge of wood and stone situated on the north bank of the River Avon where the Lairig an Laoigh track fords it, but again it is too far from most cliffs to be useful.

Shelter Stone (Map Ref 001 016). Situated under Shelter Stone Crag, there is a cave under a large boulder which provides shelter. This boulder has several paths converging on it, a cairn on its top and a distinctive pink scar on its downhill side. There are also in the area several other howffs in the jumble of boulders below the cliff many of which are cleaner and more pleasant than the Shelter Stone itself. In winter however, they may fill up with snow and be difficult to find. There are several good camp sites on the valley floor.

Hutchison Memorial Hut (Map Ref 024 998). An open bothy situated in Coire Etchachan makes a reasonably convenient base for climbing on the cliffs at the head of Loch Avon, but it is normally approached from the south. Although in a fine location, the hut is somewhat spartan, especially in winter.

STACAN DUBHA

(Map Ref 013 017)

These crags, situated to the east of the Beinn Mheadhoin–Carn Etchachan col, look quite good from a distance but are disappointing on closer acquaintance. They are broken, consisting of many short ribs and buttresses which from further away give the impression of much more continuous rock than actually is found. The rock itself is poor in places. There are several winter routes, but they generally lack continuity. The crag also has long approaches, which tends to deter most except the hardiest of explorers and seekers of the esoteric.

Zigzag 140m Very Difficult   (1969)
This route lies on the obvious slab at the left side; a bit wet and vegetated. Start below a large overlap.
1. and 2. 80m Climb slabs trending left across the overlap.
3. 30m Climb slabs, still going left, to a rib.
4. 30m Climb the rib.

The Shuttle   100m   Very Difficult   (1957)
The highest and most prominent buttress starts with a detached
section of cracked slabs, followed by a chimney on the right of a terrace.
Above, climb the buttress with deviations on the right.

Ribbon Ridge   120m   Moderate   (1954)
At the eastern end of the crag lies a rib above a chute of red screes
and between deep gullies. The rock requires careful handling.

In the centre of the crag is a triangular buttress flanked by gullies
which join below the plateau. The right-hand one is on the left of a deep
fault capped by a chokestone and is Grade III; the left-hand gully is
Grade II. The right side of the big buttress on the left is Grade IV.

CARN ETCHACHAN
1120m (Map Ref 003 012)

This great pointed crag has two distinct faces; the Main Face which
looks north over the head of Loch Avon, and the Gully Face which drops
into Castlegates Gully. The Main Face is cut at about mid-height by The
Great Terrace, which can be reached and followed from the Beinn
Mheadhoin col until it vanishes near the junction with the Gully Face.
Above and below the terrace, the face has differing aspects. The Upper
Cliff, which holds the majority of the routes, is a complex area of steep
towers, ribs, chimneys and cracks. These rise to 100m in height and
give the best rock climbing on the crag. The Lower Cliff is more open
and slabby and scored by several left-leaning ramps, the largest of
which near the right-hand end is the Diagonal Shelf. This is a grassy
slope or a snow field depending on the season. Some of the routes in
this area climb the full height of the cliff.
The crags above Loch Etchachan are indefinite and provide poor
rock climbing. The smaller, isolated buttress on the south side of the
loch provides short problems up to 25m. The only recorded climb is
Lochside Chimney (Difficult, Grade III), in the centre of the east-facing
crag. The short and deep gully right of this crag is Grade I.

THE UPPER CLIFF, MAIN FACE

This complicated face gives some good routes and fine pitches, but it
has a gloomy appearance. The rock is fairly quick drying in spite of its

northerly aspect, but the climbs towards the right-hand side are fairly vegetated.

Passing along The Great Terrace from the Beinn Mheadhoin col and Loch Etchachan, the first main buttress houses Crevasse Route; a large diagonal ramp marks its left side. Next comes the obvious gully-fault of Equinox with a steep, square-cut tower on its right. To the right of this tower is an upper amphitheatre whose left wall is cut by the prominent final crack of Boa. Next is the square pink spur of Python, and where it meets the face on the right is the corner crack of Nom de Plume. Right of this is the long slanting chimney of Pagan Slit, then a more broken spur of pinkish rock. This area of pink rock, the larger of the two, provides a reasonable landmark on the left side of the main Battlements groove.

The Great Terrace merges into the face about this area, but ledges trend up to the large V-groove of the Battlements. This climb, once located, provides a convenient means of descent to the routes. Its top is situated close to a rock window near the highest part of the crag. From the top of the cliff, the return down to Loch Etchachan can involve awkward route finding and scrambling because of the slabs and outcrops which litter the hillside. The descent down the county boundary from the actual summit is the easiest line.

1 Inside Edge 75m V,6   (1987)
This route takes the wide sloping shelf on the left edge of the buttress. Start just right of the mid-line, as for Crevasse Route. Climb steep rock to a rock crevasse (20m). Continue up for 20m, move into a corner on the right and climb to a large leaning block at the foot of the wide shelf. Follow the shelf on the left, entering a chimney at mid-height, to a small overhang. Surmount the overhang and traverse left to the extreme edge of the buttress. Climb this with difficulty to a large ledge, then finish up easy ground.

In summer this route is Severe, and was originally a variation finish to Crevasse Route. An independent first pitch climbs cracks direct to the start of the shelf at about VS.

2 Crevasse Route 75m Mild Severe **   (1955)
A charming and exhilarating route on the first main buttress that is characterised by a rock window which is well seen from the Beinn Mheadhoin col. Start from the lowest rocks in the centre of the buttress. Climb steep rock just right of the mid-line to a rock crevasse (20m).

Continue up for 20m, move right into a corner on the right and climb a large leaning block. Layback the overhanging curving crack above (crux), then step left and climb huge flakes to a crevasse. A queer contorted chimney exits through a hole to a fine eyrie. Climb the first crack above for 25m, veering right at the top up a nose to the true finish of the buttress.
Winter: V,6 *   (1981)
Follow the summer route.

3 Poison Dwarf 75m E1 *   (1978)
A good route which reaches the rock window from the right-hand side. Start about 5m up the gully of Equinox.
1. 35m 5a Climb the left-sloping overhung ramp until a ledge on the left can be gained. Climb the corner above to a ledge.
2. 15m 5b Climb the wide crack above to the rock window.
3. 25m 4c Go up the wide groove above to a recess, then use a large flake to gain the arete on the right and follow it to the top.

4 The Poison Trail 100m V,6   (1979)
A counter-diagonal to Crevasse Route. Climb the first pitch of Poison Dwarf, using tension to gain the upper corner. Traverse left under the contorted chimney of Crevasse Route and continue left on ramps to easier ground.

5 Time Traveller 80m HVS *   (1978)
A good route following the thin crack system high on the right wall of the buttress. Start at the foot of the Equinox gully.
1. 30m Climb the gully to a huge block.
2. 15m 5a Step left and go up the groove and crack to a ledge. Alternatively, climb the flake crack as for the winter route.
3. 25m 5a Continue up the crack system.
4. 10m Finish *via* the short corner.
Winter: VII,7   (1987)
Climb Equinox to just above the first chimney. Chimney up to gain a ramp on the left wall which leads to a fine flake crack above a roof. Climb this (1 rest), then continue up the wall above and go over a final bulge to a small ledge. Continue up the crack (as in summer) and a gradual easing in difficulties.

6 Solstice 90m VI,8   (1992)
This climb takes the crack line between Time Traveller and Equinox.
Start about 10 metres right of Equinox.
1. 35m Climb a turfy fault to a huge ledge. Go left to belay on Equinox.
2. 20m Climb the crack line with a very thin start, then sustained
climbing leads to a ledge.
3. 35m Continue more easily up the crack line, then step right and go
up a corner leading to steep snow and the cornice.

7 Equinox 75m VS   (1954)
The gully line on the right of the first main buttress; often greasy. Climb
the main gully line, then shelving slabs on the right of the groove. Where
this steepens, traverse back into the gully. Climb a vertical corner on
the right and continue direct to an obvious chimney with a constricted
top. Climb this to a ledge the finish up the chimney on the left.
Winter: VI,6 *   (1981)
A good winter climb following the summer line.

   Apogee (90m V,7) takes the right side of the Equinox recess the
whole way. It starts as for Solstice and shares sections with Equinox.

8 Pythagoras 90m VS   (1978)
A route on the left wall of the upper amphitheatre on the right of the
Equinox gully. Poor lower pitches lead to an excellent upper section.
Start left of the pink spur of Python.
1. 30m Follow a grassy groove leading left to where it splits.
2. 30m Continue up right-facing corners and pass right of a huge flake
to a large platform below the final wall.
3. 20m 4c Climb the fine crack until it ends, then traverse left to an
exposed stance on the buttress edge.
4. 10m Go up the left-slanting groove until it is possible to move right
and so to the top.
Winter: VI,7   (1986)
A winter ascent based on the summer route. Climb the summer route
to below the final wall, where corners formed by its base lead rightwards to a large platform. Climb the fine crack to where it bends right,
and climb the wall on the left to the exposed stance. A rising rightwards
traverse then leads round a slight edge to the finish.

9 Boa 60m Severe   (1954)
The main feature of this route is the superb crack in the left wall of the
upper amphitheatre. Start below the amphitheatre left of the pink spur
of Python. Zigzag easily to the foot of a wide chimney on the immediate
left of the Python spur. Slant left by ledges and corners to easier ground
in the upper amphitheatre. Move left and climb the wide crack passing
a hanging chokestone about 20m up. A fine exposed pitch.
Winter: VI,6   (1981)
A different start was taken to gain the upper crack. Start up ledges left
of the summer route, leading past a perched block to a belay in a corner.
A corner crack on the right rib of the corner leads to the summer line;
follow this to the top.

10 The Guillotine 75m Mild Severe   (1955)
An interesting route with the crux right at the top. Start as for Boa.
Zigzag to the foot of the wide chimney, climb it direct and continue into
the amphitheatre. Take the second chimney on the right which cuts
deeply into the spur and passes below a huge blade of rock. Exit by a
tunnel roofed with blocks to the platform on the spur. Climb the chimney
above with an overhang at the top (crux).
Winter: V,6 **   (1979)
Follow the summer route throughout; a good and interesting climb.

11 Python 75m VS   (1954)
This takes the pink spur in the centre of the Upper Face. Start at the
right side of the spur below a huge flake high on the face.
1. 10m Climb a wide crack in the red rocks to a ledge.
2. 25m 4c Climb the corner, then curve up and left to a ledge on top
of the great flake.
3. and 4. 40m Walk left to the left side of the spur and climb the first
chimney to a platform and finish up the chimney above as for The
Guillotine.
Winter: V,6   (1981)
Sustained and technical climbing following the summer route.

12 Snakebite 100m HVS   (1990)
A direct version of Python taking the corner left of Nom de Plume and
inset in the right of the pillar containing Python. Start just left of Nom
de Plume.

1. 40m 4c Follow Python to the top of the great flake.
2. 35m 4c Traverse right along horizontal cracks in the vertical wall, then continue up the corner to the ledge below the final chimney of The Guillotine.
3. 25m 5b Climb the rib on the right of the chimney, including a short overhanging crack.
Winter: V,7 *   (1990)
Climb the summer route to below the Python/Guillotine chimney. Descend Nom de Plume a short way, then finish up right by mixed ground (sometimes an icefall).

13 Nom de Plume 75m VS   (1956)
The chimney-crack in the corner formed by the right side of the Python spur. Follow the chimney line until near the top to a huge diamond-shaped block. Pass this on the left wall to a platform and finish up the final pitch of Python.
Winter: VI,7   (1982)
Steep and strenuous by the summer line. Finishing by Snakebite is also logical.

14 Pagan Slit 75m Hard Severe   (1955)
Between the spur of Python and the next rocks is a prominent right-slanting chimney which gives the line of the route. It is broken by several ledges and is somewhat vegetated.
Winter: V,5   (1980)
Climb the initial section on the right, thereafter follow the summer route.

15 The Hairpin Loop 110m V,6   (1982)
A route on the wall right of Pagan Slit. Start 35 metres right of Pagan Slit at a left-slanting fault. Follow the fault and exit right onto a large ledge. Go up and right to a triangular recess, then traverse back left about 10m above the belay until it is possible to go up then right to the crest overlooking The Battlements groove. A short crack now leads left to easier ground and the top.
Variation:
Avoid the loop by climbing directly up grooves to gain the rib; better than the ordinary route.

16 The Battlements 120m Moderate   (1954)
Once located, this route provides a handy descent to reach the climbs
on the Upper Cliff. Near the right end of the Great Terrace the cliff
becomes more broken. From near the end of the terrace, ledges trend
naturally up to a large V-groove; climb this on its right wall. The long
pink streak on the rock is to the left of this groove. Above, easier
climbing leads left then right to finish near the top of Carn Etchachan
by a rock window.

THE LOWER CLIFF, MAIN FACE

The face below The Great Terrace is open and characterised by several
left-slanting ramp lines, the largest of which by far is the Diagonal Shelf.
Right of this in a huge bay is the big chimney of Red Guard, which
marks the junction with the Gully Face.

17 Eastern Approach Route 100m Difficult   (1955)
Near the left end of the crag is right-slanting slanting fault line consist-
ing of a number of short pitches and vegetation.
Winter: IV,5   (1979)
Follow the summer line.

18 The Silent Approach 110m IV,6   (1989)
This right-slanting line, parallel to Eastern Approach Route, crosses
Western Approach Route and finishes in the trough below The Guillo-
tine.

19 Western Approach Route 110m III *   (1989)
A series of left-slanting ramps lead to The Great Terrace near the start
of Equinox. Start left of the lowest point of the buttress, left of a mound
of huge blocks and climb the three narrow ramps and a short chimney.

20 The Crystal Maze 160m VI,7   (1994)
This route takes a line crossing the Diagonal Shelf to end on the
Terrace. There is a choice of starts which lead to a prominent corner
system on the steep wall left of the snow basin of Route Major. Start
just left of the Diagonal Shelf and climb a slab slanting left into the base
of a big groove topped by overhangs (25m). From near the base of the
groove, climb a turfy crack up the steep wall on the right, then go left
up a slabby corner to the Diagonal Shelf (45m). Traverse the shelf until
below the big groove (20m). Climb the corner direct in two pitches to
the Terrace.

CARN ETCHACHAN

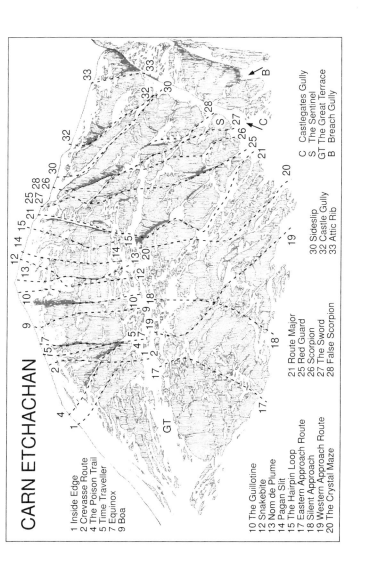

1 Inside Edge
2 Crevasse Route
4 The Poison Trail
5 Time Traveller
7 Equinox
9 Boa

10 The Guillotine
12 Snakebite
13 Nom de Plume
14 Pagan Slit
15 The Hairpin Loop
17 Eastern Approach Route
18 Silent Approach
19 Western Approach Route
20 The Crystal Maze

21 Route Major
25 Red Guard
26 Scorpion
27 The Sword
28 False Scorpion

30 Sideslip
32 Castle Gully
33 Attic Rib

C Castlegates Gully
S The Sentinel
GT The Great Terrace
B Breach Gully

Variation Start:
A more direct start up a shallow gully (often icy) on the left leads to the shared belay at the base of the groove (25m). A line of corners to the right of the turfy crack leads to the Diagonal Shelf, then to the base of the big corner.

21 Route Major 285m IV,5 ***   (1957)
A long climb with complex route finding; a classic Cairngorm winter route with good situations. It starts at the Diagonal Shelf and uses The Battlements in its upper section. Climb easily up the Diagonal Shelf for about two pitches until it is possible to move up and right on a ramp to reach a snow basin. Exit from the basin by the obvious tapered chimney, moving left where it constricts. Another ramp now leads to more broken ground. Go diagonally right for two pitches to the deep V-groove of The Battlements (this is difficult to see from below but lies to the right of the long pink streak on the rock). Follow the groove, steep at first, to a bend and continue up and left more easily. Now take a chimney leading up right to finish.
Variation:
The initial snow basin can be reached by climbing the narrow ramp lines leading left from the foot of Red Guard. More interesting than the normal start.

22 The Winter Palace 120m V,7
The fault in the steep wall about 10 metres left of Bastille crux. Climb the variation start to Route Major (as for Bastille in winter) (75m). The fault bulges and slants left at the start; next is a boulder problem overhang (25m). The fault continues steep and flaky and slants right to The Great Terrace (20m).

23 Bastille 285m VS   (1978)
This route keeps close to the left arete of Red Guard, then continues up the prominent two-tier corner above. The lower pitches, which are good in dry conditions, can be used to reach the Upper Cliff. Start at the foot of the ramp of Route Major.
1. 45m Climb a short corner to a higher ramp, continue up and right to the edge overlooking Red Guard, then go up and left to belay.
2. 40m Climb cracks close to the right edge, then follow a left-slanting groove to a grassy bay.

3. 20m 5a Go up right over a chokestone, then move left to the foot of a two-tiered corner. Climb the lower one with an awkward exit left.

4. 25m 5a Climb the second corner or, if wet, step round the left arete, climb a short groove, exiting on the right to a ledge system.

5. and 6. 80m Trend slightly right to land on a ramp at the point where Red Guard breaks off.

7. 30m Move left, then go up to the prominent collar-shaped overhang. Climb this by the central crack, then continue up the crack.

8. 45m Easy climbing leads to the top.

Winter: V,7   (1982)
Start as for the summer route but climb a shallow groove, then a well defined easier groove which slants left into the bay of Route Major. Move right and climb the two-tiered corner (Friend 3 for aid). Above The Great Terrace, a right-trending line of ledges and short chimneys leads past the top end of the ramp of The Sword.

24 The Kremlin 260m V,7   (1986)
Start 10 metres left of Red Guard and climb steep steps right, then follow a groove to a terrace. Ascend steep turfy cracks above. Follow the continuing weakness up the wall to the left of the arete to a bay. Belay on the right below a steep wall on top of the arete. Climb a steep crack with a block at half-height to a niche. Traverse right into an easier groove to reach The Great Terrace. Move up left and crawl under a chokestone. Follow the right-slanting groove to join Red Guard or Route Major.

The previous two routes could be combined to give an ascent of the Bastille summer line all the way.

THE GULLY FACE

This face starts where the cliff bends round to overlook Castlegates Gully. The Great Terrace fades out just as the Gully Face is reached. Near the bottom of this face is the deep chokestone-filled chimney of Red Guard, then comes a prominent vertical triangular wall about 15m high. This is the Sentinel, which marks the start of the gully proper. Continuing up Castlegates Gully, first is the wide broken fault of False Scorpion, then the large buttress distinguished by a great pink ramp formed by a huge rockfall scar. On its right is the fault of Castle Gully, after which the cliff diminishes in height.

The rock on this face is generally inferior to that on the Main Face. Much is vegetated and some is loose. However, in winter this face comes into its own with a fine selection of long and interesting climbs. These are often in condition and are of good quality.

25 Red Guard 250m Severe   (1977)
Follows a natural line the full height of the cliff. Start below the obvious block-filled chimney just above the Diagonal Shelf. Enter the gully and climb cracked slabs on the left to below a steep blank wall. On the left margin the obvious chimney gives excellent climbing, including two through-routes to land in a grassy bay. The continuation groove looks dirty, so move down and right into an exposed groove. Follow this, which becomes more broken, to a ledge system traversing the cliff. Ahead is a steep cracked wall forming the left flank of a clean and wide cracked pink shelf. Scramble rightwards along the ledge to reach the shelf. Climb this as far as a short corner on the right-hand side, leading to a balcony stance atop the prominent square-cut overhang. Easier progress can now be made as the cliff tilts back to meet the plateau.
Winter: VI,6 **   (1978)
An excellent and interesting route. Above the deep chimney, follow the dirty continuation groove to ledges, then go right for 10 metres and follow the left-rising ramp and open corner to a small bay. Traverse left to a line of weakness which leads right to an open groove above; follow this to the top.

26 Scorpion 240m V,5 ***   (1952)
This classic route, aptly named, takes a line near the boundary of the Main and Gully Faces before finishing up the huge square-shaped fault. Start about 15m below the Sentinel, mid-way between it and the initial chimney of Red Guard. Climb a steep corner left of a V-groove and, at about 20m, continue left for 10 metres to below a steep wall. This is cut by a slanting crack which is difficult to find. Enter the subterranean crack (harder on the outside), then from its exit climb an overhung wall on the immediate right on good holds. Go round a corner to the right and move up in a left-trending line to cross left over a slab by a crack in its lower margin. The next pitch is obvious to below the upper fault. A long chimney below a leaning wall leads back right into the main fault which is climbed to the top. It may contain several ice pitches and be heavily corniced.
    In summer this route is Very Difficult and has a fair variety of pitches.

27 The Sword 285m V,5 *   (1978)
A good sustained route, initially climbing the buttress overlooking False
Scorpion then finishing by a ramp on the upper buttress. Start at an
open groove on the left of the Sentinel. Climb the groove and continue
up the buttress above the Sentinel, first by a open groove, then by short
walls (50m). Go diagonally left on ramps and up short steps to reach
an area of ledges (50m). Go a short way up the chimney of Scorpion,
then gain and follow the ramp leading up left (the summer ramp of Red
Guard). At its top, climb the steps and the corner system to the final
slopes.

28 False Scorpion 240m V,5   (1970)
The main fault, which starts just inside Castlegates Gully above the
Sentinel, usually holds more ice but has less variety than Scorpion.
Climb the main fault, keeping to the left to reach the main gully above
a narrower and steeper section. Finish as for Scorpion.
   In summer it is a loose and unpleasant Very Difficult.

29 Siberia 210m IV,5   (1979)
The main feature of this climb is the hanging gully right of the Scorpion
fault. It is reached by following the bottom edge of the pink-scarred
buttress. Start below this buttress. Follow ramps easily up and left for
two pitches to below the first steepening. Go right and climb ramps,
which lead left and overlook the main fault, to reach a *cul de sac* level
with two large blocks on the right skyline. Move onto the rib on the right
and descend to gain a groove which leads to the hanging gully. This
funnel-shaped fault leads to the plateau. Needs a good build-up.

30 Sideslip 150m III *   (1975)
This takes the pink rockfall scar and hanging gully on the left of the
buttress. Climb the ramp to its top, go round the corner and traverse
left into the foot of the gully. Climb this to the top (as for Siberia).

31 Revelation Arete 140m V,6   (1988)
The arete left of Castle Gully. Start about 10m up the big ramp of
Sideslip. Climb the wall to a small ramp which leads left to an awkward
exit onto slabs. Go diagonally right to below a steepening. Return
diagonally left to the crest at a small pinnacle. An exposed groove just
left of the crest leads back to a flake on the crest. A short easy pitch
finishes the route.

32 Castle Gully 150m III   (1964)
The gully on the right of the pink-scarred buttress. The lower section is
open and slabby but becomes more defined towards its top. An
alternative start lies further right and comes in along an obvious snow
ledge.

   In summer this route is Very Difficult, but it keeps more to the crest
on the left in the top section.

33 Attic Rib 100m II/III   (1977)
This lies to the right of Castle Gully. Start left up a ramp, then move
right and go up a short step to gain the left side of the arete. Follow this
to the top. Graded as a pure snow arete; it is harder under powder.

SHELTER STONE CRAG
(Map Ref 001 013)

This 270m high cliff, with its distinctive flat top, is one of the most
impressive in the Cairngorms. Sometimes known as the Sticil, it thrusts
out boldly between Castlegates Gully on the left and Pinnacle Gully on
the right; these are fairly unpleasant scree-filled scrambles in summer
and simple Grade I climbs in winter. The crag consists of a main north
face and two lesser triangular faces which overlook these gullies.

   Although at first sight the crag appears as a great unbroken tower of
granite, there are several well defined and distinct features. Starting in
Castlegates Gully is the rib of Castle Wall, separated from the tapering
tower of Raeburn's Buttress by the curved fault of Breach Gully.

   Right of Raeburn's Buttress and left of the chimney line of The Citadel
is the impressive and near flawless area of boiler-plate slabs set in the
middle of the cliff between the Low and the High Ledges, two distinctive
vegetated horizontal breaks. These are the Central Slabs.

   Right again is the Main Bastion, where the cliff is at its highest,
steepest and most continuous and some superb long climbs are to be
found. This part of the crag fades out in the region of Clach Dhian
Chimney, the obvious fault near the right side of the crag. After this, the
face takes a turn to overlook Pinnacle Gully and diminishes in height
and quality.

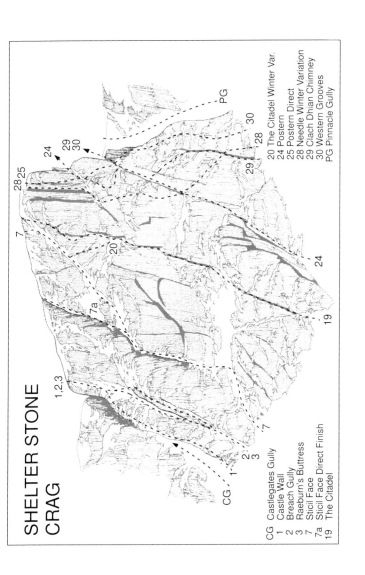

SHELTER STONE CRAG

CG Castlegates Gully
1   Castle Wall
2   Breach Gully
3   Raeburn's Buttress
7   Sticil Face
7a Sticil Face Direct Finish
19 The Citadel

20 The Citadel Winter Var.
24 Postern
25 Postern Direct
28 Needle Winter Variation
29 Clach Dhian Chimney
30 Western Grooves
PG Pinnacle Gully

1 Castle Wall 210m III *   (1970)
This is the initially well defined arete which starts near the foot of
Castlegates Gully. Follow the ridge throughout, the lower 90m being
the most difficult. Above, the ridge merges into the upper rocks and
gives interesting climbing with fine situations. In summer it is Difficult
with much scrambling.

2 Breach Gully 240m IV,5   (1977)
The prominent gully between Castle Wall and Raeburn's Buttress. Pass
the very blank steep section at about 20m above the initial snow bay
on the right and regain the gully above. A through route followed by a
traverse right leads to the upper couloir which leads more easily to the
plateau. The route can occasionally be all ice, when it will be IV,4.

3 Raeburn's Buttress 240m IV,5   (1971)
This route takes the left side of the tower-like buttress; the difficulties
ease with height. Start in the deep bay on the left. Traverse right to follow
a line slanting slightly right for a pitch. Go diagonally left to gain then
follow the main vegetated fault which leads to a deep narrow chimney.
Climb this or its right rib to the shoulder at the top of the buttress. Climb
the line on the left of the buttress to the top.
   In summer the route is Severe, vegetated and dangerous.

4 Pointlace 250m E3   (1986)
A direct line up the buttress left of Consolation Groove. Start 3m up left
from the lowest point of the buttress.
1. 45m 5b Move up then right to climb a waterworn groove-flange to
ledges, then step up right and using a crack move across to the right
and go up to a ledge. Continue up cracks in the blunt arete to a small
triangular niche.
2. 45m 5c Move up onto the arete and follow this to climb twin cracks
up a steepening, then pull out right to cross a groove and reach a loose
block. Continue up right a short way until it is possible to step left just
below a tiny overlap to a crack. Climb the crack in the slab to where it
blanks out and make a move up and left to a grass ledge. Step back
right and climb the slab to another grass ledge.
3. 30m 5b Continue directly above to follow a fault line and crack to
below a small roof. Pull right over the roof to grassy ledges, then move
up left to higher ledges.

4. 30m 5c Step left, climb a flake and continue up a right-trending groove until beneath the left end on the obvious long roof. Traverse right under the roof to surmount it at its mid-point and continue up to the wall just above.
5. and 6. 100m Gain grassy ledges above and continue to the upper part of the buttress. Climb this easily by cracks and grooves in the crest.

5 Consolation Groove 150m HVS   (1969)
A worthwhile route which takes the groove line on the crest of Raeburn's Buttress. Start at the right side of the buttress.
1. 20m Climb the groove and break left to a grass ledge.
2. 30m 5a Step right onto the slab and go up to an overhang. Traverse right under it and continue traversing until moves up and right lead to ledges (poorly protected). Go up and return left to a steep groove.
3. 25m 4c Climb the groove to a ledge.
4. 35m 5a Continue up the groove system to a grassy ledge.
5. 15m Scramble up to the foot of a wall with a long overhang.
6. 25m 4c Climb a crack at the right end of the overhang and go up to a large ledge. Move left and up to easy ground. Scramble to the top.
Winter: VI,7   (1987)
Only constructed loosely round the summer line. Start up Raeburn's Buttress. Just above where it traverses left, and below a steep blind groove, make a diagonal abseil right back to the summer line and reach it just right of a small pinnacle. Continue up to the long overhang where a chimney on the left leads to the large terrace. Finish without difficulty on the left of the upper buttress.

6 Rib Tickler 150m E2 **   (1991)
This route takes a groove system right of Consolation Groove. Start by scrambling a short way up the grass leading to the Low Ledge until an unusual flake column is seen on the left below the shallow groove of Threadbare.
1. 20m 5a Climb past the flake to a groove curving up left. Climb clean rock to the left of this vegetated groove. Break back right onto a short rib leading to a grassy ledge.
2. 40m 5b Climb straight up a blocky rib just left of the main groove system to a block. Move into the groove and follow it until below a short overhanging section, well seen from below.

3. 25m 5b Above the overhang the line curves leftwards into Consolation Groove. Quit it before this and follow flake cracks right to overlook
Threadbare and climb a groove in the crest overlooking it.
4. 15m 5b Go up the easy corner to a ledge, then climb a blocky
overhanging groove to below the roofed corners of Threadbare.
5. 25m 5c Climb the roofed corner until forced right to a sensational
belay, a superb pitch.
6. 25m 4c Go up the big flake crack to a ledge which spirals round to
the top of the tower. Either finish up Raeburn's Buttress or descend left
and abseil into Castlegates Gully.

Threadbare (280m VS) takes a line on the right side of Raeburn's
Buttress starting a short way up the grass leading onto the Low Ledge.
The lower section is vegetated and a fair amount of aid was used in
the upper part.

THE CENTRAL SLABS

These are the magnificent and unmistakable high-angle slabs set in
the centre of the cliff. They are defined on the left by the open vegetated
corner of Sticil Face and on the right by the lower chimney of The
Citadel. They lie between the grassy breaks of the Low Ledge and the
High Ledge and route lengths are given between those two ledge
systems. The Low Ledge is most easily approached from the left; from
the High Ledge, either the top of Raeburn's Buttress or the last section
of Sticil Face can be used to gain the plateau. Both are equally exposed
and unpleasant. Abseiling back down is also an option; there may be
in situ gear above Run of the Arrow and The Pin.
    The main feature and reference point in the middle of the slabs is
the diagonal diedre of Thor. It faces right and its lower end finishes in
an overlap which runs leftwards into Sticil Face. The lower corner of
the diedre is reached *via* a left-facing corner system which marks the
start of several routes.

7 Sticil Face 240m V,6 ***   (1954)
An excellent long route with varied climbing, following the angle
between Raeburn's Buttress and the Central Slabs. Start at the bottom
left side of Low Ledge. Climb up right to Low Ledge, then traverse it to

Time Traveller, Carn Etchachan (Climber, Steve Blagbrough)

a shallow depression trending slightly left. Climb this to a big ledge below a steep wall. Climb the steep ice corner on the right (usually the crux) and continue more easily to below a narrow chimney. Climb this awkward chimney to easy ledges. Now go up and right across High Ledge to its top. Climb the wide fault above until it is possible to move left into another break leading to the top. The narrower 30m chimney left of the main fault gives a harder finish.

Direct Finish: 120m V,6   (1986)
From above the awkward chimney, climb without difficulty to a corner directly above and climb this and a short wall to easier ground and the top. This variation needs ice.

   In summer the route is Hard Severe, wet and vegetated. The crux is the steep edge overlooking the winter crux, a wet slabby holdless gully.

8 The Harp 100m E3 **   (1983)
A very good route which starts at the left of the slabs and runs diagonally rightwards. Start from the left-hand end of Low Ledge.
1. 20m Climb grassy corners as for Sticil Face, usually wet and very unpleasant.
2. 15m 5c Move right to a ledge on the slab, then go up a thin crack to the overhang, pull over this and go up 5m to a ledge.
3. 40m 5c Follow the thin crack in the slab for 30m to below a steeper wall, move right to cross the crack of Snipers to a ledge, then go up a crack system to a small ledge and peg belay on Run of the Arrow. A superb and generally well protected but sustained pitch.
4. 25m 5b Follow the obvious right-slanting line to a junction with Cupid's Bow just below its final flake crack and finish up this.

9 Snipers 105m E2   (1969)
A fine line, a bit dirty, but it should improve with traffic. It takes the thin crack on the left of the slabs. The overlap constitutes the crux, but above it the climbing is quite bold. Start at the left-facing corner system which leads to the foot of the Thor diedre.
1. 35m 5a Climb the corner to an overhang, move left then go up to below the overlap above a loose flake.
2. 25m 5b Cross the overlap (2 pegs for aid or free at 6c) and climb the thin crack to a niche.
3. 45m 5a Continue up the crack to High Ledge.

The Missing Link, Shelter Stone Crag (Climber, Murray Hamilton)

10 Aphrodite 95m E7 **   (1990)
A really big route in every way. Start at the corner as for Snipers.
1. 35m 5a Climb the left-facing corner system to below the overlap.
2. 60m 6c Cross the overlap free, then move up and right to a
weakness leading into Run of the Arrow. Follow Run of the Arrow to its
crux, then move up, then right then up again to a small ledge. Continue
straight up to good footholds in the scoop where Cupid's Bow traverses
in. Finish as for that route.
   If there are rope length problems, do pitch 2 as for Snipers and belay,
then descend to gain the line; practical, if not aesthetic.

11 Thor 110m E5 ***   (1968/1989)
A stunning route which climbs the eye-catching diagonal diedre in the
centre of the slabs. Start at the left-facing corner system as for Snipers.
1. 40m 5b Climb the corner and traverse right to the base of the main
diedre. Climb this to a small stance and peg belay.
2. 25m 6b Continue up the diedre to awkward RP placements beneath
an obvious sidepull flake above the overlap. Gain a good sidepull in the
alcove (old bolt and peg runner) and cross this (crux) to belay on a flake
at a clutch of pegs.
3. 45m 6b Continue across beneath the overlap, past a peg runner, to
reach a good jug, then a good horizontal crack and a further peg runner
above the overlap (Friend 2 also). Traverse right above the overlap with
a long reach and follow a series of rising ledges passing a line of Rurps
to reach The Pin. Climb this to a belay.
4. Now finish up The Pin, or abseil from 10m up and left of the belay.
Variation: 6a
An easier alternative to pitch 3 is to hand traverse the lip of the overlap.

12 The Missing Link 105m E4 **   (1981)
This takes a diagonal line right across the slabs; sustained and serious
for both climbers on pitch 3. Start at the left-facing corner system as
for Snipers.
1. 35m 5a Climb the corner system to belay above a loose flake under
the overhang.
2. 25m 5b Go up the Thor diedre to a hanging stance below a ledge.
3. 45m 5c Traverse right and go up to follow the long narrow overlap
(poor peg runners) to reach a hollow flake. Traverse this to its end and
pull into The Pin and move up this. It also possible to move down The
Pin to belay.
4. Finish up The Pin.

SHELTER STONE CRAG

CENTRAL SLABS

RB	Raeburn's Buttress	11	Thor
C	The Citadel	12	The Missing Link
L	The Low Ledge	13	The Run of the Arrow
H	The High Ledge	14	Cupid's Bow
8	The Harp	16	The Pin
9	Snipers	16a	The Pin Variation Start

13 The Run of the Arrow 100m E5 **   (1982)
Another excellent route with some bold climbing, taking the faint crack line in the slab between Snipers and Cupid's Bow. Start at the foot of the left-facing corner system.
1. 40m 5a Go up easily right for 10m, move left round the rib and follow a crack up to the base of the Thor diedre. Climb this a short way to a belay on pegs.
2. 35m 6b Swing left onto the rib and move up left to a thin crack line. Follow this and the slab above to reach a small overlap on the right (RP and a large wedge-shaped nut runners). Make a delicate move left from the runners, go up into the scoop, then follow a crack to sloping ledges on the left.
3. 25m 5a Follow the obvious right-slanting line to a junction with Cupid's Bow just below its final flake crack. Finish up this.

14 Cupid's Bow 85m E4 ***   (1978)
A fine difficult route which takes the bow-shaped corner above the upper part of the Thor diedre. Start below the left-facing corner system leading to Thor.
1. 40m 5c Climb up about 5m to belay in a small niche. Gain the grassy bay above and climb out of this *via* cracks on the left. Move right into a shallow corner and climb this to a pull out onto the rib. Go up and left to a hanging belay below a ledge in the Thor Diedre.
2. 45m 6b Climb the diedre to a ledge at the foot of the 'bow'. Climb the corner with difficulty past a peg until it is possible to gain the arete. Go up this to climb an awkward bulging section at the top of the corner, then follow the continuation of the bow to where it curves right. Step left and climb the steep slabby section to traverse right below the headwall. Finish back left by the obvious, not very large flake crack.

15 Realm of the Senses 35m E7 6c **   (1993)
An extremely difficult slab route taking the left-facing corner left of The Pin. Start as for Cupid's Bow and follow the variation start to The Pin to belay at the top of its first pitch. Climb the left-facing corner running up and left with increasing difficulty (RP protection) to the overlap (good protection). Move left on non-existent holds past two peg runners to join the Missing Link at its first peg. Climb this route past the down pointing peg to gain a standing position on the hollow flakes and place crucial runners above the overlap. Reverse the last couple of moves before traversing left above the overlap to gain a flake leading to the Thor belay. Finish as for Thor.

16 The Pin 85m E2 ***   (1968)
This route takes the striking crack line near the right margin of the slabs
and gives very fine sustained climbing. Start high on the Low Ledge
below the crack.
1. 20m 5b Climb the crack directly up the wall to a stance.
2. 25m 5b Continue up the crack, crossing an awkward bulge, then go
slightly right and continue to a good thread belay.
3. 40m 5a Go up and climb the overhanging wall to reach then follow
the continuously interesting crack to the High Ledge.
Variations: E3 5c
An alternative start takes a long curving line coming in from the left
across the top of the wall forming the first pitch. Start as for Cupid's
Bow to belay under a steep wall, then continue in the natural line to the
top of pitch 1.
Variation to pitch 2:
Where the crack becomes more difficult go diagonally right under a
steep wall, then return left above this section to the thread.

17 L'Elisir d'Amore 50m E7 6c **   (1994)
Another desperate which is serious for both leader and second. It takes
a diagonal line going left across the upper section of the slab. Start
above the top end of the Thor overlap, gained either *via* that route or
by reversing the last section of Thor from The Pin (a line of old Rurps
marks the way). Gain the old peg in a pocket 8m above the top of the
Thor overlap. From the peg, move right then go up to a hanging flake
(good nut for a side runner). Move back to the peg and make hard
moves up left to a hold at the top of the pale streak (good, crucial nut
in the back of the hold). Move left up a flake to its termination. Make a
desperate and bold move left to a good foothold in the red streak. Move
precariously up the streak to a line of poor pocket holds that lead *in
extremis* leftwards to a rest in a short groove (the continuation of the
fault line of The Harp) and some poor RPs. Climb the left wall of the
groove to easy ground, traverse 20 metres left to Run of the Arrow and
belay.

THE MAIN BASTION

The centrepiece of the cliff, this magnificent sweep of rock is nearly
300m high and steepens from slabs at its foot to vertical rock at the top.
The left side is defined by the chimney of The Citadel and its continuation fault, and the right side, with its two distinct steps high up, is the

edge overlooking Pinnacle Gully. These lines bound a narrowing and steepening wedge of good continuous rock, although the right side, is cut by Clach Dhian Chimney, is more broken. The main features low down are the right-facing corners of Steeple starting near the toe of the buttress. High up are two large and impressive right-facing corners; the left one fails to reach the top of the cliff and is taken by Steeple, the right-hand one rises to a distinctive notch on the skyline and is taken by The Needle. Although there are few large horizontal features, there are several lines of ledges which partially cross the bastion. These and the tapering nature of this section of the cliff means that some routes share stances, particularly in the upper reaches.

18 Blockbuster E2 5b   (1976)
High on the left side of the Main Bastion, starting from the upper right end of High Ledge, is an obvious chimney line with huge chokestones. Gain the chimney from the left and follow the fault to the top. It can be gained by the lower part of The Citadel or used as a finish to routes on the Central Slabs.

19 The Citadel 270m VS *   (1958)
A traditional Cairngorms classic with all that that implies. The lower section takes the conspicuous chimney bounding the right side of the Central Slabs; the upper is on the steep nose on the left of the great upper bastion. Start below the chimney line. Grassy cracks lead in two pitches to Low Ledge. Above, a further three pitches lie up the chimney until overhangs force an exit to ledges on the left. The next pitch is the lower crux. Go up and left on slabs, then make a right traverse to a corner with a crack in the right wall. Move up this, then go right again to gain the slab above and a grassy fault leading to a belay (4c). Traverse right into an open corner, climb this and the corner into which it develops, to gain a ridge. Follow this, then go left to a stance by a huge flake. Next is the upper crux. Hand traverse left, then climb the crack and chimney system above to a good stance (4c). Continue up the crack above, then traverse right with a step down to ledges. Climb the ensuing right-slanting fault until the left of two short chimneys leads to the plateau.

Winter: VII,8 ***   (1980)
An extremely hard and sustained route, particularly in the upper section. Follow the summer route throughout. Good conditions are

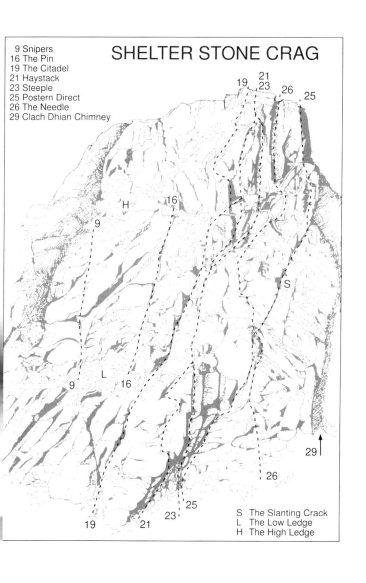

SHELTER STONE CRAG

9 Snipers
16 The Pin
19 The Citadel
21 Haystack
23 Steeple
25 Postern Direct
26 The Needle
29 Clach Dhian Chimney

S The Slanting Crack
L The Low Ledge
H The High Ledge

rarely found; it requires ice on the slabs below the lower crux (1 peg for aid, only freed once) but not so much snow that the upper slabs are too deeply buried.
Variation:
The Moonlight finish makes a left traverse across slabs from above the second crux to a ledge system which leads into the final chimney of Sticil Face.

20 Citadel Winter Variation 270m VI,8 **   (1975)
A logical and worthwhile winter line. Follow the summer route to above the lower crux, then go up and left to finish up Sticil Face. Aid may be needed at the lower crux depending on conditions.
Variation Independent Finish: (1987)
After joining Sticil Face, move up 10m to below an obvious thin ramp trending slightly left up the headwall, and climb this to the top.

21 Haystack 280m E2 ***   (1971)
A varied, steep, strenuous and generally superb route up the nose of the buttress. Start at the toe of the buttress.
1. 30m 4c Climb the right-facing corner to below a short corner. (This is often wet and can be avoided by going 5m up the grassy gully as for Steeple).
2. 30m 4b Climb the short corner and exit left onto slabs. Continue up and left to a good grass ledge below a shallow corner.
3. 40m 4c Climb the corner, then move right and cross the overlap above *via* a prominent crack. Move left, then go up a right-sloping corner to terraces.
4. 40m Follow short walls and grassy ledges left (approximately as for Steeple) to below a steep wall. The ramp pitch of Steeple goes rightwards from above here.
5. 40m 5c Climb the steep line of weakness (as for Steeple) and continue straight through the slight break, then move right up a ramp (above the Steeple ramp) to a slight recess.
6. 45m 5a Make delicate moves left onto a ledge and climb pleasant cracks left to a break in the arete. Follow a crack, steep initially, to a ledge below an overhanging wall.
7. 30m 5b Climb a spectacular overhanging crack-groove, passing a prominent flake at the start of the difficulties.
8. 25m 5a Move right and climb a short vertical crack in the wall above (common with Steeple), then finish more easily.

22 The Spire 160m E4 *** (1982)
Another fine, difficult and spectacular climb. Start by climbing the first
three pitches of Steeple or Haystack to belay on the grass terrace
midway between the crux pitches of Steeple and Needle.
1. 45m 5c Climb the shallow groove, with deviations right then left
below a small overlap. Pull right over the bulge at the top and continue
up to the Steeple belay beside a large pointed block.
2. 45m 6a The corner on the right is Steeple and an obvious ramp
leads into it (5c, sometimes climbed in mistake to make the route E3).
Above is a higher ramp. Gain this ramp with difficulty and at its top follow
a series of cracks above, trending slightly left, to belay beneath the
spectacular overhanging crack of Haystack.
3. 40m 5a Climb up right across the wall *via* grooves to the arete
overlooking the Steeple corner, then go up to ledges at the foot of the
final crack of Steeple.
6. 30m 5a Finish as for Steeple.

23 Steeple 250m E2 *** (1968)
A superb route, in many ways the finest on the crag, taking a line
connecting the obvious lower and upper corner systems. Start at a
right-facing corner rising from the toe of the buttress and from about
5m up a grassy gully on the left of the corner.
1. 30m 5a Climb the corner, crossing two small overlaps, to belay
above the second one.
2. 25m 5a Continue up the second corner and exit left.
3. 45m Climb by short walls and grassy ledges to below a steep line
of weakness which leads to a right-slanting ramp.
4. 35m 5c Climb the slabby fault to below the overhang, move right
with difficulty to gain the ramp then climb this to a belay. A superb pitch.
5. 45m 4c Go up the obvious line of layback cracks, then move up and
right to the foot of the impressive corner.
6. 40m 5b Climb the corner using a hidden crack to a niche, then
continue to ledges on the left.
7. 30m 5a Above, a thin and surprisingly difficult crack leads to easier
cracks and ledges which in turn lead to the top.

24 Postern 245m Hard Severe (1957)
This route has lots of grass, good views and interesting route-finding,
and takes a somewhat diagonal line up and right to reach the prominent
Second Step on the skyline. Start at the grassy gully just right of the
Steeple corner.

1. 45m Climb the grassy gully (unpleasant) and move left to below a smooth right-facing corner, right of and parallel to the Steeple corner.
2. 30m 4c Climb the fine corner, then follow broken ground to a terrace.
3. 35m Go up and right to the next terrace.
4. and 5. 60m Above lies the Slanting Crack running right. Climb this fault easily to where it develops into a deep chimney.
5. Climb the chimney and traverse left to a long wall and groove pitch which ends at a narrow ledge.
6. A short left catwalk, then an obvious right-trending line leads to the Second Step.
7. Finish out right on a fan-shaped slab staircase overlooking Pinnacle Gully, as for Clach Dhian Chimney.
Variation:
A good finish is the obvious groove (the Direct Finish to Clach Dhian Chimney) rising directly above the Second Step.
Winter: VII,7   (1980)
Follow the summer route throughout. However, it may be necessary to climb pitch 2 of Steeple if the fine corner of pitch 2 is bare.
Variation: VI,6*
This is more usually in condition than the summer line and is the usual way that the route is now climbed. Start just right of Clach Dhian Chimney, climb up, cross the chimney and follow a left-slanting ramp to the terrace.

25 **Postern Direct** 255m VS   (1969)
The generally uninspiring climbing in the lower section is followed by a better and airier finish in the region of the prominent brown cave near the top of the cliff.
1. to 4. 170m Follow the normal route to the deep chimney.
5. 35m 4c From a short way up the chimney, move left into a deep groove (the right-hand of two). Climb the groove past some bulges and a wide crack and move left at its top.
6. 15m 4b Climb the steep slab above to the Second Step.
7. 35m 4c Above is a huge brown rectangular recess. Climb wide cracks in the left wall of the recess (this may be dangerous because of rockfall damage), until moves left round the edge in a dramatic position allow blocks and cracks to be climbed to the top.
Winter: VII,8   (1988)
The summer route was followed after a start up Clach Dhian Chimney. On the final pitch climb the wide crack rather than moving onto the arete.

26 The Needle 265m E1 *** (1962)

A classic climb; long, varied and extremely good but not too high in its grade if the correct line is taken. The main feature is the imposing top corner. Start directly below the corner about 30m up and right of Steeple.

1. 30m 4b Climb straight up the slab, then a step left to a nose at 20m to reach a ledge and block belay.

2. 45m 5b Above are twin zigzag cracks. Gain these from the right and follow them to a steep wall at 40m. (Possible belay on the right side of the ledge below this wall). Climb the steep rib on the right to a stance below a grassy terrace.

3. 25m Cross the terrace and climb a slab until a flake leads left to a huge block.

4. 30m 5b Go up left for 5m, then move right into a flake crack. Climb this until a narrow ledge leads left to a bulging crack. Follow this crack to a stance.

5. 20m Go up from the left end of the ledge to gain a slabby ramp and climb this diagonally right to ledges, then move right.

6. 35m 5a Climb the left-facing corner *via* 'the crack for thin fingers', break out right, then go up and left by blocks and ledges.

7. 20m Go up grooves to the foot of the chimney-crack.

8. 35m 5a Climb this, the Needle Crack, to a ledge.

9. 25m Continue by the line of the chimney to thread a pile of chokestones and emerge on the plateau.

27 Stone Bastion 265m E4 ** (1992/94)

A magnificent line up the obvious leaning corner in the upper wall right of the Needle crack, gained by mainly independent climbing. Start just up right from The Needle.

1. 50m 5a Climb easily to a small overlap. Cross this to gain an obvious groove line slanting up left. Follow this to a junction with Needle just below its stepped corners, then traverse right beneath a wall to gain another obvious left-slanting corner line which is climbed to a small ledge.

2. 45m 5c Continue up the corner a short way, pull up a flange on the right to reach a ledge, then awkwardly pull up right to another ledge beneath a leaning wall. Step round the edge on the right and go easily up a ramp to a thread belay on the terrace, as for The Needle.

3. 30m 5a Follow the fault of Postern up right for a short way, then traverse left and along beneath a leaning wall to gain the top of a huge

block beside The Needle belay. Step right, pull onto the wall and gain a ledge, traverse right, then go up to another ledge.

4. 35m 5a Move up a short way, then go left into a corner-groove and pull up into a recess beneath a roof. Exit from the recess up and out left, then go up a short corner to reach easy ground leading up right to below the 'crack for thin fingers' of The Needle.

5. 15m 5a Climb the 'crack for thin fingers' to the groove above.

6. 35m 4b Exit from the groove and follow the grassy shelf up right beneath the upper bastion to join Postern. Continue up a loose blocky groove to some blocks just below and left of the Second Step.

7. 15m 5c Pull over a short wall to a shelf beneath a thin steep and hard-looking crack (above is a peg and a possible entry to the upper groove). Traverse the shelf left into the base of the corner and climb this to swing out right onto a sloping ledge occupied by some blocks. The hold at the top of the corner is best avoided.

8. 30m 6a Climb the tapering corner to its top, the crack on the right providing some useful but awkwardly placed protection. Continue up the wall in a fine position to a small niche up on the right, where Postern Direct comes in. Move up a short way to a niche just below the top.

9. 10m Pull out right and scramble to the top.

28 The Needle (winter variations) VIII,8   (1985)
The route started up the big left-facing corner just left of Clach Dhian Chimney, then took a ramp slanting left to the terrace. The Needle was followed for three pitches (1 rest on crux), then the layback cracks pitch of Steeple (1 rest) to the base of Steeple corner, bivi site. The Needle was rejoined. A peg for aid was used to start the Needle crack, which was left at mid-height for a ledge on the left. The arete above was climbed and The Needle rejoined for the last pitch.

29 Clach Dhian Chimney 220m Very Difficult   (1947)
A mountaineering route with some loose rock but fine situations. It starts up the big chimney just left of Pinnacle Gully. Climb the wide chimney; the first chokestone pitch is climbed by a crack on the left which leads to a groove then easier ground. Two more pitches up the chimney, here virtually a gully, lead to below a steep wall. Exit left, then zigzag up for 60m to meet the Slanting Crack of Postern. Follow this up right to take an easy but sensational horizontal shelf which leads to the lower step on the horizon. Continue up to below the final wall and

finish up right by the fan-shaped slab staircase overlooking Pinnacle Gully.

Variation: Severe
Climb the prominent V-groove which runs up the final wall.
Winter: V,5 (1972)
A good long route which follows the summer line, but further traversing right is employed on the top pitch.

30 Western Grooves 220m IV,4 (1978)
The easiest winter line up the Main Bastion, basically a variation to the lower part of Clach Dhian Chimney but more often in condition. Start midway between Clach Dhian Chimney and the edge of the face. Climb wide shallow grooves into a short deep red chimney. Climb this, awkward exit and continue in a groove until a ramp leads left into the slanting fault of Clach Dhian Chimney. Follow this to the top.

31 West Ridge Route 240m Difficult (1969)
This is the ridge overlooking Pinnacle Gully. Start just left of the gully. Climb a broken rib for 120m to below a steep triangular wall. Abseil diagonally right or climb down to a gully (40m). Climb the right edge of the buttress to the first step, then finish as for Clach Dhian Chimney.

32 The Impostor 240m VII,7 (1986)
Climb West Ridge Route to a steep wall where the abseil is. Traverse left on a ledge to a niche, ascend this *via* a jamming crack to a small ledge below steep cracks, then climb them. Climb up to an obvious groove, Clach Dhian Chimney Direct Finish, and follow this to the top.

33 Unknown Gully 150m III (1979)
The obvious gully starting about halfway up Pinnacle Gully and running up to the First Step on the skyline. Above, climb to the Second Step then go diagonally right to finish as for Clach Dhian Chimney.

34 Games of Chance 90m VI,7 * (1991)
The most obvious line up the centre of the face right of Unknown Gully gives a variety of climbing in a short way. Start in the big snow bay. Climb up and left to below the steep wall. A steep crack with bulges leads to the foot of the big wide chimney. Climb the chimney, mostly on ice in the right corner.

FOREFINGER PINNACLE

This curious rock formation, shaped like a hand with the index finger pointing heavenwards, is unique for Cairngorm granite. It lies at the head of Pinnacle Gully, itself a wide scree corridor in summer and a simple snow plod in winter. The pinnacle has been climbed from all sides, but the combination of the blocky structure and time is making most of the routes a bit shaky.

(a) The normal route is up the back or short side by an crack between the main wall and a subsidiary buttress on the right.

(b) About 3 metres left of the normal route close to a corner; Difficult.

(c) The face opposite Shelter Stone Crag; Difficult.

(d) The west face, passing dangerous loose blocks; Hard Severe.

(e) From the lowest point in the gully, stepping left where the face becomes very steep, to finish by a crack on the east face.

(f) Direct from the lowest point. Moderate rock leads to a large block, then move up the left edge of a vertical wall. Traverse right to a shelf, then go up on the right of a crack to finish up a shallow chimney with an overhang at the bottom; Mild VS 4c.

GARBH UISGE CRAG

This is the smaller, more broken cliff on the right of Pinnacle Gully. It is not a summer cliff but does give some pleasant winter routes which, because of their northerly aspect, can be in condition when other routes in the area are not. Garbh Gully, a deep Y-shaped fault in the centre of the cliff, is the most obvious feature.

Blunderbuss 135m III   (1978)

This route follows the buttress on the left of Garbh Gully. Start at the foot of the buttress on the immediate left of the gully and climb a steep chimney (45m). Continue by grooves and short walls to finish by an open snow slope.

Garbh Gully 150m III *   (1972)

This is the Y-shaped gully in the centre of the crag. Climb the gully and the right branch, the crux being the tapered ice corner after the fork.

Quartz Gully 90m II   (1972)

Climb the slabby open gully on the right of the crag direct. The top section may give a long but easy-angled ice pitch.

HELL'S LUM CRAG
(Map Ref 995 017)

This is the smooth, clean crag which lies between the Allt Coire Domhain and the Feith Buidhe. It looks south-east across the head of the Loch Avon basin and has a very fine selection of routes in the middle grades on excellent rock.

The crag's name is taken from the huge gully on its left-hand side. This cannot be seen easily, except from the south as it cuts deeply back into the cliff. Deep Cut Chimney, however, is more conspicuous, a thin black fault cutting the upper cliff. It has a curious diagonal introduction which runs across the lower part of the centre of the cliff. These two features divide the crag into three main sections: the rocks left of Hell's Lum; the grey buttress between Hell's Lum and Deep Cut Chimney; and the frontal face.

In winter, this crag with its south-easterly aspect, seeps and springs can give excellent climbing especially in cold weather when ice in quantity builds up. Vast amounts of snow can also accumulate, banking out the lower slabs and shortening many of the routes. Bergschrund and randkluft may even form, creating a barrier to the rocks in spring and early summer. During sunny or thaw conditions however, the face is liable to dangers of avalanche and ice fall, particularly on the smooth frontal face. On the left section the cornices can be huge.

Approaches
The approach from Loch Avon is obvious. The approach from the north is to descend some way down the track from Coire Domhain to the loch, then cut diagonally under the cliff. In winter, this slope and the slope under the cliff can be avalanche-prone and a sensible avoiding line should be taken when conditions are hazardous.

THE LEFT-HAND SLABS

This is the slabby area left of Hell's Lum. The rock is best near the gully, as it becomes more vegetated further left. Unfortunately it is very slow to dry because of the many seeps, but when these disappear this area offers excellent climbing on superb, clean, pink granite. On the left, three obvious faults split the slabs and give reference points for this area. Down and left of these is The Glasnost Slab, a clean area of slab giving some single pitch routes which could be lengthened by a scrappy pitch below and a traverse right to finish near Styx. An abseil descent is more appropriate however.

1 Glasnost 35m VS 5a *   (1991)
Start from a ledge at the bottom left of the slab and climb straight up to join and follow a left-slanting crack line.

2 Perestroika 35m E1 5c   (1991)
Start as for Glasnost, but from the left-slanting crack line climb straight up clean red rock to follow another left-slanting crack line.

3 Independence 40m E1 5b   (1991)
Start down and right from the ledge. Climb up to a niche, leave it by the crack line above and follow it curving leftwards to finish.

4 Raw Mince 75m Very Difficult   (1969)
This route takes the slabs left of the three faults. Start 15 metres left of Puke at the lowest rocks.
1. 30m Climb straight up cracks and after 10m trend right to a belay.
2. 45m Go up thin cracks and a slab, then continue right and go up a wall of blocks.

5 Sic 75m Very Difficult   (1969)
The leftmost of the three faults. Start from a long grass shelf about 25 metres left of the Lum.
1. 30m Climb the fault to a sloping ledge under a 3m chimney.
2. 45m Climb the chimney (crux) and continue to an overhang. Pass this on the right and continue to finish up the wall of blocks of Raw Mince.
Winter: III   (1969)
Follow the summer route, except pass the overhang on the left.

6 The Gullet 130m III   (1969)
The central and best of the three faults. Start about 20 metres left of the Lum and climb the fault, shallow and slabby at first, to reach the deeper central section. Continue this with occasional diversions to the left. The cornices can be large and difficult.

7 Puke 75m Very Difficult   (1969)
The right-hand fault.
1. 25m Climb a wall, then follow cracks to a huge glacis.

2. 25m Climb the crack, then go up to the right to below a chimney fault. Pull up left, then climb the fault to huge ledges below the final wall.
3. 25m The chimney and slab on the right lead to the top. The final wall can be climbed at VS.
Winter: III   (1970)
Basically follow the summer route.

8 Arc of a Diver 115m E2 *   (1988)
This fine route takes slabs and overlaps left of Hell's Lum and finishes up the blunt rib which overlooks the gully. Start 2 metres left of the Lum.
1. 45m 5a Climb a thin diagonal crack slanting left, then go easily up slabs to a deep right-facing corner.
2. 35m 5c Go up to below the big overlap, then right to break through it by the wide fault. Trend right to near the edge of the slab.
3. 35m 5b Climb to below a roof, move up and right to a thin crack in a fine red slab, then go up to below the steepening. Step left onto the edge of a hanging slab, then climb the steep groove. Move left, then go up, turn the next overlap on the right and finish up the slabby wall; an excellent pitch.

9 Firewater 110m VS   (1988)
A route on the slabs and overlaps on the left of the Lum. Start at the lowest rocks left of the corner of the wall.
1. 45m 4b Climb the wall just left of the edge, then go up to a corner by a huge block.
2. 35m 4b Climb the slab to the first overlap and cross it by the break just left of where Styx goes through the W-shaped overlap. Go diagonally right to below the steeper wall.
3. 30m Climb the right-facing corner on the right of the pillar and finish up easy slabs.

10 The Bengal Lancer 110m HVS   (1988)
This route takes the big corner in the upper rocks and approximates to The Chancer. It is really an independent finish to either Firewater or Styx.
1. and 2. 80m Climb the first two pitches of Firewater or Styx, then move right under the steep wall to the corner.
2. 30m 5a Climb a small corner right of the main one, then move left round a rib to a ledge. Move left to a crack, go up this, then move back right to a thread and a jammed block. Follow the crack to the top.

The last pitches of The Bengal Lancer and Arc of a Diver can be gained by scrambling down the top of Hell's Lum, then traversing round under the steep upper rocks, from where they can be climbed as excellent single pitch routes.

11 Styx 105m VS *   (1969)
A good route but often wet. Start 15m up the gully on the left wall.
1. 35m 4b Climb an obvious slanting groove to an easing, then move right to an ochre slab and climb this to a corner.
2. 35m 4c Climb the corner, then a short slab to below the overlap. Surmount this *via* the left-hand break, then trend right to turn the next overlap. Trend back left to a niche in the next overlap.
3. 35m 4b Leave the niche on the left, then gain the crack in the wall above. Follow this to an easing in angle. Scramble to the top.

In good conditions there may be three parallel icefalls here. The left is wide and forms a chimney, the middle one is The Chancer and the right one is a thin pencil which gives a route of VI,6.
Boke (IV,5) takes a diagonal line from the foot of Hell's Lum to reach the headwall left of The Chancer. It then climbs this by a slightly right-trending line to the top slopes.

12 The Chancer 90m V,6 **   (1970)
A short steep ice route on the left wall of the Lum. Start at the top of the main ice pitch in Hell's Lum and climb ice into a cave below the large overhang. Climb the icicle (crux) to easier-angled ice, then gain the upper snowfields.

13 Hell's Lum 150m II/III ***   (1956)
This classic route up the major fault which splits the crag gives interesting climbing through superb scenery, but with a noticeable lack of good protection. It can vary from high-angle snow to having up to four ice pitches. The cornice, which can be huge, can normally be turned on the right.
In summer this is a drainage line with some steep pitches separated by scree slopes. The main pitch is climbed by cracks, firstly by the right crack on the inside, then move left to the outside. It is Severe and normally a waterfall.

THE GREY BUTTRESS

This is defined by Hell's Lum on the left and Deep Cut Chimney on the right. It has an impressive left wall leaning over the Lum, and is very quick-drying in summer because of its detached nature. Deep Cut Chimney cuts behind the buttress to appear near the top of the Lum as **The Pothole**, a deep and obvious slit with chokestones (Very Difficult, Grade III), which can be approached by descending the Lum. There is little build-up of ice on this buttress in winter.

The climbs on the front face of the buttress have excellent pitches low down but are easier higher up where the angle lies back and the lines become less well defined.

14 Chariots of Fire 45m E4 **   (1991)

A sensational route with flaky rock to add to the excitement. The route overhangs all the way but the crux is short and well protected. Start immediately above the pitch in the Lum which can be reached by abseil from the viewing block overlooking the gully.

1. 15m 5b Climb out right into a shallow corner, actually a big flake. Follow this briefly, then go right again into another corner and climb this to below a roof.

2. 15m 6a Make a high traverse left onto the overhanging wall, then pull up to good holds (crux). Traverse left to a spike, then go up a line of flakes leading left to a small ledge.

3. 15m 5a Continue up the flakes, then go straight up over the bulge to the viewing block.

15 Drop Out 110m E2   (1969)

This route follows the rake on the wall overlooking Hell's Lum. Start at broken green rocks just right of the Lum.

1. 35m Climb easy broken ground to a ledge below the overhang on the edge of the buttress.

2. 30m 5a Traverse left under the overhang, then go round onto and climb a ramp (loose in places) to a ledge at 20m. Continue up the ramp to a stance; a serious pitch.

3. 25m 5b Climb the continuation crack to where it curves left and follow it to the left edge. Go up into corners above.

4. 20m Continue by the same line to the top.

16 Good Intentions 120m VS *   (1969)
The main feature of this climb is the isolated groove on the edge of the
buttress. The difficulties are short and well protected.
1. 20m Climb broken ground and a short wall to gain the ledge below
and right of the groove.
2. 35m 5a Go diagonally left to gain the groove and climb this to a
ledge.
3. 35m Go diagonally left to a ledge below the wall with a prominent
groove.
4. 30m Climb this, exit over blocks, then climb the final short wall direct.
Winter: VII,7   (1986)
Climb the summer route; the slabby ramp is the crux and the groove is
technical but with overhead protection.

17 The Exorcist 100m E1 *   (1975)
This route is based on the left-facing corner high in the centre of the
face. Start at the foot of the buttress.
1. 20m Climb the right-facing corner to grassy ledges.
2. 35m 5b Climb the wide crack in the recess above, then go diagonally
right to gain the corner *via* a shallow groove. Climb the corner to the
roof, then break out right to a ledge on the rib.
3. 45m Climb the rib above to easy ground.

18 Evil Spirits 110m E2 *   (1986)
This route gives some good climbing up the diagonal line between
Good Intentions and Hell's Lump. Start between these routes.
1. 15m 5a Climb green rock just right of the corner to a horizontal crack,
go right to a corner, then continue to the large flake.
2. 35m 5c Climb into a deep crack (as for Hell's Lump) and continue
directly into the corner above. Climb this to the roof, traverse left, then
go up to the next corner which leads to a ledge above the corner of The
Exorcist.
3. 15m 5a Go diagonally left, then descend to an obvious overlap and
pink rock. Climb diagonally up this to its end and go up to a stance
above the crux groove of Good Intentions.
4. 45m Finish as for Good Intentions.

19 Hell's Lump 100m Hard Severe *   (1961)
A good little route. Start at the pink and green slab about 45 metres
right of the Lum.
1. 15m Climb the quartz band up the slab to a large flake.

HELL'S LUM CRAG

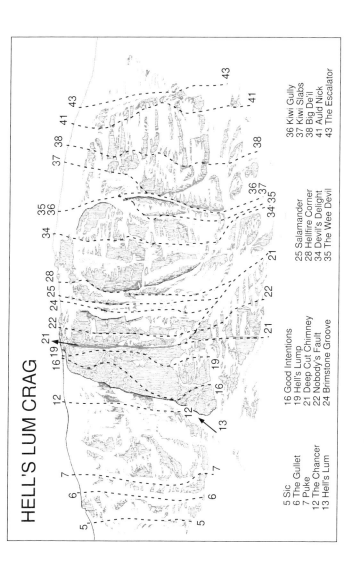

5 Sic
6 The Gullet
7 Puke
12 The Chancer
13 Hell's Lum

16 Good Intentions
19 Hell's Lump
21 Deep Cut Chimney
22 Nobody's Fault
24 Brimstone Groove

25 Salamander
28 Hellfire Corner
34 Devil's Delight
35 The Wee Devil

36 Kiwi Gully
37 Kiwi Slabs
38 Big De'il
41 Auld Nick
43 The Escalator

2. 30m Continue by the groove and crack above for 12m, then move up right and turn the square roof by the crack on the right. Gain a grassy bay, then climb up to the recess above (crux pitch).
3. 25m Climb cracks and corners trending slightly right, then gain the rib adjoining Deep Cut Chimney.
4. 30m Finish up Deep Cut Chimney.
Winter: V,6   (1986)
Start below the main groove of The Exorcist, climb a shallow left-facing corner and move left to a groove which leads to a flake roof on the summer line. Climb the groove and cracks rightwards to below the square roof, turn this on the right, then go up to climb a bulging chimney. Move right and up by grooves to a left-slanting rake which leads to the top.

20 Lion of Judah 175m VS   (1990)
This follows the rib left of Deep Cut Chimney. Start left of the direct start.
1. 45m 4c Climb layback cracks up the left edge of the slab to a ledge. Climb the clean green slab above, moving left to a small ledge.
2. 40m 4a Go straight up over ledges, then follow a crack line slanting left to large blocks.
3. 20m 5a Step out right to a slab, then go right to gain and climb the short cracked corner to a small stance overlooking Deep Cut Chimney.
4. 20m 4c Go straight up a short way, then work diagonally left to climb a short hanging chimney.
5. 50m 4b Finish as for Hell's Lump, climbing the rib adjoining the chimney.

21 Deep Cut Chimney 150m Very Difficult   (1950)
An impressive slit, vegetated in its lower part but with walls close enough for using back and foot to avoid the greenery. A pleasant route nevertheless, with a spectacular and unexpected finish. Start either directly below or by the easy terraced fault cleaving the lower slabs. Once in the chimney, the way is defined until the top where the chimney cuts well back and there are chokestones jammed well out between the walls. Back and foot out to a pile of wedged boulders in the outer jaws, after which the finish comes with startling suddenness.
Winter: IV,4***   (1958)
An excellent and highly recommended route. The fault can be approached in a variety of ways, depending on the build up. Once gained, the way is obvious, but it does have its surprises.

HELL'S LUM CRAG

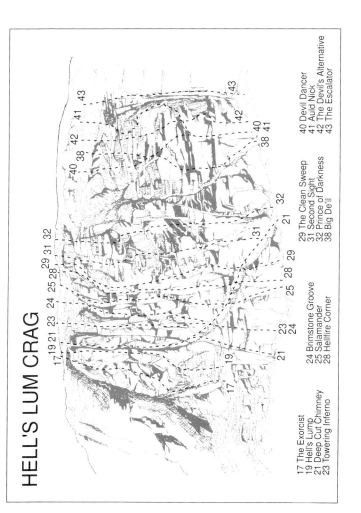

17 The Exorcist
19 Hell's Lump
21 Deep Cut Chimney
23 Towering Inferno

24 Brimstone Groove
25 Salamander
28 Hellfire Corner

29 The Clean Sweep
31 Second Sight
32 Prince of Darkness
38 Big De'il

40 Devil Dancer
41 Auld Nick
42 The Devil's Alternative
43 The Escalator

THE FRONTAL FACE

This is the largest and most important part of the crag, reaching 200m in height in its central section. It gradually steepens from bottom to top and the rock is clean and sound. There are few really large features, but Hellfire Corner, the left-facing corner system in the centre of the face, is a useful landmark.

Further right is the fault of Kiwi Gully, whose shape is roughly similar to Deep Cut Chimney with a diagonal lower section. Midway between these two features and above half-height is The Haven, a series of grassy ledges where a number of routes converge.

Near the right edge of the cliff is the broken fault of The Escalator, and between this and Kiwi Gully is an area of fine pink slabs crossed by overlaps. To the right of The Escalator, the cliff is cut by a broken terrace and soon merges into the hillside.

In winter, much of the lower section of the cliff can bank out, making route identification difficult, especially in bad visibility. However, The Escalator and Kiwi Gully both usually show as lines of ice while the big left-facing corner of Wee Devil and the main corner system of Hellfire Corner should both be fairly obvious. Left of Hellfire Corner, large amounts of ice usually accumulate.

22 Nobody's Fault 150m IV,6 **   (1979)
The shallower fault parallel to and right of Deep Cut Chimney gives a fine winter route. Start as for Deep Cut Chimney, then follow the corner-chimney to the top. The initial bulge and the hanging chimney at mid-height are of considerable technical interest.

23 Towering Inferno 200m Severe *   (1978)
This route lies on the pillar just right of Nobody's Fault and is characterised by two large rectangular roofs. Start directly below the pillar and right of a straight fault.
1. and 2. 80m Climb cracked green slabs to the easy terraced fault.
3. 40m Go up to the pink rock above and move left to a red vein. Follow this to the corner leading to the lower roof, swing right onto the rib and go up into a shallow chimney.
4. 35m Climb the corner to below the next overlap and move left onto the nose. Regain the fault and follow it to a grassy recess.
5. 45m Continue up cracks and the blocky wall to the top.

Variation: VS 4c
On pitch 3, instead of moving left, go straight up to a roof and cross it
to climb a shallow inverted V-chimney to regain the ordinary route.
Winter: VI,6 *   (1986)
The summer line gives a sustained climb, poorly protected in the lower
part. In the upper section follow the left-leaning fault by the rock beak.

24 Brimstone Groove 170m Severe   (1985)
This route takes the very wide upper fault between the enormous beaks
of rock. Start as for Towering Inferno.
1. and 2. 80m Climb cracked slabs to the diagonal fault.
3. 40m Work right into a steep left-facing corner, make a few moves
up this, then pull onto the right rib (crux). Continue up the line of corners
to a belay.
4. 50m Climb up into the huge fault of blocky fine-grained rock and
follow this to the top.
Winter: IV,4   (1970)
In winter, a fine sheet of ice forms on the rocks left of Hellfire Corner.
This route follows the left edge of the ice to break through the steep
upper rocks by the largest and widest fault on the left, as for the summer
route. A good ice climb.

25 Salamander 155m HVS *   (1971)
This direct line, on good rock parallel to and left of Hellfire Corner, gives
fine climbing but it is often wet. Start below an obvious right-facing
corner about 30 metres left of The Clean Sweep's green whaleback.
1. 40m 4b Climb into the corner and follow it to a ledge. Continue in
the same line to climb a steeper section by a bulging slab to a platform.
2. 20m Follow easy rocks to the diagonal fault.
3. 20m 5a Climb twin cracks up steep slabs left of an obvious corner
to a platform.
4. 20m 4b Go through the overlap by the short black corner, then follow
the crack to the obvious recess.
5. 30m 4b Continue to a shallow groove and follow this to break through
the upper overhangs by a striking chimney slit.
6. 25m Continue up the open funnel to easy ground.
Winter: IV,5 *   (1973)
A fine ice route which follows the centre of the ice sheet left of Hellfire
Corner, breaching the upper rocks by the steep chimney slot. Above,
easier ground leads to the top.

26 The Vacuum 60m Severe *   (1968)
A short climb which only goes to the diagonal fault, so it can be used
as an alternative start to other routes in the vicinity. Start about 10
metres left of The Clean Sweep where two parallel cracks run up into
an overlap at about 30m.
1. 25m Climb mostly the right-hand crack.
2. 35m Continue past an overlap to a platform, cross right and go up
a corner crack until the slab on the right can be gained and followed to
the fault.

27 Damien 175m E1 *   (1984)
An eliminate with some fine climbing between Hellfire Corner and The
Clean Sweep. Start at a thin crack left of Hellfire Corner.
1. 40m 5a Climb the thin crack and its continuation into the left-facing
corner.
2. 40m Go easily right, crossing the diagonal fault, to the huge block
belay of The Clean Sweep.
3. 25m 4b Climb the grassy cracks to the foot of the obvious corner.
4. 40m 5b Climb the corner to a junction with The Clean Sweep and
continue up this into a large bay.
5. 30m 4b Move back right onto the front face and climb to the top.

28 Hellfire Corner 185m VS **   (1958)
This excellent route, usually wet at the crux but graded for damp
conditions, follows the main left-facing system of corners in the middle
of the face. Start at a crack (arrowed) about 30 metres left of the easy
terraced fault leading to Deep Cut Chimney.
1. and 2. 60m 4b Climb the crack which runs into a left-facing corner,
then go up this to the diagonal fault
2. 45m 4a Climb the short deep left-facing corner into another corner
system, then climb this to below a large overhang.
3. 20m 4b Go up the depression and the continuation corner until an
awkward move leads to a platform where this merges with the main
corner.
4. 20m 4b Climb the steepening corner, then go through the overlap
by airy chimneying moves before moving right to easier ground.
5. 40m Climb the big fault to the top or, better, finish up the right-facing
corner left of the big fault.

Winter: VI,7 *   (1985)
An excellent route by the summer line with ice on the lower pitches and a spectacular crux through the steepening.

29 The Clean Sweep 160m VS ***   (1961)
A great route up the pink leaning corner overlooking Hellfire Corner. Start at a green whaleback buttress left of Deep Cut Chimney's diagonal fault.
1. 30m 4c Go up the corner on the left of the buttress for a short way to gain a groove. Either go up the groove to cracks on the crest, or go right to cracks. These lead to the top of the buttress.
2. 45m 4a Step over the fault and climb slabs and corners to a huge block below the pink corner.
3. 45m 4c Climb the corner and the continuation fault; a superb pitch.
4. 40m 4a Continue by cracks, corners and bulges up the round grey edge above to the top.
Winter: VI,7   (1978)
Follow the summer route.

30 The Omen 180m HVS   (1976)
This route lies to the right of The Clean Sweep. Start at the base of the diagonal fault of Deep Cut Chimney.
1. 30m 5a Gain the slab above the short vertical wall and follow this in a left-rising traverse.
2. 20m 4c Go left then back right on the ledge above and climb the thin crack in the slab to below the obvious left-facing corner (just left of an enormous block in a triangular niche).
3. 20m 5a Climb the corner to the huge block on The Clean Sweep.
4. 30m 4b Climb the crack 5 metres right of that route.
5. 20m Move up and right over a bulge, then climb a quartzy crack to reach The Haven, a series of grassy ledges.
6. and 7. 60m 4c Climb to the top of a huge block, then go up a series of cracks in the pink rock. Finish up easier rocks.

31 Second Sight 170m HVS *   (1982)
A good but often wet climb which takes the crack lines running up to the left side of the huge triangular niche. Start about 10m up the diagonal fault of Deep Cut Chimney.

1. 40m 5a Cross the steep wall and gain the right-hand of the two cracks above. Climb this, then follow a short shallow corner to an enormous triangular block.

2. 30m 5a Climb the block to exit from the recess, then work left and into the crack (often wet) which leads to the bottom left of the huge triangular niche.

3. 25m 4b Follow the same fault line by corners to reach The Haven.

4. 35m 4c Go left and climb the crack line left of the pink crack (taken by The Omen). Trend up and left *via* bulges and cracks to some jammed blocks.

5. 40m Climb directly up the fine grey pillar above, then follow easy rocks to the top.

32 Prince of Darkness 150m E1 **   (1984)

This line left of the corner of Wee Devil has a particularly fine pen-ultimate pitch. Start by the foot of the diagonal fault.

1. and 2. 70m 4b Climb the thin crack in the green slab and follow cracks and corners to below the prominent red slab.

3. 30m 4c Climb cracks in the big red slab to a good ledge.

4. 20m 5b Work up into the right-facing corner with overlaps, then climb this to a ledge on the left.

5. 30m 5a Return right into the continuation corner and crack, which leads to the top.

33 The Underworld 185m VS   (1976)

A long route linking some well separated features around the main corner of Wee Devil. Start as for Prince of Darkness.

1. 40m 4b Climb the thin crack in the green slab about 5 metres left of The Wee Devil and follow cracks and corners.

2. 35m 4b Go up left then over a roof by the obvious crack, then continue more easily right to below a corner down and right of the main corner of The Wee Devil.

3. 35m 4c Climb the corner. Just below the top, move right onto the rib, then go up slabs and walls.

4. 40m 4b Move left into and climb a short pink corner, then continue up the cracks on the edge overlooking the main corner of The Wee Devil.

5. 35m 4b Traverse left on a hanging slab, gain the fault on the left of the tower and climb this *via* an obvious overhanging niche to the top.

Winter: V,4   (1994)

Follow the summer line.

34 Devil's Delight 165m Hard Severe   (1957)
This route is on the slabs left of The Wee Devil and is characterised by
a large wet triangular niche. Start at the vegetated fault leading into the
left-facing corner. Climb cracks and shallow corners up left to a big
recess in a glacis (60m). From atop a 3m block, climb into the triangular
niche. Leave this *via* a crack to reach The Haven. On the right is a wide
shallow chimney fault. Follow the cracks, passing some awkward
bulges, to chimney behind a huge block. Finish straight up.
Winter: V,5 **   (1973)
A superb ice route when in condition. A cascade of ice leads into the
triangular niche, then on to The Haven. Above, narrow ice runnels in
grooves and corners follow the summer line and constitute the crux.

35 The Wee Devil 150m IV,5   (1971)
This follows the prominent left-facing corner system halfway up the
face. There is an obvious red slab on its left. Climb the discontinuous
gully into the corner, move up this, then exit left below the overhang.
Above, go up and right *via* a large flake until a right-facing corner line
right of a steep tower can be followed to easier ground and the top.
    In summer this route is Hard Severe.

36 Kiwi Gully 150m IV,4 *   (1972)
The obvious gully gives quite a good route. It slants left in its lower
section and is deepest at about two-thirds height. Climb the gully direct,
and where it fades out, trend left to finish up the top right-facing corner
of The Wee Devil.

37 Kiwi Slabs 150m IV,3   (1959)
An interesting ice route which first follows Kiwi Gully to the deepest
section. From there, break up and right on easier-angled ice smears.
These lead to a slanting left-facing corner which is normally ice-filled.
This leads to the snow apron and the top.
    In summer this is Very Difficult. The original start, Hard Severe,
climbs the green buttress directly below the chimney and can be used
as a start to Big De'il.

38 Big De'il 145m VS *   (1971)
A nice little route which climbs the left of the slabs initially, then goes
diagonally right into the centre. Start at the foot of Kiwi Gully.
1. 45m Scramble up Kiwi Gully, then climb a vertical crack to below the
overlap.

2. 20m 4b Gain the continuation crack above and go left into the deep two-tiered right-facing corner.

3. 20m 4c Climb the corners, then go right into a circular depression.

4. 40m 4c Go diagonally right, then work up by a corner system which leads to the break on the right of a long low roof. Climb this and belay above.

5. 20m 4a Work diagonally right across the grey walls above.

Winter: IV,4   (1980s)

As usual with this part of the crag, the build-up of snow and ice makes this route very open to variations, but the summer route can be followed throughout.

39 Beelzebub 110m HVS   (1988)

This route takes the left side of the slab right of Big De'il. Scramble up Kiwi Gully to beneath the big overlap halfway between Big De'il and Devil Dancer.

1. 35m 5c Surmount the overlap (crux) and go up the crack line above to the second of two horizontal breaks. Traverse right beneath the big overlap to under a shallow left-facing corner.

2. 25m 4c Go over the bulge, climb the corner, then continue to the base of the Devil Dancer corner.

3. 25m 4c Move right and climb the arete of the corner to join Devil Dancer and follow this to a belay.

4. 25m Finish by Devil Dancer or The Devil's Alternative.

40 Devil Dancer 145m HVS *   (1977)

A pleasant route which climbs the centre of the slab, then goes diagonally left. Start about 10 metres right of Kiwi Gully at an obvious crack.

1. 45m 4b Climb the crack and the corner continuation to below the first overlap.

2. 45m 4b Climb the right-facing corner in the overlap and the continuation crack to the next bulge, then follow the crack through it to the glacis. Continue diagonally left to below the deep left-facing corner.

3. 25m 4b Climb the corner and continue to the recess at the left end of the long low roof.

4. 30m 5a Gain a horizontal flake and from its left end go up the pink streak to a diagonal crack (hidden protection) and climb this to a ledge. Go left and climb an easy corner. Scramble to the top.

41 Auld Nick 160m Severe ***   (1965)
A excellent, open and sustained route on the right of the slabs. Start about 10 metres right of Kiwi Gully. The first 60m are shared with Devil Dancer, and all the pitches can be split.
1. 45m Climb the crack to below the first overlap.
2. 45m Climb the right-facing corner and the crack to the next bulge, go right on a horizontal crack, then move diagonally right.
3. 20m Climb the left-facing corner by a series of steps to below a right-tapering roof.
4. 30m Go past the roof on the right and continue leftwards, passing a big block, to a big ledge. Climb the wall above the centre of the ledge by a thin crack to below the huge grey block.
5. 20m Finish on either side of the big grey block. Scramble to finish.
Winter: III   (1971)
A very variable route which can give good climbing. The lower slabs to the second overlap often bank out and the route follows short ice walls and snowfields by the corner. Finish either side of the grey block, then *via* the upper snowfields.

42 The Devil's Alternative 180m HVS *   (1981)
This direct line on the right of the slabs gives interesting climbing on excellent rock. Start at a greenish buttress just left of The Escalator.
1. 45m Climb shallow cracks in the greenish rocks to a huge terrace.
2. 45m 5a Twin cracks rise above the overlap; gain these from a scoop on their right and follow them to the next overlap (Auld Nick crosses rightwards here). Work left through the overlap onto the glacis.
3. 45m 5a Above is a stepped wall. Zigzag up this to a short left-facing corner, above which moves up and right lead to the next glacis.
4. 45m 5a Climb into a niche in the grey wall above, go left to a horizontal crack, then follow easier ground and a rib to the top.

43 The Escalator 150m Moderate   (1955)
The watercourse fault on the right of the cliff; the route is obvious up pink water-worn rocks. Easy scrambling up the initial gully leads to a large platform below the steeper section, where an easy shelf runs off to the right. Pleasant climbing follows, finishing just left of the water-course.
Winter: II/III *   (1960)
A good ice route up the summer line. The initial gully is usually straightforward, but ice in quantity can form in the upper fault.

44 Squirk 135m Very Difficult   (1975)
This lies to the right of The Escalator, starting at a crack and groove
between that route and the big open corner of Sneer. Climb the crack
and groove and continue through overlaps to cross the diagonal break.
Gain and climb the left-hand of the two obvious cracks.

45 Sneer 120m Very Difficult   (1963)
A varied although broken route on clean rock. Start 30 metres right of
The Escalator. Climb the big open corner which leads to easier rocks
and a diagonal terrace. Climb the right-hand crack through overlapping
slabs (often wet).
Winter: II/III   (1966)
Although the lower pitches usually disappear, the upper slabs often
become sheathed in ice, offering a choice of good single pitches.

Hell's Lum Crag is also crossed by a girdle (Severe), which starts up
The Escalator and finishes up Hell's Lump, crossing at about the level
of The Haven.

THE STAG ROCKS
(Map Ref 003 022)

The Stag Rocks is the collective name for the cliffs lying on the south
side of Cairn Gorm between Coire Raibert and Coire Domhain. They
look out over the head of Loch Avon and face south towards Loch
Etchachan. The rock is rough and quick drying, and rock climbing may
be possible here in the spring when other cliffs are still in winter
conditions. In winter however, the cliff is less likely to give good
conditions away from the main faults, although in cold weather and
early in the season mixed buttress routes can be good.
    The rocks consist of two sections, separated by Diagonal Gully (Map
Ref 001 022), a long open chute whose screes almost reach the loch.

Approaches
    The approach from Loch Avon is obvious. From the plateau it is
possible to descend Diagonal Gully, but care is needed, particularly
down the steep and grassy top section. For climbs on the Left Sector

Hell's Lum

a descent down the prominent Y-shaped gully (Map Ref 000 022) at the left-hand side is convenient. Alternatively, descend either Coire Raibert or Coire Domhain and traverse round under the cliffs.

THE LEFT-HAND SECTION

The bulk of this lies between the open Y-shaped gully on the left and Diagonal Gully on the right. It consists of several well defined ribs separated by grassy faults. To the left of the Y-shaped gully is a short clean steep wall midway between Coire Domhain and the Left Section proper. This can hold a lot of ice in winter.

1 The Overflow 45m III   (1986)
The groove immediately left of the main wall, on which Cascade forms, can give a good ice pitch.

2 Cascade 45m V,5 *   (1977)
Climb the obvious steep icefall direct. It is generally just less than vertical but very sustained.

3 Cascade Right-Hand 45m IV,4
The right-hand ice fall may have several steep steps but it is generally easier than its companion.

4 Afterthought Arete 150m Moderate ***   (1956)
The best route of its grade in the area, following the left-hand and most regularly-shaped arete bounding the right side of the wide scree-filled Y-shaped gully. The first pitch from the lowest rocks is harder than Moderate but it can be avoided. After this, the rocks develop into an excellent knife-edge which maintains its interest to the top.
Winter: III   (1969)
Gain the arete from the right and follow the summer route. The groove left of Afterthought Arete is Grade III/IV in winter.

5 Open Caste 150m III   (1989)
This route takes an obvious ridge just left of Quartz Digger's Cave Route. Start at the foot of Afterthought Arete and slant up rightwards for two long pitches to below the crest and about 20m left of the quartz digger's cave. Bypass the steep crest by going right and back left to belay near it (30m). Now follow the crest to easy ground.

Steeple, Shelter Stone Crag (Climber, Bruce Jardine)

6 Quartz Digger's Cave Route 80m Very Difficult   (1957)
On the buttress immediately right of Afterthought Arete is an artificial
cave hollowed out by the gemstone seekers of the past. The climb
starts on the rib to the left of the cave and 5m beneath the entrance.
1. Follow the rib until forced left into an open groove. Climb this on its
right wall, then trend up and left to a stance.
2. Climb the wall above into a large open groove. Move left at its top
and climb the clean rib to the top.
Winter: III   (1986)
Follow the summer route.

7 Gemstone 95m V,5   (1988)
Start 8 metres right of the quartz digger's cave. Climb a vague groove
up a slab, passing a triangular roof on the right. Follow a ramp left to a
block belay on the crest. Traverse right over the block, go up a groove,
along a ledge and up a V-groove to a roof. Swing right under the roof
and climb to a ledge. Take the upper corner leading back to the crest.

8 Stag Route 135m II   (1969)
This route follows the shallow gully left of Triple Towers, the central of
the three ribs, and enters a narrow snow runnel below the final tower.
The lower gully contains several ice pitches, the largest of which is
avoided on the right. If all the pitches are climbed direct the climb is
Grade III (1971).

9 Triple Towers 135m Moderate   (1954)
The central of the three aretes is formed by three discontinuous towers,
each of which is climbed on or close to their right edges.
Winter: II   (1969)
Climb the summer route.

10 C M Gully 135m II/III   (1970)
The gully between Triple Towers and Serrated Rib curves up and left
below the impressive left wall of Serrated Rib and finishes up a narrow
snow runnel (common with Stag Route).

11 Serrated Rib 135m Moderate   (1930)
The left wall of Diagonal Gully is mostly scrambling, but higher up it
narrows to an arete on its left edge.
Winter: II   (1969)
Climb the summer route.

STAG ROCKS

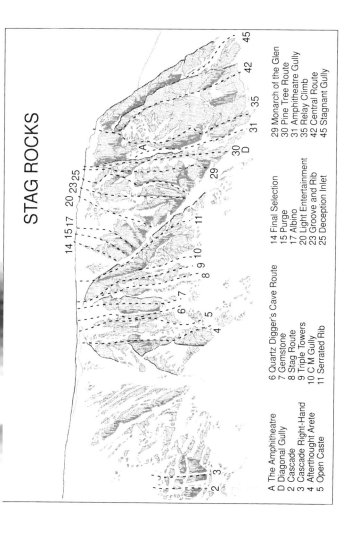

A The Amphitheatre
D Diagonal Gully
2 Cascade
3 Cascade Right-Hand
4 Afterthought Arete
5 Open Caste

6 Quartz Digger's Cave Route
7 Gemstone
8 Stag Route
9 Triple Towers
10 C M Gully
11 Serrated Rib

14 Final Selection
15 Purge
17 Albino
20 Light Entertainment
23 Groove and Rib
25 Deception Inlet

29 Monarch of the Glen
30 Pine Tree Route
31 Amphitheatre Gully
35 Relay Climb
42 Central Route
45 Stagnant Gully

12 Diagonal Gully

The long open gully is chiefly scree in summer and is a means of access to routes on its right wall. In winter, it is a long and generally easy slope, although it does have a steeper section near the top and a cornice may form on its right side.

THE RIGHT-HAND SECTION

The rocks here are more massive and divided in two by Amphitheatre Gully. On its left is the inverted triangular Pine Tree Buttress, with its grooved face forming the right wall of Diagonal Gully. This is itself divided in two by the shallow but large rambling fault of Apex Gully. To the right of Amphitheatre Gully is the larger flat-faced Longbow Crag. This cliff does not extend all the way to the plateau but is topped by about 60m of broken scrambling. In winter this cliff is rapidly stripped of snow by any mild weather or sunshine.

13 Final Groove 80m II/III (1988)

The large right-facing groove at the top of the gully wall.

14 Final Selection 60m Difficult *** (1956)

An excellent little climb on the last defined arete near the top of Diagonal Gully. The right side is steep and the left side is a cracked slab angling into the big right-facing groove. Start up the large groove, then break out right to the arete. Continue up the edge and cracks on the left of the edge to a platform on the right, just below the level of the obvious overhang. A corner on the right then leads to the top.
Winter: III (1969)
Follow the summer route.

15 Purge 90m Very Difficult (1969)

The groove below Final Selection. Climb the wall and groove for 45m, then go straight up the slabs above to finish.
Winter: IV,4 (1986)
Climb the right-hand of twin slabby grooves, then the left one to below a wall. Traverse left, then climb a continuation groove.

16 Alb 85m Very Difficult (1969)

Start at a slab corner below Purge and climb the slab for 35m. Move up steepening slabs for 20m and traverse right below an overhanging wall. Go along a ledge, then climb a steep wall to easier ground.

17 Albino 80m IV,4   (1986)
This route takes the slabby corner immediately above Apex Gully.
Climb the corner to the wall, then traverse right to a stance. Move round
the corner, climb onto the crest of the buttress and follow a faint groove
to the top. (This may correspond to Alb.)

18 Apex Gully 150m III   (1971)
The obvious icefall and fault about halfway up Diagonal Gully. Iced-up
slabs lead into the snow gully, which is followed to its fork. The right
branch leads to the top at about Grade II. The left fork contains a good
ice pitch.

19 Faintly Amusing 135m III,5   (1995)
This route takes the ill defined buttress on the right of Apex Gully with
a steep start and finish. Start at the foot of the turfy groove just right of
the ice boss of Apex Gully. Climb the groove and move right below the
triangular tower. Continue up the blocky crest to gain a wide groove-
ramp on the left of the final steep tower of Light Entertainment. Climb
this to a steep exit up the blocky corner.
Variation Start: 40m III,5
Start below Apex Gully where a horizontal ledge goes out right (as for
Light Entertainment). Gain the diagonal line going back left (crux) and
follow this to a wide crack behind a pinnacle. From its top, continue up
the blocky crest.

20 Light Entertainment 135m III **   (1989)
A fine climb up the line of defined grooves. Start a short way below
Apex Gully and traverse right on a low ledge to climb a V-groove. Follow
a line of grooves and chimneys just left of the crest to finish up the fault
in the final steep tower.

21 Barndance 50m HVS   (1988)
Left of the first pitch of Flakes of Fear is another corner.
1. 20m 4c Climb the corner and the cracks above to a ledge and loose
flakes.
2. 20m 5b/c Climb to a ledge on the arete, step right and go up to a
niche. Pull over the bulge to a ledge.
3. 10m 5b/c Climb the thin crack above to easy ground. Either
scramble down left into the gully or go up to the plateau, Very Difficult.

22 Flakes of Fear 55m E3   (1987)
Left of Groove and Rib are two large roofs. Start below the left end of
the right roof.
1. 5b Climb a long groove system to small heather ledges.
2. 5c Climb the wall above, finishing just right of a triangular niche *via*
some hollow-sounding flakes; serious.

23 Groove and Rib 135m Hard Severe   (1962)
Start in Diagonal Gully at about the level of the lowest rocks on the left
and below the leftmost and cleanest of three large open grooves.
1. 30m 4b Climb a 5m left-facing corner and move delicately right
(crux) to join the main groove just above the level of the big roof. Climb
the main groove to a stance.
2. 35m Go up the groove, becoming grassy, then right onto the rib.
3. and 4. 70m Climb the crest, then finish by steeper cracks and flakes.
Winter: V,6 **   (1985)
Climb the summer line, except gain the main groove from the right up
an ice smear. If climbed up the summer start it is protectionless and
has a technical grade of 8.

24 Honest Outlet 150m IV,5   (1986)
The straight and often icy groove right of Groove and Rib merges with
Deception Inlet after 65m.

25 Deception Inlet 135m Severe   (1960)
The third curving groove is very vegetated. Start at a groove on the left
of a small rock mass. Climb the groove, then go easily into the main
groove. Above, the groove widens to an amphitheatre. Go straight up
over ledges and blocks to a wall and climb a corner up it. Continue up,
then veer left up a wide depression to a short arete leading to the top.
Winter: IV,5   (1979)
Climb the summer route. Above the amphitheatre there is a choice of
lines; trending right is fairly obvious and interesting.

26 Optical Illusion 80m E1   (1989)
Start up Deception Inlet, as for Lonesome Pine.
1. 20m 5a Climb Lonesome Pine, pitch 1.
2. 45m 5c Climb the left-hand crack into a deep groove. Continue over
the roof above to a small wide crack.
3. 15m 4b Climb up left to a roof, cross this *via* deep cracks and go up
to belay. A pitch of Very Difficult scrambling leads to the top.

27 Lonesome Pine 90m E1   (1987)
1. 20m 5a Climb Deception Inlet for a few metres, then step left into a crack and go up to a left-trending ramp. Climb this and go right up a wall to under a leaning crack-groove system.
2. etc. 70m Climb the groove system to easier ground, then follow the continuation corner to easy ground

28 Wee Timorous Beastie 150m V,7   (1995)
This route climbs the wall just right of Deception Inlet and left of Monarch of the Glen. Start by Deception Inlet.
1. 50m Work up right into a narrow roofed groove split by twin cracks and belay under the roof.
2. 30m Climb twin cracks and continue to below a cracked slab.
3. 20m Climb the undercut slab above by an awkward roof crack.
4. 50m Follow easier ground to the top.

29 Monarch of the Glen 160m VS   (1992)
This route follows a system of grooves up the left edge of Pine Tree Buttress and is independent until the last pitch. Start 15m below Deception Inlet at the base of a steep wall with red streaks and a flake belay.
1. 30m 5a Climb the groove line up the right side of the wall to reach the right end of a diagonal roof. Move left under the roof and break through at a V-notch. Climb the groove above and go up rightwards to a small stance between two grooves.
2. 30m 4b Pull up into the left-hand groove and climb it, finishing up steep blocky rocks to gain the ledge.
3. 40m A steep crack in a short wall above leads awkwardly into another groove system. Follow this to a ledge overlooking Deception Inlet.
4. 30m Climb the obvious cracks in the wall above.
5. 30m Follow the easy ridge to the top.
Winter: VI,7 *   (1991)
Follow the summer route, except that on pitch 2 swing left after about 7m into an easier groove.

30 Pine Tree Route 180m Difficult   (1949)
The broad rib overlooking Amphitheatre Gully is of more interest to the botanist than the climber. It starts from the lowest rocks and wends it way up the edge, becoming steeper near the top.

Winter: III   (1970)
Start up the broad lower rib, which may be coated with ice spilling out of Amphitheatre Gully. The upper section is steeper and rockier, but is climbed keeping fairly close to the right edge.

31 Amphitheatre Gully 225m V,5 **   (1971)
The obvious gully which splits the Right Section gives a good winter route. Follow the gully into the upper amphitheatre, which gives at least one long ice pitch. The final two pitches lie up the left corner of the large wedge-shaped wall which backs the amphitheatre. The lower of these is usually the crux and can be hard for the grade. The final pitch may exit through a rock window.

32 Amphitheatre Wall 60m Hard Severe *   (1977)
A pleasant route which makes a reasonable finish to the climbs which end lower down. It can also be reached by scrambling down from the plateau and traversing in from the right.
1. 35m Climb the corner crack on the left to a grassy bay, then move up and right onto a blocky ledge.
2. 25m 4b Step left from the blocks and climb the crack into the tapered chimney, and so to the top.

33 Amphitheatre Gully, Right-Hand Finish 75m V,7   (1986)
The first corner right of the normal finish. Go up the corner until it is blocked by a roof; move right, then left to gain the corner and cracked slab above the roof. Climb this to the large ledge of Amphitheatre Wall. Finish up the groove-chimney on the right.

34 Maranatha 75m IV,6   (1988)
This climb starts in The Amphitheatre and climbs the wall right of the Right-Hand Finish. Traverse right under a large flake and climb to the right-hand and larger of two grooves. Climb this, passing roofs on their left (crux). Just before a wide chimney, go left by a flake crack to a platform and finish up a corner.

LONGBOW CRAG

This crag lies right of Amphitheatre Gully and takes its name from the large roof about halfway up the crag on its left side. It has generally slabby rock, very quick to dry, but the absence of big easily identified features makes some of the routes awkward to follow. The climbs generally end on broken ground well below the plateau. This face loses its snow very quickly in sunny weather, and can give dry rock early in the year. Some care is needed however, as there is some brittle rock.

35 Relay Climb 200m Hard Severe (1955)
This route follows the left edge overlooking Amphitheatre Gully. Start at the gully edge. Work up the edge to below a bulge at mid-height (60m). From the extreme left edge, go up to a ledge below a large overhang. Go right on this to gain and climb a groove (crux). Continue up the line of the edge to the top.

Winter: V,7 (1981)
Follow an iced groove system right of the summer line, climb the summer crux, then take the line of least resistance.

36 Shotgun 135m VS (1978)
The line of cracks which pass close to the left end of the Longbow Roof. Start about 15 metres left of a pink water-worn fault left of centre, Longbow Direct.
1. 30m Climb a rounded pocketed rib to a large block.
2. 35m Move up left and cross an overlap, go up broken slabs, then continue up a fault left of a steep reddish wall to below obvious cracks.
3. 25m Move left about 5 metres and climb a bulging wall by a small flake to gain a groove above. Follow this, then go left and back right to a large recess by the roof.
4. 45m Climb the corner, then follow the chimney fault.
Winter: V,7 (1992)
Climb the summer route; a thin first pitch and a strenuous third.

37 Longbow Direct 140m VS * (1962)
A varied route taking a line leading to the Longbow roof, the largest overhang on the left side of the face. Start at the pink water-worn fault left of centre.
1. 30m Climb the right side of the fault to below a steep wall.
2. 25m Traverse across the wall for 2 metres, then go up and left to below the obvious steep red wall.
3. 20m 5a Climb an improbable line of jugs and blocks up the wall, make a short traverse left across a slab, then follow a thin crack to a stance. (An easier alternative is to climb the left margin of the red wall).
4. 20m 4c Hand traverse right and go up a short corner to a ledge, climb to below the roof, traverse right again and swing round an arete to a good stance.

5. 45m Climb the layback crack above or follow the fine crack on the slab to its left to reach easier ground. There is now a choice of routes, but the square chimney above is an appropriate finish.
Variation: VS
An alternative start runs up the right side of the water-worn fault to join the route above the level of the Longbow Roof.
Winter: V,7   (1986)
Basically follow the summer line, except bypass the red wall on the left.

38 The Windpiper 170m VII,7   (1988)

A route based on Windchill and Sand-Pyper Direct. Start at the foot of Longbow Direct. Climb the fault for about 10m, then traverse right under a bulge. Go up to the diagonal overlap, descend 5m and traverse right to a good ledge. Gain a higher ledge which leads back to the right end of the diagonal overlap. Cross this, go diagonally left, then climb to a ledge. Traverse right past a jutting block and climb a small right-facing corner system to a good ledge. Traverse this ledge to its end, step right, then go up to a bigger ledge. Traverse right and climb a vegetated wall to the left end of grassy ground, then return left to belay in the diagonal fault. Climb pitch 4 of Sand-Pyper Direct. Go left and climb the wide crack and groove of Windchill, then finish easily.

39 Windchill 170m HVS   (1977)

This route follows the vague rounded rib just right of the pink water-washed fault and gives some pleasant if devious climbing. Start 5 metres right of a chipped arrow.
1. 35m Climb the slab to a diagonal overlap, cross this on the right and continue to a stance below a shallow corner in the next overlap.
2. 40m 4c Traverse 4 metres left to a left-facing corner, climb this a short way, then traverse back right to a flake below a roof. Continue slightly right to a stance below a long diagonal roof (common with Sand-Pyper).
3. 25m 5a Climb the roof on the left, then move down and left until a fault and crack leads up and right to a grassy ledge (common with Sand-Pyper).
4. 30m 5a Move left for 6 metres to a smooth recess by a small natural arch. Climb the recess into a scoop and go up this until a ledge leads right. Go up the steep slab and into a juniper-filled bay.
5. 40m 4b Traverse right past blocks to a groove with a wide crack. Climb this and a fine crack to a good ledge and belay. A chimney and a scramble lead to the finish.

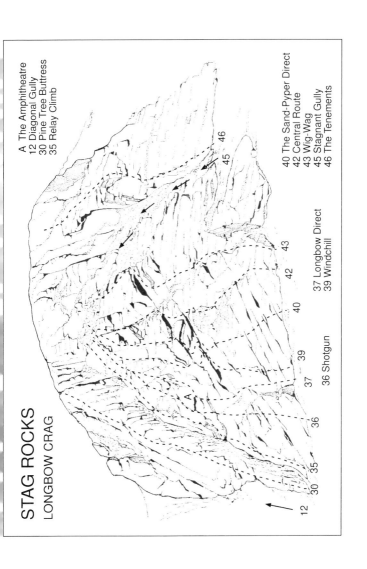

STAG ROCKS
LONGBOW CRAG

A The Amphitheatre
12 Diagonal Gully
30 Pine Tree Buttress
35 Relay Climb

36 Shotgun
37 Longbow Direct
39 Windchill

40 The Sand-Pyper Direct
42 Central Route
43 Wig-Wag
45 Stagnant Gully
46 The Tenements

40 The Sand-Pyper Direct 150m HVS **   (1962)
A fine climb which increases with difficulty and interest with each pitch. Start near the centre of the frontal face about 30 metres right of Longbow Direct.
1. 25m 4a Go left over slab shelves and climb the rounded rib to below a long low diagonal overlap.
2. 30m 4b Go between overlaps, traverse left, then climb up to a small right-facing groove. Climb this, then trend left to a ledge below a large cracked overlap.
3. 25m 4c Traverse right and climb slabs for 12m, then cross the overlap near its right end. Go back diagonally left to a grass ledge.
4. 25m 4c Follow the diagonal fault right over the block (the ordinary route follows this diagonal fault for a further two pitches). Step left over the overlap and follow the groove left to a grassy ledge.
5. 45m 5a Climb the short corner above to the roof, swing right into the next corner and return left as soon as possible (crux). Follow this corner and finish by a pleasant crack and easier ground.
Variation: **The Blue Serge** E1   (1989)
Follow the diagonal fault to the point where the Direct leaves it.
1. 15m 5a Move right to gain an awkward crack and follow this up to a poor stance.
2. 5b Continue right across the slab, then climb over the overlap to an awkward corner. Follow this to a good stance.
3. Follow cracks and grooves left then right to easier ground.

41 Addenda 140m VS   (1972)
A right-slanting diagonal route which starts just left of the vegetated depressions in the centre of the cliff. Climb up and left for two pitches to cross the overlap on the third pitch of Sand-Pyper and belay on the grass ledge as for that route. Finish with the last two pitches of Windchill.

42 Central Route 140m VI,7   (1979)
Climb the series of vegetated depressions up the centre of the cliff to the diagonal fault of Sand-Pyper. Finish up the continuation of the line.

43 Wigwag 150m Severe   (1962)
An interesting although somewhat contrived route on clean rock between the vegetated depressions and the grassy gully on the right margin. Start below and left of the obvious wide corner-crack.

1. 30m Climb the right edge of the slab to Juniper Ledge, then go left to behind a flake.

2. 30m Continue up to overhangs, avoid them on the left, then traverse rightwards along a shelf and go up to belay on the left of the prominent triangular overhang.

3. 30m Climb good rock above.

4. 25m Go right for 10m, then climb up and left to the top of a large flake. Continue to the left end of the flake and go along a narrow shelf to a large vegetated groove and the grassy amphitheatre.

5. 35m Climb short walls on the left, then scramble to the top.

Winter: V,6   (1978)

The route followed in winter is loosely based on the summer line, where ice forms and where the turf exists. The final short corner to gain the amphitheatre can be hard.

44 Flock of Chickens 140m VI,7   (1986)

This route starts in the depression below the wide corner-crack and takes the rib to the right of Central Route. It then finishes up the obvious direct continuation as for Central Route.

45 Stagnant Gully 180m IV,4   (1995)

This is the large grassy fault which higher up becomes an amphitheatre. Climb the fault, sometimes on ice and grass or on snow, for 90m. (By going left above the main face the climb is Grade II.) Trend up and left into an obvious V-groove. Climb the groove, thread the chokestone, then continue more easily to the plateau.

The slab on the left flank of the obvious roofs overlooking the grassy amphitheatre gives a two-pitch VS which finishes up a groove.

46 The Tenements 155m Very Difficult *   (1955)

On the right side of Stagnant Gully is a cleaner rocky buttress which gives the line of the climb. Start at the left edge of the rocks.

1. 20m Climb cracked slabs and blocks to a ledge.

2. 35m Go left into a recess, exit right awkwardly and work up left on fine bubbly rock to easier ground.

3. 35m Climb the big open groove above.

4. 30m Turn the steep overlap above on the right and go back diagonally left.

5. 35m Continue diagonally left to the top.

Winter: V,6   (1979)

Follow the summer route.

47 Diamond Groove 70m V,6   (1995)
This climb takes the crest of the buttress to the right of The Tenements.
Climb a large turfy groove 5 metres up and right from the lowest rocks,
then follow blocky ground to another groove capped by a small tower.
Climb the groove then the difficult left-trending continuation to finish.

STAC AN FHARAIDH

(Map Ref 014 030)

These cliffs lie on the south flank of Cairn Gorm overlooking Loch Avon
near The Saddle at the head of Strath Nethy. It is an area of glaciated
slabs which give climbs up to 140m in length on rough and generally
sound granite. The slabs themselves are divided into east and west
flanks by a shallow grassy fault, Rectangular Gully, which gives a Grade
I/II winter climb but is unpleasant steep grass in summer.

Approaches
From the north side of Loch Avon walk uphill to the slabs. From
Strathspey go to the top station of the chair lift, contour round the east
side of Cairn Gorm (or go over the top) and descend to the top of the
cliffs near the stream which flows down to their east. Either descend
by the easy slopes overlooking The Saddle and traverse back west
below the level of some broken rocks to the crag, or descend by the
west bank of the stream which drains south-west into the loch. This is
the most convenient descent but it can be very wet and slippery or
involve some scrambling down the initial steep section.
   In winter the East Flank can bank out completely leaving only
high-angled snow and a few ice bulges, but early in the season or in
lean conditions more interesting climbing can be found; Pippet Slab is
Grade II/III and Pushover follows thin ice smears at IV,4. The West Flank
can hold a lot of ice and gives some good climbs, although being
south-facing they are adversely affected by the sun and are consequently better early in the season. The approach down the line of the
stream can be an avalanche risk at times.

WEST FLANK

This section of the cliff is characterised by a diagonal wall which cuts
the slabs at about mid-height and increases in size from right to left to
finally merge into a steeper pillar on the extreme left. The climbs on the

bulk of the cliff tend to suffer from the fact that crossing the central wall is often much harder than the slabs above and below. A good reference point for the leftmost climbs is a long block lying some way up the initial very easy-angled slabs.

Left of the main slab is an area of gullies and smaller buttresses lying just below the plateau. Some of the gullies here, although short, are well defined and give interesting short routes of about Grade I to II. The deep lower section of Narrow Gully is obvious.

1 Shallow Gully 160m III   (1985)
Left of Narrow Gully is a broad, broken buttress. This route climbs the obvious shallow gully immediately left of the broken buttress, keeping right at the top where it is better defined.

2 Narrow Gully 180m II/III
This is the gully on the left of the main slabs. The bottom section is narrow and deep-cut with an awkward step at its head. Above, it is straightforward.

3 Rectangular Rib 120m Difficult   (1952)
The rib just left of the main slab which overlooks Narrrow Gully gives slabby climbing which gets more interesting with height.
Winter: II/III   (1981)
Follow the summer route, starting up the shallow, tapered chimney.

4 Mack's Dilemma 130m VS *   (1969)
A good climb which follows the left edge of the West Flank. Start at the left edge of the slabs.
1. 30m Climb cracked slabs to belay 6m below a right-facing corner.
2. 20m Climb the corner and continue up the rib, with a short excursion to the left before reaching a block platform.
3. 20m 4c Continue over an awkward bulge and go up the rib to a ledge.
4. 25m 4b Go a short way up the right side of the arete, move left onto the edge and continue to a large ledge.
5. 35m Climb easier ground in the same line to the top.

5 Speakeasy 120m VS   (1978)
This takes a line parallel to and right of the left edge of the slabs. Start at the left end of the long block. Climb the slab over two small overlaps to a belay in a corner in the large overlap. Exit left from the corner onto the ledge and traverse on the shelf above to a small corner. Climb the

corner, move right then back left with an awkward mantelshelf (5a), then go straight up to a grassy ledge. Follow the fault above into a short deep chimney. Climb this and the crack above; a short easy pitch then leads to the top.

6 Spirit Voices 120m VI,8   (1991)
A winter route based on Speakeasy. Climb the first pitch of that route to belay in the corner. Traverse right under the roof, then follow ice smears up and back left to below the upper rocks. Work up into the short V-chimney and climb it to the roof and exit left. Climb a short wall, then continue more easily up and right to finish.

7 Sermon 120m VS   (1969)
This route takes the frequently very wet line of parallel cracks which lead up into the big recess at the left side of the diagonal wall. Start by the long block and climb the cracks into the recess. Continue up the deep crack in the corner in the same line to the top.
Winter: V,6 **   (1986)
A good route which follows the summer line, firstly up thinly iced slabs leading to steeper walls and bulges into the big recess. Finish by the main corner.

8 Cherry 140m E1   (1975)
A line up the slabs whose main interest is in crossing the diagonal wall by an arrowhead-like formation with an obvious corner on the left. Start below the line at a left-facing corner. Climb the slabs for two pitches to below an obvious corner. Move left for 6 metres, gain a ledge above, traverse back right, make a blind move onto the slab above and belay on the left. Climb slabs to the left, then finish up the corner above.

9 The Deluge 140m E3   (1971)
A very unbalanced route. Start below the shallow chimney fault left of Apres Moi.
1. 40m Climb grassy slabs.
2. 25m 4c Climb the fault, with a slight excursion onto a rib to below the overlap.
3. 45m 6b Climb the bulging chimney (crux) and continue trending slightly leftwards to the apex of a slabby recess.
4. 30m Either descend slightly rightwards and finish up dirty slabs or, better, take the top part of Apres Moi.

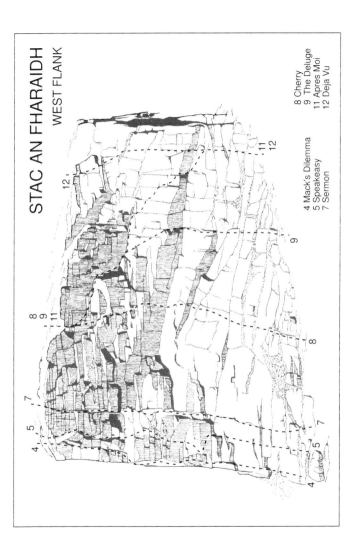

STAC AN FHARAIDH

WEST FLANK

4 Mack's Dilemma
5 Speakeasy
7 Sermon

8 Cherry
9 The Deluge
11 Apres Moi
12 Deja Vu

10 Hoity-Toity 160m IV,4 *   (1980)
A diagonal line on the lip of the diagonal wall which eventually breaks
through the steep upper walls by an icefall just left of the top corner of
Apres Moi. Start as for Apres Moi to above the diagonal wall.

11 Apres Moi 150m VS   (1969)
A rather wandering line which makes the best use of the right-hand
side of the slabs; the upper section is slow to dry. Start at cracks near
the right edge of the slab.
1. 30m Climb the cracks to below the steep central wall and move left
to a small recess.
2. 40m 4c Go up the recess, break left at the top and move left to a
shallow corner. Climb this until it ends, move left, then climb cracks.
3. 25m Go diagonally left over easy slabs to a large right-facing corner.
4. 45m 4b Climb the corner and continue leftwards.
5. 10m Continue in this line to the top.
Winter: III *   (1980)
Climb the summer line; the top corner often holds a lot of ice.

12 Deja Vu 120m Hard Severe   (1971)
The cracks on the right edge of the slab are unfortunately a bit grassy.
Start just left of the gully, as for Apres Moi.
1. 25m Climb the cracks to a steep wall.
2. 40m Follow the continuation crack to a grassy ledge.
3. 35m Trend up and left *via* cracks and slabs.
4. 20m Climb the easy left-sloping corner to the top.
   In winter, the climb is Grade III,4.

EAST FLANK

The right-hand section of the cliff gives some good, well balanced slab
climbs on rough granite. However, there is some scope for interchang-
ing pitches as there are gentler-angled sections of slab which allow
fairly easy horizontal movement. Belays can be difficult to arrange and
ropes of at least 45m are necessary. A large boulder near the centre
of the base of the crag is an obvious reference point.

13 Whispers 135m VS **   (1969)
A pleasant, popular and quick-drying route following cracks on the left
edge of the slab. Start at the second crack system from the left.
1. 45m 4a Climb the crack, vegetated at first, to an easing in the angle.

2. 45m 4b Continue up the same crack system, very close to the left edge at one point, to a huge flake below a steep grey wall.
3. 45m 4c From the top of the flake, traverse about 6m right, then move diagonally right through the bulge onto the slab above. Go diagonally left, then straight up to finish.

14 Throwover 135m VS   (1971)
This route starts to the left of Bellows then crosses it. Start at the crack 5 metres right of Whispers.
1. 45m Climb the crack.
2. 30m Move diagonally right to a sloping ledge on Bellows, then break through the overlap, 1 nut for aid, and belay left of the rib.
3. 30m Climb the thin rib to reach then follow the crack directly above. Climb straight over the bulge, 1 peg for aid, about 5 metres right of the crux bulge of Whispers, then continue up to a belay.
4. 30m Climb a rounded crack, then go right up an awkward wall right of a grassy recess and a wet step to finish.

15 Bellows 140m HVS *   (1970)
Another good route up cracks parallel to and about 12 metres right of Whispers. Start 6 metres left of the large boulder. Climb an easy vegetated crack to below a bulge. Climb the corner crack through the bulge and continue up the slab to an enormous scoop below the main overlap. Climb a series of slabs diagonally left to a crack, cross the final bulge (5a), and continue up the cracks to the huge flake. Alternatively, after the bulge, go right on pockets to a small corner, then trend up and left to the huge flake. Go up the crack, then move diagonally right through the bulge (as for the crux of Whispers). Continue to the top.

16 Nosey Parker 135m HVS   (1981)
An eliminate between Bellows and Pushover, but worthwhile nevertheless. Start up Pushover. Climb the initial crack, break out left to an overlap, climb this *via* a small corner, then go up to below the main overlap. Move left and climb back right across the wall of the overlap until it can be surmounted, then go up to the next overlap. Climb direct to the top in two pitches.

17 Pushover 140m HVS **   (1969)
The most substantial route here, taking a line up the centre of the slab. Start at the crack on the left of the large boulder.
1. 45m 4c Climb the sustained crack to the crescent-shaped overlap.

2. 15m 5a Pull onto the overlap and move left until the upper slab can be gained, then move up to a ledge.
3. 40m 4c Trend up and left to a steeper wall, and climb this by a series of cracks to below mossy blocks.
4. 40m 4b Climb over the blocks and go up slabs to a chimney. Finish up the wall above.
Alternative finish:
From the top of the second pitch, climb up and right to surmount a nose of rock by a seam and continue up the slab (45m). Continue up a corner, then move up and go left to the chimney and so to the top.

18 Yin and Yang 190m E1   (1990)
Good but disjointed climbing finishing spectacularly up the left side of the big prow overlooking Rectangular Gully. Start just right of Pushover below a blank slab with a scoop at 5m.
1. 20m 5a Climb the slab to a ledge and move left to climb a shallow left-trending crack. Cross the slab on the right to belay on Pushover.
2. 45m Trend back left over an overlap and climb corners to an easy slab which leads to the corner on Bellows at the start of its crux pitch.
3. 45m 5a Step onto the nose on the right at head-height, then traverse right and pull onto the slab above (long reach). Climb easily up and left to near Whispers.
4. 20m Move easily left round the corner into the gully.
5. 15m 5a Move up to a fine flake leading up left, quit this after 3m and climb straight up the overhang on good holds to easy ground.
6. 45m Easy climbing leads to the top.

19 Rockover 130m E1   (1994)
A fine and fairly direct line between Pushover and Pippet Slab. Start at the base of the slab between those two routes, as for Yin and Yang.
1. 45m 5a Climb the slab to an obvious groove line and follow it to near the left end of the initial left-slanting crack of pitch 2 of Pippet Slab.
2. 25m 5c Move up, then right onto the slab above (as for Pippet), traverse halfway along the slab and reach over the overlap to gain a faint ledge. Rockover to gain the slab (crux). Move up then left to a mucky groove, and pass this by the slab on the left to gain a belay just above.
3. 40m 5a Continue right up a slab to an overlap with an obvious crack above. Climb the crack to a ledge. Climb up on the right and move left slightly to a belay.
4. 20m 4c Continue up to the right to finish as for Pippet Slab.

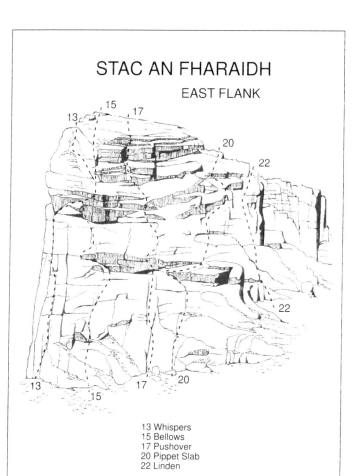

STAC AN FHARAIDH

EAST FLANK

13 Whispers
15 Bellows
17 Pushover
20 Pippet Slab
22 Linden

20 Pippet Slab 135m Mild Severe **   (1970)
A good route but sparsely protected in places. Start at the crack on the right of the large boulder.
1. 45m Climb the crack system to below the steep wall.
2. 30m Go diagonally left until a move can be made onto the slab above the wall, cross this, then regain the line of the crack and bear slightly left to below an overlap.
3. 45m Go up the shallow stepped right-facing corner system to a niche in the steeper section.
4. 15m Continue in the same line to the top. It is necessary to continue some way back to find anchors.
Variation: Hard Severe
Climb the wide crack in the overlap above pitch 1.

21 Shielden 80m Very Difficult   (1970)
This climb lies to the right of Linden and starts at the left-hand chimney 10 metres left of the chimney of Jillden.
1. 20m Climb the chimney.
2. 25m Go straight up easy slabs to below an obvious slabby corner.
3. 20m Traverse 4m left and climb diagonally right to a crack. Climb this and continue up the wall to a sloping ledge.
4. 15m Traverse left across the wall, mantelshelf and continue to the top.

22 Linden 60m Very Difficult **   (1970)
An excellent little route which lies on the right of the slab and high up takes the obvious sloping ramp. Start in the large grass bay on the right where a narrow grass ledge runs to a right-facing corner crack.
1. 30m Climb a short crack 5 metres right of the corner and follow thin flakes up the blunt arete. A short steep crack leads to a sloping stance.
2. 30m Climb the ramp by the layback crack, then the continuation corner.

23 Jillden 55m Difficult   (1970)
The obvious chimney on the right of the slabs. Start in the grassy bay below this at the right-hand of two cracks.
1. 25m Climb the rib left of the crack to below an obvious sloping corner.
2. 30m Walk along a sloping ramp to below the chimney, then climb it.

The Ben Macdui Massif

Although Scotland's second highest mountain is mostly rounded in character, Ben Macdui (1309m, Map Ref 989 989) provides some fine and remote climbing in its secluded corries.

COIRE SPUTAN DEARG
(Map Ref 000 988)

Coire Sputan Dearg lies at the head of Glen Luibeg, high on the south-eastern flank of Ben Macdui. In spring and early summer, its dark buttresses stand out boldly against the old snow and are often clearly visible from as far away as the road between Braemar and Linn of Dee. 'Sputan' is an unique corrie with a charm all of its own. The south-facing crag is a rarity in the Cairngorms and the granite is rough, clean, sound and very quick to dry. The corrie's open and sunny situation lends an unusually friendly atmosphere; the routes are short (30-150m) and descents are quick and easy, making it possible to accomplish many routes in one visit. Few climbers could fail to enjoy a day climbing on Sputan Dearg, but it is not the place for the hard man since its slabby nature and good holds preclude the modern technical route. For the lower grades, however, there is no better place in the Cairngorms.

Winter
With a cliff base at 1100m, Sputan is one of the highest corries in the area. A considerable build-up of snow may accumulate during the season and many of the rock features may be buried. The climbing is of a less exacting nature than on Creagan a' Choire Etchachan, but it serves as a useful alternative to that cliff when the freezing level is above the 1000m mark, or during periods of hard frost and sunny weather when the snow in Coire Sputan Dearg consolidates more quickly. In late season the buttresses are quickly stripped of snow by the sun, but they can give good climbing after a fresh fall of powder any time between October and May.

Approaches
1. From Braemar via Derry Lodge and Glen Luibeg.
From Braemar, take the public road to the Linn of Dee and go back towards Braemar on the north side of the Dee for 200m to a new

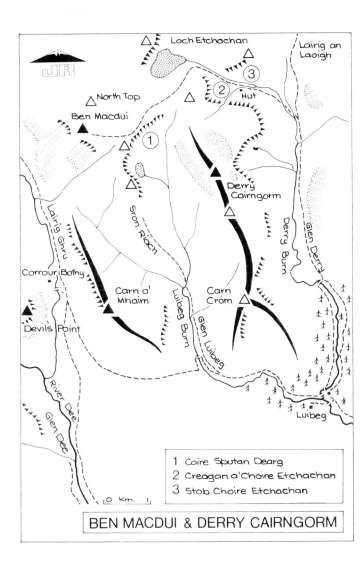

1 Coire Sputan Dearg
2 Creagan a'Choire Etchachan
3 Stob Choire Etchachan

BEN MACDUI & DERRY CAIRNGORM

carpark in the woods. A signposted path leads from here to join a track from the Derry Gates (locked) to Derry Lodge, 5km. On bike, the track is best followed throughout. Then follow the Lairig Ghru track for 3km and fork right up a rising path until some 150m short of the Luibeg burn. Follow the path up the burn; it gradually peters out. (8km from Derry Lodge.)

2. From Hutchison Memorial Hut (see Creagan a' Choire Etchachan). Follow the stream coming down the wide grassy basin to the left of the cliffs of Creagan a' Choire Etchachan and go over the col between that top and Derry Cairngorm (2km).

Accommodation
The Hutchison Memorial Hut (see Creagan a' Choire Etchachan) is the closest reliable shelter for Coire Sputan Dearg, but there are one or two draughty 'howffs' amongst the boulders in the corrie which are suitable for dry summer weather. Further from the crags, but still a good base, is Bob Scott's bothy. Bob Scott was the keeper at Luibeg for many years and a great friend of climbers. A new bothy has been built by Aberdeen climbers; the good relationship with the estate is worth maintaining. In the woods (now partly felled) just before Derry Lodge, take the road left towards Luibeg. On reaching the bridge, walk downstream for a short way to the bothy (Map Ref 042 932). There are good camp sites at Robber's Copse, a stand of old Caledonian pines at the ford over the Luibeg (3km from Derry Lodge), and also further up Glen Luibeg on the raised green shelves at the confluence of the Allt Carn a' Mhaim on the left bank. There is excellent camping just beyond Derry Lodge itself. It is also possible to camp just below the crag.

Descents
Descents present no problem. Glissade Gully (scree) is the easiest and centrally situated.

THE RED SLABS

These are the gently inclined glaciated slabs approximately 200 metres left of the leftmost buttress (Pinnacle Buttress). The slabs are affected by melt water well into the summer and it is doubtful whether they are ever completely dry. However, the granite is very rough and may be climbed at almost any point, even when wet. They freeze up readily and provide good ice practice at the start of the winter before banking out quickly.

The large prominent corner on the upper left-hand section of the slabs is **Rainmate** (Severe, Grade III). **Umbrella** (VS) takes a fairly direct line up the slabs, starting at an undercut crack just right of the lowest rocks. The best rock climb, however, is Sundance.

Sundance 120m VS 4b   (1970)
The route is a rising traverse across the slabs below the big overlap, crossing Umbrella. Start 15m up from the lowest slabs on the left at an obvious corner. Climb the corner, go right across the glacis, surmount the overlap and continue to a ledge below the vegetated corner crack (30m). Traverse horizontally right and climb a slab to a ledge. Go up to the main overlap, then traverse right below an overhanging block studded with quartz crystals and work up right to the edge of the upper slab. Step across a corner and continue to a ledge. Climb a vertical crack to the roof. Move right under the roof and go up to a belay below the final corner. Climb the corner to easy ground.

A winter ascent has been made at Grade III, but the route is usually banked out.

THE BUTTRESSES

These start high on the left of the corrie, adjacent to The Red Slabs, and they extend north in a descending line, merging gradually into broken rock near the low col leading to Loch Etchachan. They are intersected at three points by wide scree gullies (The Red Spouts) which provide easy means of descent.

Pinnacle Buttress 110m Moderate   (1948)
The first buttress from the left is easily recognised by a ledge of easy ground coming in from the right, halfway up. In winter this looks like a notch. Start at an obvious line of weakness at the foot of the buttress. Climb this initial weakness to reach a long groove forming an angle between the true crest on the right and a 30m cracked slab on the left. Start up the groove but leave it soon to slant up the slab to reach its top left corner. Scramble to the plateau.
Variation: **Direct Route** Severe
The true crest of the buttress overlooking the cracked slab gives a pleasant airy climb. A variation start, Severe, has been made to the right of the crest up a smooth slab bounding The Red Gully.

Winter: II   (1950)
An enjoyable winter route. The lower rocks are easy, but the long groove may contain ice (crux).

The Red Gully 120m I
A straightforward snow climb.

Crystal Ridge 90m Difficult **   (1948)
A grand and popular little climb. As closely as possible, follow the crest of the great slab angling into and bolstering up the upper left flank of Grey Man's Crag. The ridge has a steep left wall bordering The Red Gully.
Winter: III   (1949)
An attractive snow arete provides the finish to the route.

Slab Chimney, Right Branch 120m II/III *   (1949)
This good gully cuts deeply into the flank of Grey Man's Crag, showing up as a perfect Y from the Luibeg approach. Easy snow leads to the junction. The right branch contains two chokestones which give awkward ice pitches, but the difficulty eases with an increased build-up of snow. The left branch gives a good introduction to snow climbing in a scenic position (Grade I, 1949). Unpleasant and Difficult in summer.

GREY MAN'S CRAG

This is the largest buttress in the corrie, and it includes some of Sputan's longest and best climbs. It is defined by Slab Chimney on the left and Anchor Gully on the right. The frontal face is split by numerous grooves and narrow slabs which tend to lean left towards the very steep wall above Slab Chimney. High on the left, overlooking Slab Chimney, a remarkable crack can be seen cleaving the steep face, The Plumb-line. A girdle traverse of Grey Man's Crag has been made (Hard Severe), starting in Anchor Gully and finishing up The Plumbline.

1 Sapphire 50m E1   (1986)
This route takes the wall to the right of the striking arete on the far left of the buttress. Low in its grade. Start by climbing the first 15m of Crystal Ridge to a ledge, then traverse to a grassy niche below an obvious green corner.
1. 20m 5a Move onto the wall to the right of the niche. Climb into a short groove diagonally right, then exit left to a slab leading to a grass ledge.

2. 30m 5b Climb the groove and overhang, then continue steeply and slightly left until the angle eases. Move right to join the crack of The Plumbline. At the top of its chimney, move left along a ledge to finish up the exposed arete and the wall on its right.

2 The Plumbline 40m Hard Severe   (1956)
This remarkable crack cleaves the steep face overlooking Slab Chimney. It is normally started *via* Amethyst Wall, leaving after its short slab and going up left *via* a groove to the crack.
Winter: 100m V,7   (1991)
With sufficient build-up, Slab Chimney can allow direct access to the route. Start 10m above Amethyst Wall (winter); this is 10m above the ledge where the first slanting pitch of Amethyst Wall (summer) ends.
1. 10m Climb up easily right to belay below a steep groove which descends from the Plumbline crack.
2. 10m Climb the groove and belay on the left.
3. 35m Make a hard move on to the wall above to enter the crack. Climb this to the top, exiting steeply right.
4. 45m Continue up the crest to the top.

3 Amethyst Wall 120m HVS   (1956)
This meandering route on the steep wall right of The Plumbline crack has been superseded in quality by Amethyst Pillar. Climb the prominent chimney-crack slanting low above Slab Chimney to a grass ledge. Scramble up 6m, then traverse down and right to a ledge on the face. Work up right *via* three flake cracks to a large ramp ascending from the depression on Pilgrim's Groove. Go left on the ramp to a stance. Move around the corner on the left and climb a short slab to a grass ledge and block belay. Directly above is a corner, and to the left is the crack of The Plumbline. Go right for 5 metres to below an overhang, then climb it (crux) and follow a vertical crack before moving right and finishing up slabs.
Winter: VI,7   (1988)
The winter route turns the summer crux by a devious line on its left. Start by climbing directly to the ledge above the slanting chimney and climb the next two pitches of the summer route. Go up left to the foot of The Plumbline crack and make a slightly descending right traverse to a small ledge directly above the last belay. A short corner and exit right on flakes regains the summer line.

COIRE SPUTAN DEARG

GREY MAN'S CRAG

5 Amethyst Pillar
6 Pilgrim's Groove
7 Lucifer Route
8 Grey Slab
9 Ferlas Mor
10 Hanging Dyke
11 Ghost Slab
12 Ardath Chimney
13 Aurora

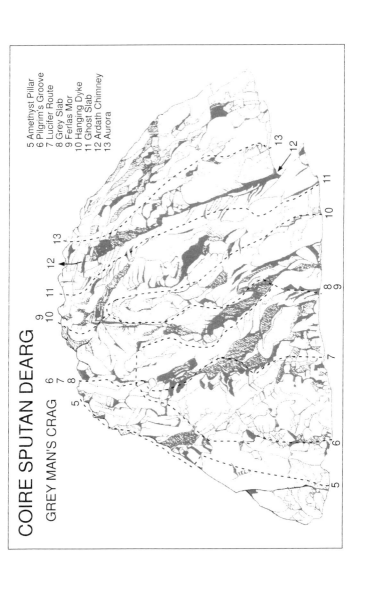

4 Zircon 120m E2   (1992)
An eliminate line left of Amethyst Pillar gives good sustained climbing, high in the grade, with pitch 4 needing a forceful approach. Start 10m below the chimney of Amethyst Wall.
1. 10m 4c Step onto the slab on the right and climb to a large ledge.
2. 35m 5c Follow Amethyst Pillar for a few metres, then take the crack system trending left. Pass below a narrow rectangular roof, climb the steep crack system 3 metres to its left and make a strenuous exit on large holds to reach a ledge.
3. 25m 5a Continue up the left-facing chimney-groove directly above. This is left of the flake pitch on Amethyst Wall.
4. 20m 5c This takes the steep wall between the crux pitch of Amethyst Wall and Amethyst Pillar, pitch 3. Gain a small sloping triangular ledge from the right and follow a line of flakes diagonally left across the wall to a steep finish on the left arete.
5. 30m 4a Easy cracks and grooves lead to the top.

5 Amethyst Pillar 100m HVS ***   (1964/79)
This direct line to the right of Amethyst Wall gives an excellent steep climb. Start at the foot of a prominent slanting chimney-fault.
1. 40m 4c Move out right to steep slabs, starting about 5m below a curious round niche. Alternatively, climb into the niche and exit right. Climb up the wall above (Pilgrim's Groove crux is now 3m to the right). Go left and pull over a bulge into an obvious hanging corner. Step left at a small roof, then go down left and traverse along a flake ledge to its end.
2. 25m 4c The flakes of Amethyst Wall can now be seen to the left. Above is a shallow cracked groove with a bulge. Climb the groove and exit right onto a ramp which ascends from the depression of Pilgrim's Groove. Alternatively, climb diagonally right across the steep wall above the flake ledge to gain the same ramp lower down. Follow the ramp up left to its top.
3. 35m 5a Go up right to an obvious vertical crack above a rock pedestal. Use a loose jammed flake to overcome the initial bulge and continue directly up the crack to slabs which lead to the top.

6 Pilgrim's Groove 120m Hard Severe   (1949)
Situated just left of centre on the buttress and to the left of the lowest rocks, this route follows a defined groove developing into a prominent chimney. It is somewhat vegetated and the chimney is usually wet. The

fault right of and parallel to Pilgrim's Groove is Lucifer Route. Start in the groove. Climb moderate rock to a stance about 10m below a triangular overhang. Continue up the groove to the overhang, turn it on its left wall and climb steep rock to a large grassy depression. The next pitch is the continuation chimney which rises for 20m in four steps, each progressively more difficult. The remainder is easy.

Variation Finish: VS 4b
Better than the original. Start from the grassy depression and climb a groove and chimney line on the left, finishing by a swing out left under an overhang.

Winter: V,7 *   (1981)
A natural winter line with a very technical but well protected crux. The upper chimney is occasionally a fine icefall. Follow the summer route to the grassy depression. On the only known ascent, in lean conditions, the Variation Finish was followed, using tension below the overhang to gain the summer line.

7 Lucifer Route 120m Severe   (1956)
This vegetated route (with a clean crux) follows a fault parallel to and right of Pilgrim's Groove. The fault is blocked by a large overhang. Climb the fault to belay under the overhang. Go up the vertical right wall on good flake holds (crux), then continue up the fault to belay beside the large depression of Pilgrim's Groove. Climb to the right over a huge detached block onto Grey Slab and go up to a belay on a ledge near its top. Move left and step down into the chimney of Pilgrim's Groove. Follow this to the top.

Winter: VI,7   (1983)
Climb the summer line, using 1 peg for aid at the crux.

8 Grey Slab 115m Hard Severe ***   (1963)
This excellent route follows a conspicuous corner trending left up the centre of the buttress. Near the top, it climbs the right side of a large slab which gives the route its name. Scramble up broken rocks to a good platform 10m below the corner.
1. 10m Climb a shallow depression and move awkwardly right to below the corner.
2. 20m Climb the corner to a grass platform.
3. 40m Continue up the corner to an overhang. Turn this on the left and go up to a ledge (possible belay). Climb by the corner at the right edge of the Grey Slab, until forced to move left at its top.

4. 45m Step down and enter the chimney of Pilgrim's Groove on the left (as for Lucifer Route). It is better (but 4c) to climb a short slab and enter Pilgrim's Groove higher up. Finish by Pilgrim's Groove.
Winter: VII,7 ***   (1984)
A superb sustained route by the summer line. A pitch up the centre of the upper Grey Slab is perhaps the highlight. One peg for aid on pitch 2.

9 Ferlas Mor 125m Hard Severe **   (1971)
A direct line between Grey Slab and Hanging Dyke. The climbing is as good as Grey Slab and the standard similar, but the line is less prominent. Start as for Grey Slab.
1. 10m Climb Grey Slab, pitch 1. For an independent start, climb the layback corner right of the normal start (5a).
2. 30m Swing up right and climb grooves and ribs on the edge overlooking the Grey Slab to a basalt fault. Climb the fault to a ledge and belay below the crux of Hanging Dyke.
3. 40m Move left and continue up grooves, exiting onto the crest on the right, level with the top of the Grey Slab.
4. 45m Continue to the top on the skyline, *via* a short easy chimney and an arete.
Winter: VI,8 *   (1990)
A sustained and technical route with a fierce second pitch. Follow the summer line for 3 pitches, then take the natural continuation up the groove and chimney of Hanging Dyke to gain the summer line above.

10 Hanging Dyke 120m Very Difficult *   (1949)
A popular route following the backbone of the buttress by a geological dyke. The crux is delicate and exposed. Start to the right of the lowest rocks at the foot of a broad slab; the dyke goes up the centre of this slab. Follow the dyke to a small ledge, then climb a grass-filled crack to a good stance. Climb a wide slab inclining left by a series of parallel cracks to a sloping corner. The dyke steepens and forms a rib to the left of the groove. Climb the rib for 20m on small holds (crux) until the dyke falls back into a chimney. Follow the continuation of the dyke up left on the crest for a further 30m.
Winter: V,5 *   (1971)
A sustained climb. The crux is the steep rib, as in summer.

Zircon, Coire Sputan Dearg (Climber, Simon Richardson)

11 Ghost Crack 90m VS   (1972)
This is the shallow crack slightly left of the crest between Hanging Dyke
and Ardath Chimney. Technically interesting climb but a little artificial.
1. 40m 4b Climb the crack to a ledge and go slightly right by a short,
deeper crack to another ledge below obvious stepped overlaps.
2. 45m 4c Surmount the overlaps and climb the thin crack above until
a smooth wall forces a traverse up right to a slab overlooking Ardath
Chimney. An easier alternative is to step round the arete on the left
and follow cracks, initially overlooking Hanging Dyke, to reach the slab.
Climb a crack in the slab, then easier rock to a belay.
3. 5m A short pitch leads to scrambling. In dry weather it is possible
to descend Ardath Chimney (Difficult).

12 Ardath Chimney 120m III *   (1955)
A good winter climb, best climbed early in the season or after a thaw
when the chimney holds plenty of ice. A short ice slab about 30m above
the chimney may prove to be the crux. In summer, the climb is Difficult
for the first 45m of the chimney, then scrambling.

13 Aurora 150m Hard Severe   (1993)
Takes the well defined buttress between Ardath Chimney and Anchor
Gully. Start from the bottom of Ardath Chimney.
1. 30m 4b Move right to the base of a right-facing groove. Climb this
to a roof, move right using a flake and continue up the continuation
groove to its top. Step right and move up to a ledge.
2. 45m 4b Follow cracks straight up to a grass depression at 15m.
Continue straight up on blocky rock.
3. and 4. 75m Easier slabs lead to the top.
Winter: IV,6   (1991)
Climb pitch 1 of the summer route. After 10m of pitch 2, move left into
a groove system which leads to easier ground.

14 Anchor Gully 120m I
The gully between Grey Man's Slab and Anchor Route is named after
the formation of snow at its foot in spring. There may be a pitch early
in the season. Later, the gully becomes quite straightforward except
for the cornice which can usually be outflanked on the right. Moderate
in summer.

The Dagger, Creagan a' Choire Etchachan (Climber, John Swift)

15 Anchor Route 120 III

This route lies on the two-tiered buttress bordering Anchor Gully on the right. In winter the rocks of the lower tier tend to bank out and it is best to start in Anchor Gully. On the upper tier, start and finish right of the crest, but there is an excursion onto the steeper gully wall in the middle.

In summer the route is pleasant but a little scrappy, Difficult.

16 Glissade Gully

Set near the centre of the cliff, this is a natural highway between plateau and corrie floor in both summer and winter. In summer it is scree-filled, in winter a snow slope. There may be a cornice which is avoidable on the left. The small buttress on the left of Glissade Gully is Glissade Buttress, Grade II.

SNAKE RIDGE

On the right of Glissade Gully are twin ridges. The left-hand ridge, which is split into two sections low down, is Janus and the right-hand ridge is Snake Ridge.

Hackingbush's Horror 130m VS   (1956)

This route starts by the steep rib on the left of the chimney (the left leg of Janus). Above the chimney, it takes the upper buttress which has a notched terminating ridge. The first pitch is good, but afterwards the climbing is Difficult, scrappy but interesting. Climb the groove from the foot of the rib to a ledge, then move right to the crest. Step awkwardly left and move up to a platform. Climb the shallow depression above to the foot of a vertical crack with an overhung top. Use a good layback and traverse right to the crest (4b). Follow the ridge to easy ground below the upper buttress. Climb the upper buttress on the left side above Glissade Gully by going round a ledge to the left past an initial groove. When the ledge peters out bear sharp right up a second groove to the crest.

Janus, starting by the right-hand rib is Difficult and in winter, Grade III with 2 pegs for aid in the second groove. The chimney which splits the two ribs in the lower section is **Janus Chimney** (Very Difficult, Grade III).

Snake Gully 130m II *   (1963)
The dividing fault between Janus and Snake Ridge gives a good
natural winter climb. The gully starts as steep snow and curves up left
to an ice pitch. This will vary in length according to the build-up. Easier
climbing leads to the level of the upper buttress of Janus. Go up the
right side of the upper buttress *via* a short arete and an ice groove.
Thereafter, snow slopes lead to the plateau.

Snake Ridge 130m Hard Severe *   (1949)
One of the original classics of the corrie, with a short crux. Snake Ridge
is the second of the long ridges to the right of Glissade Gully, so named
for its fancied resemblance, when seen from the top, to a snake head
down. For easier recognition, its lower rocks fan out into three ridges
giving a fair impression of inverted Prince of Wales feathers. The left
side of the ridge is low and angles easily into a grassy gully running
alongside. Start on the left feather.
1. and 2. 60m Follow the crest directly to a platform below a step on
the ridge.
3. 15m Climb this on the left to a stance on a spike on the right.
4. 25m Go up to a short wall and use good holds to pull into a groove
(crux). Continue right up the groove to the crest or, easier, leave the
groove and climb to a good hold on the left.
5. 30m Continue to the broken upper buttress.
Winter: V,5   (1985)
A sustained and technical route under early season powder, but parts
bank out later on.

THE CENTRAL BUTTRESSES

Immediately to the right of Snake Ridge is a slender gully, The Ladders,
Grade II. To the right again is the well defined Narrow Gully, Grade I.
The compact buttresses forming a close-set trio to the right of Narrow
Gully are, from left to right, **Cherub's Buttress**, The Black Tower, and
Flake Buttress. They are separated by wet slabby depressions which
become icefalls in winter. Cherub's Buttress is Difficult, Grade III, by a
line close to the crest on the left overlooking Narrow Gully. **Flying
Ridge**, Grade II, takes the separate leg on the right in the lower section
and joins the parent route at the amphitheatre below the upper
buttress.

Dark Horse 100m HVS   (1993)
This route takes the steep left edge of Cherub's Buttress. Start at some
pale rock just left of a short crack with a chokestone.
1. 25m 5a Climb the wall on knobbly holds until it is possible to make
a difficult traverse above an obvious square-cut overhang to gain more
knobbly holds out on the right. Go straight up, then move slightly left
and follow a groove to find a pull out right to ledges on the crest.
2. and 3. 75m Climb the blocky edge, then finish more easily.

Left-Hand Icefall 90m IV,4   (1977)
This short steep icefall, in the depression between Cherub's Buttress
and The Black Tower, presents difficulties concentrated in the steep
ice-filled groove hard against the left wall of The Black Tower. Above,
an easy snow gully leads to a col behind the Black Tower summit. An
attractive snow arete leads to the plateau.

The Black Tower 110m Severe *   (1952)
This short climb is excellent and of great character. Unfortunately it
also has a very unpleasant approach pitch. 'From the corrie floor, the
buttress is squat and compact; its finer and truer form is best seen from
Cherub's Buttress where it appears as a tapering, twisted spire having
a curious, square summit block reminiscent of the greater Aiguilles'.
Start to the left of the buttress. Climb into an unpleasant basin oozing
with wet vegetation (Left-Hand Icefall in winter). From the right side of
the basin, about 20m above the lowest rocks, follow a groove developing into a narrow chimney (25m). Climb broken slabs on the left for
10m to a platform at the foot of a steep 6m groove on the edge of the
tower. Enter the groove on the right and climb it to a platform and a
block (crux). Move round a corner on the left and climb a crack to the
base of a short arete. Thence, by a delicate traverse across a slab on
the right, it is possible to regain the crest and summit of the tower by
a short steep crack. The tower is linked to the plateau by a short broken
arete.
Winter: V,7   (1988)
Follow the summer route.
Variation: V,5   (1979)
Climb the first pitch as for summer, then gain the summit by a line well
to the right of the summer crux section.

Right-Hand Icefall 80m II ** (1967)

A prominent cataract of ice between The Black Tower and Flake Buttress.

Flake Buttress 110m Moderate * (1949)

An interesting variety of pitches. More difficult variations have been made in the lower section. Start just right of the lowest rocks, and follow a grassy depression right to a stance on the broken crest (20m). Continue in the same line until a flake crack leads back left to a short right-angled corner. Swing up left on good holds, go up a chimney on the right, then follow easy ledges to a stance below an overhang on the crest. Behind a huge flake on the left climb a vertical crack on grand holds and continue up slabby blocks to a gap. Ignore the easy ground on the right and take the arete straight ahead to the plateau.

Winter: 120m III * (1950)

The buttress gives a fine climb which should be possible under almost any conditions.

Winter Direct: 120m V,7 (1993)

The triangular front face of the buttress is cut by a right-facing corner crack.

1. 35m Gain the crack from the left, and follow it past an awkward bulge to an impasse formed by a roof. Pull through the overhang on the left and continue up a crack to a ledge.

2. 35m Climb to a prominent left-facing groove and climb it, making a difficult exit at the top. Move up easily to belay by the flake of the normal route.

3. and 4. 50m Follow the normal route to the top.

Joker's Buttress 40m HVS 5c (1992)

The three-tiered triangular slabby wall between Flake and Spider Buttress gives a fun route on perfect granite, but it is much harder than it looks. Start in the centre of the buttress and climb a chimney formed by a large flake. Continue up the crack on the left and make an awkward mantelshelf onto a ledge. Surmount the next wall by a fierce layback (crux). Climb the final tier by a left-trending ramp which leads to the apex of the buttress. Scrambling leads to the plateau.

SPIDER BUTTRESS

This is the slabby buttress between Flake Buttress and the Main Spout. It has two overhangs on its left flank, the right one containing a prominent crack and the smaller left one being cigar-shaped. Right of the overhangs is a steep cracked wall containing The Fly.

The Skater 45m E4   (1984)
The left edge of the buttress, overlooking a big low-angled corner, gives good climbing with a short and serious crux; a little artificial. Start at the base of the big corner.
1. 30m 6a Climb a shallow corner just right of the right arete of the big corner. Exit right at the top to join Chebec for a move. Go diagonally left across the slab to a jug on the arete and a poor peg runner. A good hold above is tantalisingly out of reach, forcing the difficult slab on the right to be climbed to the obvious corner at the left end of the cigar-shaped overhang. Belay at the top of the corner.
2. 15m 4b Continue up and a little left over easy blocks to finish by a short overhanging crack.

The Chebec 60m VS   (1975)
This route takes a line between the overhangs on the left flank of the buttress. From the left end of the buttress, scramble up right for 10m to belay below the cigar-shaped overhang.
1. 35m 4c Move left and climb a groove to the right end of the overhang, pull out right and climb a crack, then climb a slab to a ledge.
2. 25m Go left and climb a right overhung corner to a horizontal crack, traverse right, then move up more easily to finish.

The Fly 45m VS 4c *   (1971)
A technical but well protected pitch on fine rock. The object is to reach a prominent S-shaped crack high on the steep cracked wall. Start at the base of the wall. Climb a crack up left, then move right to gain a horizontal crack. Traverse across the wall and climb easily up left to the deep S-shaped crack. Climb this, then the slab above or the deep flake crack on its right.

The Web 50m Severe   (1966)
Start in the prominent corner just right of the steep wall of The Fly. Climb the corner, then the chimney above and go left across the wall

to a small stance (20m). Traverse horizontally to the crest, move round the corner, then go straight up to a slab. Finish up the slab or the deep crack on its left.
Winter: 80m IV,4   (1987)
Short, but interesting and well protected. Follow the summer route.

THE MAIN SPOUT and TERMINAL BUTTRESS

The right flank of the Main Spout sports numerous short ribs and walls which diminish in size towards the plateau. Terminal Buttress and Terminal Wall lie on the largest piece of rock at the foot of the Spout. A grassy shelf slants down from the final crest of Terminal Buttress into the Main Spout. This offers the usual means of descent for all the routes on this section of the cliff.

A route has been climbed on the right side of the wall above the shelf, **April Wall**, Severe. It can be used as a continuation for the 'Terminal' routes. It has also been climbed in winter (V,7), starting up grooves 5 metres left of Terminal Buttress, then crossing the shelf and finishing through the depression of the summer route. Above the base of the descent shelf is a steep wall overlooking the Spout and including The Chute and The Swing. Although short, all the routes described are good.

Next to Last 30m HVS 5a   (1989)
This route takes the main groove line on the wall about 30m up the Main Spout from The Swing. Start at a distinctive recess of slabby rock. Climb up the recess, then move out of it by the overhanging crack. Continue up the groove and continuation cracks to the top.

The Swing 35m Severe   (1960)
Climb the crest of the steep rib 15 metres left of The Chute directly, then go up the obvious hanging V-corner above.
Variation: VS 4b
Climb the corner on the right of the rib, finishing by the V-corner.

Contra Flow 30m HVS 5a   (1985)
The wall between The Swing and The Chute. Start up a flake line just right of the corner start to The Swing. When this becomes blind, traverse right and finish up a crack line which is the upper continuation of a blind crack just left of The Chute.

The Chute 45m HVS 5a *   (1970)
Left of the descent shelf is a steep wall containing several grooves.
The leftmost of these grooves forms an open corner capped by a
curious jammed block. Climb the corner, going behind the jammed
block. Step left and follow an obvious left-trending crack to a shallow
groove left of a prominent overhanging prow. Climb the groove to a
good platform and scramble to the top.

Wee Heavy 45m VS 4b   (1971)
From the top of the jammed block, move up 4m to a bulge, climb a
deep crack slanting right and continue across the lip of an overhang
to follow a shallow gully to the top.

Terminal Buttress 70m Very Difficult   (1949)
Situated on the lower section of the cliff, this route follows a prominent
crescent-shaped groove. Start in a short gully at the foot of the lower
wall. Climb a fault on wrinkled and puckered rock for a steep initial 10m.
A little higher, traverse left round a rib and move up over a projecting
spur to a deep V-groove and belay on the edge. Follow the groove for
10m, passing an overhang on the left, until forced out horizontally left
around a corner to a large ledge. Climb straight up to a broad shelf,
then follow a shattered rib on the right to finish.
Winter: IV,5   (1961)
A short technical problem. Late in the season, the first pitch usually
banks out.

Terminal Wall 70m Hard Severe *   (1963)
This fine exposed route, high in the grade, ascends a series of cracks
and grooves on the left edge of the big wall right of Terminal Buttress.
Start just right of the Terminal Buttress fault. Climb straight up over an
overhang on an unusual formation of huge jugs, then go left to a
sloping ledge leading right. Go straight up from the end of this ledge
and make an awkward move left around a corner. Finish by cracks and
blocks.

The Hin'most 80m VS 4c   (1976)
On the wall right of Terminal Wall. Climb the first pitch of Terminal Wall
to the belay ledge. Make a long rising right traverse following obvious
parallel folds. Where the folds almost meet the flanking gully, go up left
to the foot of a prominent crack in the centre of the wall. Climb this
crack, starting on the wall to its right.

CREAGAN A' CHOIRE ETCHACHAN
(Map Ref 016 997)

This fine crag is situated high on the north-east and east-facing slopes of Creagan a' Choire Etchachan (1108m, a top of Derry Cairngorm), just a few hundred metres left of the tourist path to Ben Macdui. It presents a very bold straight face of granite averaging 120m in height.

The large buttress at the left-hand end of the crag, The Bastion, is defined by the hidden Forked Gully on its left and the prominent slabby trench of The Corridor on its right. Between The Corridor and the much shallower slabby gully, Square-Cut Gully, lies Juniper Buttress. Pioneer Buttress is the triangular mass of rock right of Square-Cut Gully. A prominent line of overhangs rises diagonally rightwards from the foot of Pioneer Buttress — The Meadows — across the face above two large grass depressions — The Meadows.

Finally, the dark vertical fault of Red Chimney separates The Meadow Face from the great sweep of the Crimson Slabs on the extreme right. As a general guide, the areas of The Corridor recess and the Crimson Slabs have the soundest and cleanest rock and consequently the best climbing.

Winter
As a great winter cliff, the Etchachan face only lacks height. The vegetated buttresses, wet slabby gullies and smooth slabs become liberally plastered in snow and ice and offer some of the finest sport in the area. An east-facing aspect and moderate altitude (the base of the cliff is at about 850m) account for more variable conditions than higher cliffs but this, along with the persistence of the drainage lines on the face, frequently results in very icy conditions. The Bastion is the safest place to climb if the condition of the snow is doubtful.

Approaches
1. From Braemar via Derry Lodge (see Coire Sputan Dearg).
About 200 metres beyond Derry Lodge, turn right at the public telephone, cross a bridge and follow the forest up into Glen Derry. Under powder snow it is better to follow a bulldozed road on the right side of Glen Derry. Instead of crossing the bridge, follow the right side of the shallow valley bottom for about 200 metres until the road starts just up on the hillside. A path branches left from Glen Derry to the Hutchison

hut. In thick weather in winter (in the dark), both the hut and the correct point to branch left are difficult to find. (8km from Derry Lodge.) In summer one can cycle to within 2km of the hut.

2. From Glenmore via the Shelter Stone and Loch Etchachan.
The quickest way is to ascend Coire Cas to the plateau or take the chairlift and walk over Cairngorm. In either case, descend Coire Raibert and follow the path round the head of Loch Avon to the Shelter Stone (5km from the Coire Cas car park with considerable ascent and descent). Take the track over the col between Beinn Mheadhoin and Carn Etchachan to the outflow of Loch Etchachan and descend to the cliff or the hut (8½km in total).

Accommodation
The Hutchison Memorial Hut (Map Ref 024 998). This open shelter in Coire Etchachan, built in 1954, is ideally located amidst wonderful scenery, if somewhat cold and bleak in winter.

Descents
Descent can be made at either end of the cliff. At the Bastion end, Forked Gully (Grade I) is a sporting descent but in summer it is unsatisfactory due to loose rock and vegetation; it is better to descend the steep grass and scree further away. At the Crimson Slabs side, a line of small crags beyond the slabs must be skirted before descent can be made.

THE BASTION

The largest buttress on the left of the crag has two major features; the easy-angled left-hand crest, Quartzvein Edge, alongside Forked Gully, and the very impressive gable wall overlooking The Corridor recess. The lower half of this wall is a huge slab taken by Talisman, one of the best routes on the crag. Higher up The Corridor, two great corners break the continuity of the wall.

The central area of the Bastion is rather featureless, consisting of mainly slabby ribs and grooves. Here climbing is possible almost anywhere at Difficult to Severe in standard. The routes are much better in winter as the grooves are vegetated. A number of climbs have been made in this section.

The left edge is defined by Forked Gully and left of this is a small buttress which contains **Foxy Groove** (Grade III). This climbs the groove and corner system starting from the toe of the buttress.

1 Quartzvein Edge 120m Moderate *   (1952)
A popular easy climb on reasonable rock following the left edge of the
Bastion overlooking Forked Gully. Start at the foot of Forked Gully
beyond a detached block. Climb a short wall with an inset piece of
quartz. Follow the edge at first, then find a way up slabs which develop
into a shelf leading round a false tower on the left. A scree funnel leads
to the top. Better but harder is to climb the false tower on its right side.
Winter: III   (1956)
A good choice when snow or weather conditions are doubtful as it
should be possible in most conditions. The false tower at the top is
usually the crux. No cornice.

2 Bastion Wall 150m IV,4   (1963)
This route takes a line on the left side of the Bastion and is open to
variation. Consolidated snow and ice will lower the grade to III. The
main features are long iced grooves and a 30m chimney just below the
plateau. Difficult and not unpleasant in summer.

3 Blinker 150m Severe   (1986)
This climb takes the vague crack between Bastion Wall and Original
Route. From a grassy bay some 30m up left from the toe of the buttress
climb a shallow scoop of pink rock and follow the line of the crack in
two pitches of continuous climbing to reach easy ground.
Winter: IV,4
At least three lines have been climbed in this central section of the
Bastion, all at the same grade. How separate and worthwhile they are
has yet to be investigated.

4 Original Route Direct 130m Severe   (1972)
This route follows a line of grooves just right of centre of the Bastion.
Start to the right of the lowest rocks on the right of the buttress.
Scramble left up an easy depression ending at a deep V-groove, almost
a chimney. This groove is the best means of locating the route, although
it is most prominent from the base of the buttress, left of the start of
this route. Climb the groove until it becomes grassy, then the rocks on
its left, to gain the right side of a prominent red slab in a depression.
Traverse the slab to belay on its left wall (40m). Return to the right side,
climb up and swing out right on a prominent jug. Go up then left to follow
a large V-groove to easy ground (45m).

Variation: 40m VS 5a
Very good but harder. From the left side of the red slab, step left low down and follow the arete overlooking the red slab, then overlooking the large V-groove, to easy ground.
Winter: 150m V,6 *   (1992)
The summer route gives a good winter line; the V-groove is the crux.

5 Original Route, Winter 140m IV,5   (1969)
Also a good winter line, although less direct, this route is relatively steep and sustained in the middle section. Start left of the Direct, whose line will still be visible under snow. Go up for 45m to a steep wall left of the first V-groove of the Direct. Avoid the wall on the left and work right underneath the Red Slab, crossing the Direct, to reach a large platform. Gain the left-slanting ramp above and follow it to the large V-groove of the Direct which leads to the top. Mild Severe in summer.

Red Scar Route (Severe, IV,5) takes a line fairly close to the right edge of The Bastion, touching the vein of red rock at one point. It starts from the foot of The Corridor and links chimneys to reach a choice of lines higher up.

6 The Talisman 100m Hard Severe ***   (1956)
An excellent route following the defined right edge of The Bastion on the brink of The Corridor. Steep and clean with continuous difficulties, it dries quickly after rain. Start from a platform beside a huge block set against the wall 10m up The Corridor.
1. 35m Climb the crack behind the block to a ledge. Move right and climb straight up until it is possible to traverse left across the huge slab to the crest.
2. 20m Detour left round an overhang and climb a corner to regain the crest. Move left to a groove and go up to a short overhanging corner. Climb the corner to a good stance (crux).
3. 45m Follow the crest directly, starting on the face overlooking The Corridor.
4. Scramble to the plateau.
Direct Start: 40m HVS 5b *   (1981)
Although not in keeping with the standard of the normal route, this sustained start with a well protected crux is worthwhile in its own right. The line follows the obvious corner system just left of the arete below

CREAGAN A' CHOIRE ETCHACHAN

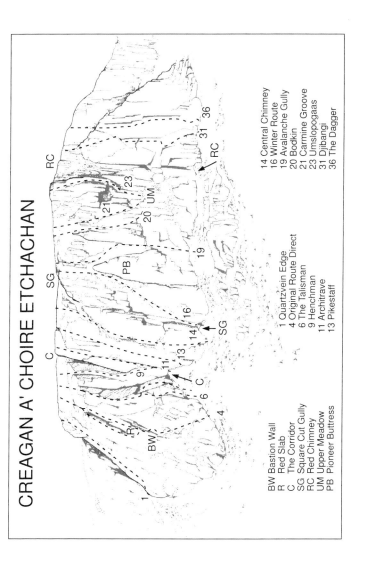

BW Bastion Wall
R Red Slab
C The Corridor
SG Square Cut Gully
RC Red Chimney
UM Upper Meadow
PB Pioneer Buttress

1 Quartzvein Edge
4 Original Route Direct
6 The Talisman
9 Henchman
11 Architrave
13 Pikestaff

14 Central Chimney
16 Winter Route
19 Avalanche Gully
20 Bodkin
21 Carmine Groove
23 Umslopogaas
31 Djibangi
36 The Dagger

Talisman. Start at the lowest rocks. Climb the corner to an overlap (peg runner), then take the continuation corner on the left. Traverse back immediately across a steep wall on good holds to reach the arete which is followed to the stance after the traverse on Talisman.

Winter: VI,7   (1965)
A sustained ascent of the normal route on snow-covered rock. Pass the final crest on the left by an iced groove.

7 Talking Drums 115m E2 *   (1986)
A spectacular finish up the steep Corridor Wall right of The Talisman.
1. 40m 5b The direct start to The Talisman.
2. 25m 4c Take the obvious thin crack leading diagonally right past a triangular block and through the girdling bulge. Move slightly left and go up to a poor belay under the headwall.
3. 25m 5a Gain the base of a shallow groove, the first feature right of the Talisman arete, *via* two shallow scoops. Climb the groove to its top, then move right and up on hidden holds to a hand traverse line leading right to a mantelshelf and an *in situ* peg belay.
4. 25m 5b Make a delicate move up to gain a small ledge and peg runner, then swing down right and across the wall to the base of a corner crack. Follow this to finish.

8 Talismanic 30m E3   (1990)
This route takes the arete between The Talisman's Direct and Normal Starts, starting at the foot of the latter. Pull onto the edge using obvious big holds and go up to a perch. Continue boldly for 4m, then follow cracks to the stance of The Talisman.

9 Henchman 50m E3 *   (1983)
The route follows the clean right-hand of the corners on the steep wall between The Talisman and The Corridor. A fine line although regrettably short. Scramble up The Corridor to below a flake on the right-hand side of the corner line.
1. 30m 5c Step left round the flake and climb the chimney formed by it to near its top. Step left into a groove and climb it round two small bulges to a V-notch. Belay on top of the roof above the V-notch.
2. 20m 5b Climb the jam crack above and move right onto the wall under a block. Climb round this and finish steeply by a crack in the right wall. The top section seems dangerously loose, but it can be avoided further right.

10 The Corridor 120m IV,5 **   (1954)
A first rate winter route, popular and variable in standard. There are
usually two major ice pitches, one leading over jammed blocks into a
cave and another immediately above. The pitch above the cave will
generally constitute the crux and may be very steep. There is often a
large cornice which is best taken on the left. Severe in summer.

11 Architrave 120m Severe   (1960)
This is the prominent groove in the slab close to the right wall of The
Corridor recess. The groove gives a good climb when dry, which is rare.
Start up the rib on its left for 45m; thereafter follow the groove and its
continuation chimney
Winter: IV,4   (1969)
In winter the groove can form an impressive ribbon of ice, a more
sustained route than The Corridor, but less steep. Climb the groove
directly on ice to a point below a chimney. Either go straight up or move
left across an obvious ramp and finish as for The Corridor.

JUNIPER BUTTRESS

Between The Corridor and Square-Cut Gully, this buttress is split by
the Central Chimney into two ribs. That on the left is Pikestaff; the right
is Juniper Rib.

12 The Hex 80m Hard Severe   (1971)
This short steep route on The Corridor flank of Juniper Buttress has
good, clean rough rock, and is sustained. Start 6m above the rock
pocket of Pikestaff (arrow).
1. 40m Climb a vague fault to the left of a system of grass cracks to
belay at the top of these cracks beneath a small bulge.
2. 40m Step left and follow the continuation crack on the smooth
Corridor wall until it becomes grass-choked. Traverse right to the crest
and finish by Pikestaff.

13 Pikestaff 120m Very Difficult   (1954)
This route on the left hand rib is a little vegetated but it has good views
of Talisman. Start just inside The Corridor at a curious little pocket in
the rock. Slant up The Corridor wall to reach the crest and follow the
rib as closely as possible, keeping to the good rock.
Winter: IV,4
A sustained but very artificial climb.

14 Central Chimney 120m II *   (1955)
A good winter climb, following the chimney separating the two ribs.
Start at a fault leading left from the base of Square-Cut Gully into the
gully proper. A more sporting start is an obvious V-cleft splitting the
lowest rocks. The chimney itself gives 60m of climbing over small ice
pitches to the foot of a right-slanting snow ramp which provides a
beautiful finish. Difficult and unpleasant in summer.

The rib on the right of Central Chimney is **Juniper Rib** (Difficult,
Grade III). It is a good choice in powder snow but not in avalanche
conditions as there is a snow slope at the top (Winter Route is safer).

15 Square-Cut Gully 150m V,6   (1966)
The gully is dominated by a magnificent pillar of ice (or icicle) at the big
overhang. The initial 80m will normally give straightforward climbing on
snow and ice. The ice pillar is climbed direct. A second difficult pitch
may be presented by the final slab if it is covered by unconsolidated
snow. Severe in summer.

16 Winter Route 150m II   (1949)
A fair winter climb taking the easiest and most natural line on this
section of the cliff. Graded for hard snow. Start up Square-Cut Gully
and take an obvious line of weakness leading up to Pioneer Buttress.
Mixed climbing leads to an ice pitch on the left near the top.

PIONEER BUTTRESS

This is the large triangular buttress between Square-Cut Gully and
Avalanche Gully. **Cambridge Route** (Severe, Grade III) was the first
recorded route on the cliff in 1949; it follows an obscure line up the
easier left edge of the buttress.

17 Cambridge Route Direct 180m IV,5   (1992)
This route starts up the original line, but continues direct where the
original escaped left to easier ground. Start just left of the initial gully
of Pioneer Buttress Direct.
1. 45m Climb a slab to gain a large groove which slants up left. Follow
this to the base of a wall. Climb the wall and continue directly up a series
of steep grooves to a snow shelf below a steep cracked wall.
2. 15m   Traverse right beneath the wall and move up to join the
left-facing corner system of Pioneer Buttress Direct.
3. etc. 120m Follow the corner to the top.

18 Pioneer Buttress Direct 95m VS   (1971)
The line generally follows the broad rib on the front face. The rib is defined by a vertical crack on the right and a vegetated groove on the left. Start up and right of the lowest rocks.
1. 20m Climb trending right to an obvious overhung bay.
2. 40m 5a Step left onto a rib overlooking a steep groove and follow it, making occasional moves into the groove, which closes at 30m. Either make a difficult move up the short corner or step onto the rib and go up *via* a small pocket (harder). The flake crack above leads to a good ledge and belays on the left.
3. 35m Climb a wall and follow a grassy ramp to easy ground, then scramble to the plateau.
Winter: 150m VI,7   (1991)
A technical climb based on the summer line.
1. 30m Gain the vegetated groove left of the summer rib and climb this to an alcove.
2. 25m The summer route takes the corner above; instead climb to the base of the corner, then make a difficult move onto a slab and up to a ledge level with the top of the corner. Move up and left across a steep wall and move round the arete (crux) to belay.
3. and 4. 95m Continue directly up the crest to the top.

19 Avalanche Gully 120m VI,5   (1985)
The steep narrow fault breaching the lower tier of overhangs is blocked at 45m by a large overhang. Climb the icicle direct, then follow an icy groove above, finishing leftwards by snowy grooves to the upper part of Pioneer Buttress. The gully is loose and dangerous in summer (VS).

THE MEADOW FACE

A barrier of overhangs rises diagonally right from the foot of Pioneer Buttress to the upper reaches of Red Chimney. Two prominent grass scoops, The Meadows, are situated below the largest section of overhangs, just left of Red Chimney. The routes follow a number of steep grooves which cut through this upper section of the face.

20 Bodkin 140m Severe   (1954)
This vegetated route makes for the upper meadow, traverses out above the lower overhangs, then goes up a groove and a rib to finish beside a curious horizontal flake well seen in profile from the right-hand side

of the crag. Start directly below a recent rock scar in the lower overhangs. Scramble up right to the upper meadow (60m). From its left edge, go left past a clean groove (Carmine Groove) and move up to a stance. To the left again is a smooth slab poised over space and angling into a large groove. Move down into the groove, ascend across the slab at its lower end and climb the rib at the far side to a stance. Move up left and climb a groove until it steepens at 10m. Step round left and climb cracks to gain the crest of a rib. Follow this to the top. The rib finish is a finer alternative to the original line which went up the grassy grooves on the right.

Winter: IV,5   (1977)

Follow the original summer route; a much better climb than in summer.

21 Carmine Groove 80m VS   (1971)

This is the prominent red groove on the upper cliff left of the big overhangs. Unfortunately the groove is often wet, but when dry it gives two excellent pitches on steep clean rock. Use the first section of Bodkin to gain the upper meadow.

1. 20m 4b Start up the groove at the left edge of the meadow, then move right to a flake. Climb straight up, re-enter the groove and continue to below an overhang.

2. 25m 4b Step left to a steep red slab and climb the corner directly to a roof. Exit right to a small ledge and climb a thin crack in the slab to ledges.

3. 35m Move right and climb a narrow grey rib to easy ground.

Winter: IV,5 *   (1974)

This excellent though short route is quite often in condition. Follow the groove throughout on ice, except for a move onto the rib on the right at the top.

22 The Red Snake 90m V,4   (1992)

This excellent line of ice, which passes the left edge of the big overhangs above the upper meadow, is unfortunately rarely in condition. Gain the upper meadow (60m) and belay just right of Carmine Groove.

1. 50m Climb ice just right of a corner, then continue direct towards the overhang. Step left to the top of a V-groove, then go diagonally left up a slab past the left edge of the overhang into a shallow groove. Go up this to a belay.

2. 40m The groove soon becomes easier and is followed by snow.

23 Umslopogaas 100m HVS   (1974)
This route takes the big slab corner, the left and more prominent of the
two corners high on the face left of Red Chimney. Gain the upper
meadow (60m). A few metres above its upper left extremity, a thin rib
separates a V-groove on the left from an open corner on the right.
1. 35m 4c Climb directly up pink rock right of the open corner. Move
right below overhangs to a moss ledge below the corner (often wet).
2. 25m 5a Zigzag up the slab for 10m to a nook on the right edge and
continue straight up cracks to the top.
3. 40m Go left round a rib and climb pleasant rocks to the top.
Winter: VI,7   (1992)
Variations on the summer line avoid the slabby base of the big corner;
ice is not required. Start as for summer at the foot of The Red Snake.
1. 30m Climb ice up the summer route, then break out right on thinner
ice to a short wall below the right-hand slab corner. (With no ice, a line
further right can be taken). Climb the wall strenuously into the corner.
2. 10m Climb the corner to where one can traverse into Red Chimney,
but instead make an improbable pull out left into the nook on the right
arete of Umslopogaas.
3. 10m Cracks in the slab lead to a big ledge.
4. 45m Step left and follow grooves parallel to Red Chimney to the top.

   The rib and V-groove left of the start of Umslopogaas is the beginning
of **The Serpent** (VS 5a), which crosses Umslopogaas, climbs a section
of the winter route up the right-hand slab corner, and follows the
traverse to enter Red Chimney near its top.

24 Flanking Ribs 150m IV,4   (1967)
An undistinguished climb, but the upper rib gives an escape from below
the top section of Red Chimney. Climb the rib on the left of Red Chimney
and cross the chimney at its easy middle section, pulling out awkwardly
onto the rib on the right. Follow this to the top. Very Difficult and
vegetated in summer.

25 Red Chimney 150m V,5 **   (1959/67)
This very fine climb, a natural ice trap, is reliably in good condition. The
lower section is usually filled with a cascade of clear ice overflowing
the Crimson Slabs, but when lean, start up turfy corners on the right.
The upper chimney becomes choked by a series of steep ice bosses
(ice screw runners).
   The lower section is Severe on sound wet rock in summer.

THE CRIMSON SLABS

These are the finest single feature of the crag, a spectacular sweep of slabs about 100m wide and up to 140m high, rising to the right of Red Chimney. They provide some of the best rock climbing in the area. Continuity of the slabs is broken by two great corners, The Dagger on the right and Djibangi on the left. Away to the right, a steep raking terrace ascends to a platform near the top of The Dagger and provides a useful but loose means of descent for those wishing to avoid the inferior upper tier of slabs.

The shorter hard routes can be combined using an abseil descent and later retrieval of the anchor (or use the *in situ* peg at the top of the Djibangi corner).

The corners of Djibangi and The Dagger are slow to dry, as they collect drainage water from above. However, the ribs on their right dry quickly and provide equally good routes.

26 Cutlass 140m HVS   (1969)
Between Red Chimney and Djibangi there is a large bow-shaped overlap. This route follows the edge of the overlap, then goes straight up parallel to Red Chimney. The crux pitch is poorly protected. Start 3m right of Red Chimney.
1. 35m Climb either of twin corners to the left end of the large platform on Djibangi and belay below the overlap.
2. 10m Step onto the edge of the overlap, climb straight up over a small bulge, then step right to a small ledge.
3. 20m 5a Regain the edge and follow it delicately to a point just right of Red Chimney. Move over a small overlap to gain a grassy corner.
4. etc. 75m Continue up a rib to join Flanking Ribs (chossy), or bear right easily to the upper reaches of Djibangi and descend the terrace.

27 Scalpel 85m E1 *   (1977/1985)
The very shallow tilted corner between Cutlass and Djibangi gives a fine sustained pitch which is quite bold at the top. Start just right of Cutlass.
1. 40m 4c Climb the arete overlooking the initial corners of Cutlass to the ledge. Climb Cutlass for 10m to the small stance.
2. 45m 5b Continue up the shallow corner to its end at an overlap. Step right to place good runners in King Crimson, then return and make a rising traverse left (crux) to the arete of a curving corner (the original route). Go up cracks just right of the arete to progressively easier

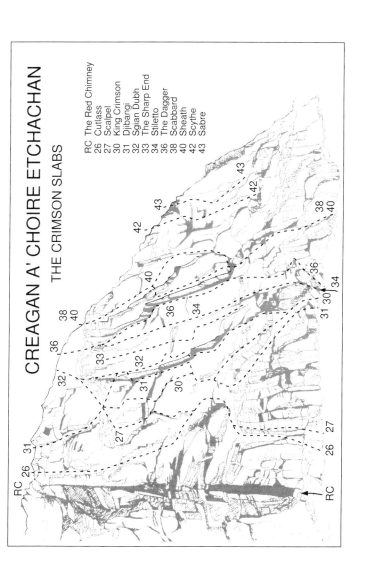

CREAGAN A' CHOIRE ETCHACHAN

THE CRIMSON SLABS

RC The Red Chimney
26 Cutlass
27 Scalpel
30 King Crimson
31 Djibangi
32 Sgian Dubh
33 The Sharp End
34 Stiletto
36 The Dagger
38 Scabbard
40 Sheath
42 Scythe
43 Sabre

ground. Now either go right to join Djibangi and descend *via* the terrace, or continue to the top.

The original route (HVS 5a) takes a left exit from the shallow corner and continues up the curving corner, joining it from the left.

28 In the Pink 45m E3 5c   (1985)
A direct but poorly protected line up the pink rock right of Scalpel, just left of the grey streak. Start from a small ledge at the top of the small corner at the top of Djibangi pitch 2. Go out left to an obvious jug, then climb the slab to a shallow flake with unexpected but crucial runners. Continue straight up until a tiny foot ledge on King Crimson can be reached on the right (this is immediately under the shallow curving overlap). Follow King Crimson left and up for 5m to the good runners below the overlap (used on Scalpel). Step left and climb straight up through the main overlap to join Scalpel on easier ground.

29 Djibooty 140m V,4 *   (1992)
In good conditions twin icefalls form in the Djibangi area. One comes down Djibangi and its direct start; this one forms down In the Pink and the normal summer start to Djibangi (which has been climbed as a winter start to Djibangi). Climb the icefall in three pitches (not technical but don't fall off!) with a deviation to belay at the base of the Djibangi corner.

30 King Crimson 125m E3   (1984)
An eliminate with a fine crux pitch on perfect pink rock between the corners of Scalpel and Djibangi; sustained with limited protection. Start from the alcove as for Djibangi.
1. 35m 4c Climb a flake crack between Djibangi and Sgian Dubh, then go left round a bulge and move up to join Djibangi. Follow its small corner to the foot of the main corner.
2. 45m 5c At the left end of the ledge a prominent streak of grey unwashed rock sweeps down from the apex of the slabs left of Djibangi. Climb straight up the pink rock on its right to fix runners under a shallow curving overlap. Go up left to grey rock and continue to below an obvious notch in the main overlap. Move right, then go up through the overlap just right of a small corner forming the notch. Continue straight up, pull left into a small groove (Friend zero runner), then follow this to broken ground below an area of clean cracked slabs.

3. 45m 5a Climb straight up the slabs by cracks going through a break in the overlap and passing right of a large block. Scramble to the top.

31 Djibangi 140m VS **   (1956)
The left-hand of the two great corners gives the easiest and most popular route on the slabs, and the most intriguingly named. The first pitch of Sgian Dubh provides a direct start, better but harder than the normal route. Start at a grassy alcove (containing a recessed right-facing corner) beneath the main corner.
1. 20m Follow a diagonal line up left to a large platform overlooking the first pitch of Red Chimney.
2. 25m Trend right and climb a small corner set in the middle of the slabs. Easier climbing now leads to a good stance in the main corner.
3. 35m 4c Climb the corner directly past an overlap. Exit by pulling out right onto the rib. (It is now possible to follow grassy grooves right to join The Dagger, then to descend the terrace.)
4. and 5. 60m Step back left into the corner and climb it for a short way. Work up left to gain an obvious groove and follow this to a huge block. Climb round the block and continue up a rib to easy ground.
Winter: V,4 **   (1965)
An outstanding route, but not always in condition (Red Chimney is a reliable alternative). To reach the foot of the main corner, either follow the summer line or, if conditions allow, directly up iced slabs. Climb the corner throughout, then work up left and climb icy grooves.

32 Sgian Dubh 110m HVS *   (1978)
The arete right of the Djibangi corner dries quickly after rain. Start at the grassy alcove as for Djibangi.
1. 35m 4c From its left side, follow a series of shallow left-facing corners (the lower continuation of Djibangi corner) to below the main corner.
2. 35m 5a Climb the arete overlooking the corner. It is easier to move away from the arete briefly in the middle section.
3. 40m Follow grassy grooves right to the terrace.

33 The Sharp End 45m E2 5c   (1985)
Start just left of Stiletto at twin cracks. Climb these, then the continuation crack to reach the traverse line of Crimson Cringe. Traverse left towards the Sgian Dubh arete, then return diagonally right to a down-pointing flake. Step right and climb over a slight bulge (crux), then finish up a shallow corner.

34 Stiletto 110m E1 ** (1966)

Midway between Djibangi and The Dagger, an impressive thin vertical crack splits the slabs. This climb gives sustained, technical but well protected climbing, near the top of its grade.

1. 25m 4b Climb the lower continuation of the crack or the first pitch of The Dagger to below the crack.

2. 40m 5c Climb the crack past two hard sections.

3. 45m Traverse right into The Dagger and follow it easily to the terrace.

35 Scarlet Fever 45m E3 6a (1985)

This unlikely line with some thin moves takes the slab midway between the crack of Stiletto and The Dagger. Climb a thin crack and move right to a small scoop, peg runner. Go up and slightly right to a porthole, peg runner. Pull through the overlap into cracks, climb these and work up left to easier ground.

36 The Dagger 130m VS * (1955)

The right-hand corner, the line of the original Crimson Slabs route, gives a classic corner pitch. Start in the grassy alcove, as for Djibangi.

1. 25m 4b Traverse right and a little up for 5m (nearly to the arete of Crimson Cringe). Move back left into a short corner, then go slightly left again to easier ground leading up and right to the base of the corner. An easier alternative is a vegetated line coming in from the right.

2. 35m 4c Climb the corner to a hanging stance on a huge spike below an overhang.

3. and 4. 70m Avoid the overhang by moving left below a bulge, then regain the grass groove above the bulge and scramble to a large platform below the last slab (the terrace descends from here). Climb the slab by a crack slanting right, then continue straight up to the top.

Winter: V,5 * (1977)

Follow the summer line, but start up the vegetated alternative. The climbing is superb, but rarely in condition as it requires ice in the corner. The final slab will usually be the crux.

37 Crimson Cringe 100m E2 (1984)

A traverse line with minimal protection for the hard sections. Start at the clean rib overlooking the initial corner of Scabbard.

1. 20m 5a Climb the clean rib, bypassing an overhang by moving left and back right to reach the foot of The Dagger corner.

2. 25m 5b Go up the corner for about 10m, then take the second

traverse line out left to meet Stiletto at a small niche. Continue traversing slightly down, then go up to the base of the main Djibangi corner.
3. 15m 5b   Climb the corner until below the lower small overlap. Traverse more or less horizontally to the small ledge of Scalpel.
4. 40m Finish up Scalpel or Cutlass.

38 Scabbard 105m VS *** (1966)
A fine exposed route following the rib to the right of The Dagger. It dries very quickly after rain. Start by a clean-cut, right-facing corner directly below the right bounding rib of The Dagger.
1. 20m 4c Climb the corner, then move left to a stance level with the foot of The Dagger corner.
2. 35m 4c Climb an obvious finger crack, then further cracks to a small overlap. Go up the edge to the huge spike at the top of The Dagger.
3. 50m 4b Move right, descend a little and pull out right to an edge. Climb cracks and blocks to reach the terrace at its highest point.
Winter: VI,7 * (1985)
Climb the summer route. The first pitch held ice but the limited protection was worrying. The second pitch was superb; sustained but very well protected.

39 Switchblade 160m VI,7 (1991)
A line of turfy cracks slanting right across Sheath gives another fine technical route, but the line is not as good as Scabbard.
1. 20m   Start as for The Dagger in winter and belay just right of Scabbard.
2. 40m   Climb the right-facing corner which bounds the right side of Scabbard, then follow a wide crack to slabs. Make a thin traverse right into a turfy left-facing corner and follow it to a turfy bay (Sheath crosses left here).
3. 45m Go over an overhang at the top right corner, climb cracks, then go diagonally left to the terrace just below its top.
4. 35m Climb a thin turfy crack left of the arete of Delicatessen.
5. 20m Easy ground leads to the top.

To the right of Scabbard are three right-facing corner systems; the left is Sheath (pitch 2), the middle one, which starts higher up and leads to a roof is Scythe and the right one, which starts higher still and has a cracked arete on its right, is Sabre.

40 Sheath 100m HVS   (1961)
The route starts at the clean-cut corner common with Scabbard and
goes up to a conspicuous red slab, usually streaked with water. The
crux is poorly protected.
1. 20m 4c Climb the corner, move right, then go up to belay on top of
a huge detached block at the foot of the red slab.
2. 35m 5a Climb a good layback crack on the left side of the slab and
continue until forced to make a delicate horizontal traverse across the
slab to a grass niche. Go up a vertical crack for 6m, move right to below
a bulge and climb a smooth corner-groove to an overlap. Break out left
and belay.
3. 45m 4b Move left to join Scabbard, then climb cracks and blocks to
the terrace.

41 Tickler 45m E1   (1986)
This route lies right of Sheath, and starts near the foot of Scythe at a
small right-facing corner.
1. 25m 5b Climb the corner, then follow the flake continuation left to
an overlap. Cross this (and Sheath), step left into a shallow roofed
corner, cross the roof and follow thin cracks until it is possible to pull
out left to gain a prominent fin of rock which leads to a belay on the
right.
2. 20m 4c Gain the obvious rib to the right and climb this until a move
right gains a hidden finger crack which leads to easy ground.

42 Scythe 50m E2 5b   (1983)
This good, sustained, but very poorly protected pitch follows the middle
corner system. Climb the slab about 3m right of the initial corner to a
prominent roof. Step right and pull over a bulge into a smaller corner.
Follow this to easier slabs which lead to the terrace.

43 Sabre 45m VS 4b   (1982)
A good pitch, useful as a filler-in. It follows the rightmost corner, starting
up an awkward pale-coloured slab and surmounting an overlap at 25m.
A cracked slab leads to the terrace.

Above the top of the terrace and descending right is an area of largely
vegetated slabs containing the finish to The Dagger and lower down
the shallow stepped corner of **The Gangway** (Severe). These slabs
are bounded on the right by a clean cracked arete about 20m down
from the top of the terrace (Delicatessen). The corner immediately right

of the arete is perhaps **Enigma** (VS), precise line unknown. Next right is a grassy fault and beyond it the corner system of **Stanley** (Hard Severe).

44 Delicatessen 40m VS 4c *   (1983)
Climb the clean cracked arete directly, keeping near the crest. It provides the best continuation for routes leading to the terrace.

STOB COIRE ETCHACHAN
1082m (Map Ref 024 005)

This is the shapely pointed top of Beinn Mheadhoin overlooking Coire Etchachan. It displays a high wedge-shaped face which is very prominent from Glen Derry. Unfortunately, the face consists of easy-angled broken ribs and buttresses, separated by scree-filled gullies and offers very little to the rock climber, although many of the buttresses have been climbed. In winter however, the open gullies and ribs make for sporting direct routes to the top of Beinn Mheadhoin.

The biggest mass of rock on the face, situated almost opposite the door of the Hutchison Hut, is **Bellflower Buttress** (100m, a loose Difficult, Grade III). Low down on the extreme left of the face, just above the Ben Macdui path, the rock becomes more continuous and the buttresses form a frieze to the skyline. Routes are 50m long. The attractive steep rib which forms the lowest rocks at the head of the corrie, and skylined when seen from the hut, is Stag Buttress (Very Difficult). The obvious corner crack at the bottom left of **Stag Buttress** (Hard Severe) provides a good start and makes the route worthwhile for an evening. On the rocks higher and to the right of Stag Buttress, and beyond a slanting gully, is the prominent **Amphitheatre Edge** (Very Difficult).

The forlorn little buttress lying high up under the 1163m top of Beinn Mheadhoin is **The Slug** (Difficult). The highest point of Beinn Mheadhoin itself is on a tor, the Great Barn of Beinn Mheadhoin. This requires a short scramble by the easiest way.

Braeriach and Cairn Toul

Cairn Toul, shapeliest of the greater Cairngorm summits, shares with Braeriach a giant arena of five corries drained by the headwaters of the River Dee. Stretching 3km across from summit to summit, with a rim edging the plateau for nearly 6km, this cirque is the most alpine of our mountain areas in terms of snow accumulation and the prolonged period of its cover (near permanent below Garbh Choire Mor). All but two of the corries lie under the great plateau of Braeriach in the lee of the prevailing winds; the plateau, itself a vast collecting area, is further backed by a gently sloping tableland extending west to An Moine Mhor (The Great Moss) above Glen Feshie. From this desert of snow, drift is carried by the wind for many kilometres and is finally driven into the corries where it piles up to great depths. The result is the longest unbroken cornice to be found on our mountains; at peak season it reaches awesome proportions over many sections of its considerable length.

Snow in such quantity and permanence gives this area an added attraction in late spring and early summer, when the buttresses, bare of snow and separated by corniced gullies, rise from unbroken snow-fields and the whole scene creates an atmosphere which is truly alpine. A mountaineering attitude is necessary to appreciate these corries. Those seeking technical rock climbing will be disappointed; those who seek a remote mountain setting can only be inspired.

The idyllic summer picture is shattered in winter. The routes, though short, match most for quality, but the challenge is the long approach into this snowy wilderness, negotiation of giant cornices and difficult descents from the most hostile of our winter plateaux. The vast cornices can present insuperable problems, but it is worth considering a visit very early in the season before the snows have accumulated.

The length of the approaches dictate that many will prefer to stay overnight in the area. There are a number of options:

1. Garbh Coire bothy (Map Ref 959 986). Centrally placed between the corries, this is a fine base. It sits on the left bank (facing upstream) of the Allt a' Garbh-choire about 1½km from the Lairig Ghru and merges well into the background. Fairly solid and reasonably watertight, though poky, it holds three to four (or six uncomfortably) but is now getting on in years and shows its age.

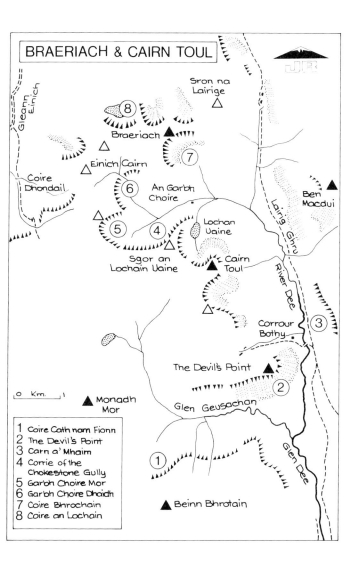

BRAERIACH & CAIRN TOUL

Gleann Einich

Sron na Lairige △

⑧

Braeriach ▲

△ Einich Cairn

⑦

Coire Dhondail

⑥

An Garbh Choire

Ben Macdui ▲

△ ⑤

△ ④

Lochan Uaine

Lairig Ghru

△

Sgor an Lochain Uaine

Cairn Toul ▲

River Dee

△

Corrour Bothy

③

The Devil's Point ▲

②

0 Km. 1

▲ Monadh Mor

Glen Geusachan

Glen Dee

1 Coire Cath nam Fionn
2 The Devil's Point
3 Carn a' Mhaim
4 Corrie of the Chokestone Gully
5 Garbh Choire Mor
6 Garbh Choire Dhaidh
7 Coire Bhrochain
8 Coire an Lochain

①

▲ Beinn Bhrotain

2. Corrour bothy (Map Ref 981 958). This lies in the Lairig Ghru on the west bank of the Dee, 5km south of the Garbh Coire bothy. At the point where the path from Derry Lodge into the Lairig Ghru joins the path up the Dee from the White Bridge, a small path cuts diagonally down to the river and a solid bridge 300 metres south-east of the bothy. The bothy holds 10 in reasonable comfort but it often becomes over-crowded at popular periods (e.g. Easter, July and August weekends) and is best avoided at these times. There is a dirt floor.

3. Camping and bivouac. There are various sites between Corrour and Garbh Coire bothy and upstream from here. There is a delectable site in Garbh Coire Dhaidh, bordering the Dee where it opens out into small pools just above the lip of the corrie. Immediately to the north-west of the pools is the Dey-Smith bivouac, a built-up cave under a large boulder (cairn on top) which can hold two.

Access
Access is very long from either the north (Aviemore) or the south (Braemar), as are the alternatives from the west from Glen Feshie and Gleann Einich.

1. The north approach is shorter but trickier in the dark. Leave the Cairngorm ski road at the Sugar Bowl, the car park at the hairpin bend where the road leaves the forest (Map Ref 985 075). From the top side of the bend, follow the path down over a bridge and continue on a reasonable path, at first along the ridge, to the Chalamain gap (Map Ref 965 052). Go through the distinctive rocky gap and descend diagonally into the Lairig Ghru. Follow this over its summit, then leave the path to traverse over the shoulder of Braeriach to the area of the Garbh Coire bothy (12km).

2. A variation to this approach, useful for a day visit to the northern corries such as Coire Bhrochain or Garbh Choire Dhaidh, is to go over the summit of Braeriach *via* Sron na Lairig.

3. In good weather, a pleasant approach is to take the Cairngorm chairlift to its top, climb over Cairngorm and the top of Coire an t-Sneachda and contour the slopes of Cairn Lochain reach the broad col between Cairn Lochan and Ben Macdhui. Head towards Ben Macdhui, then descend a vague ridge north of the Allt a' Choire Mhor into the Lairig Ghru. A slightly more direct alternative is to descend the left bank (facing down) of the March Burn, which is very steep at the top, into the Lairig Ghru. This approach in winter is also good on ski (8km).

4. The south approach starts from the Derry gates and passes Derry Lodge. Thereafter it follows the Luibeg Burn and turns north into Glen Dee. Follow the Dee, then take the western branch leading into An Garbh Choire; a tiny path follows the right bank (facing upstream) until about 400m from Garbh Coire bothy when it crosses and fades. This approach follows the main Lairig Ghru path until the last part, so it is easy walking but 17km.

5. In winter, the western approach from Achlean in Glen Feshie is the shortest for Garbh Choire Mor. Although good for a day visit, but there may not be enough daylight early season. It requires hard snow for walking or enough for skis. Ascend Carn Ban Mor, cross the north end of the Moine Mor, then ascend over Einich Cairn to find the descent into the desired corrie. This in itself can be difficult and is dependent on weather conditions and local knowledge (10km).

6. Sometimes the quickest approach, but dependent on conditions (Gleann Einich should be free of snow), is *via* Gleann Einich on a mountain bike. Start from Whitewell (Map Ref 915 086) and descend from the carpark by a path to reach a the main track from Coylumbridge which leads towards Loch Einich. Leave this 400 metres before the loch and follow a good path up Coire Dhondail. Where the angle eases, head straight for the top at 1265m. For the descent into Garbh Coire Mor, see the introduction to that corrie. On the return journey, the top of the path above Loch Einich can be very hard to find in poor visibility unless great care is taken.

CAIRN TOUL

1293m (Map Ref 963 972)

Despite its splendour as a summit, Cairn Toul itself offers little for the climber. Coire an Lochain Uaine is the symmetrical hanging corrie between the peaks of Cairn Toul and Sgor an Lochain Uaine (Angel's Peak). Harbouring only short mouldering aretes and uninteresting slabs, it is of little interest to the climber in summer. In winter, the stream which flows steeply from Lochain Uaine into the young River Dee near Garbh Coire bothy forms great sheets of low-angled ice which offer good ice practice or an interesting approach (Grade II) to the North-East Ridge of The Angel's Peak.

The two east-facing corries of Cairn Toul which overlook the Lairig Ghru, Coire an t-Sabhail and Coire an t-Saighdeir, look fine when snow-filled, but there is no worthwhile climbing in them.

THE ANGEL'S PEAK

1258m (Map Ref 954 976)

This beautiful mountain offers a classic scramble and some interesting excursions on the southernmost wall of An Garbh Choire.

North-East Ridge 300m I *
Also known as Angel's Ridge, this leads from the edge of Coire an Lochain Uaine to the summit and is the most aesthetic approach to The Angel's Peak and Cairn Toul from the Lairig Ghru. More of a scramble than a climb, the ridge narrows at the top and can be interesting. A fine easy scramble in summer.

Angel's Delight 400m IV,4   (1983)
This route takes a west-facing corner system directly up the large broken face between the previous route and the Corrie of the Chokestone Gully. Start about 150m before the face turns round into the corrie. Gain the corner from the right *via* a steep little groove (crux). Cross the snow and continue for another two pitches in the corner on the upper tier. Scrambling (120m) leads directly to the summit.

CORRIE OF THE CHOKESTONE GULLY

From some distance west of its north-east ridge, the flanking rocks of The Angel's Peak are ill-defined although continuous low down. Near the entrance to Garbh Choire Mor they recede upwards to form the headwall of a high corrie or bay. Although arguably part of Garbh Choire Mor, these are traditionally held as distinct and named after an unmistakable feature, a dark twisting gash cleaving the steepest rocks; Chokestone Gully. With the exception of the first two pitches of Bugaboo Rib, the rock varies from bad to atrocious.

In winter, apart from the routes close to Chokestone Gully, the lines are not well defined and lack major features. The routes are open to variation, the line frequently depending on the size of a generally large cornice. However, as the cliff faces north, good conditions usually persist well into April. In late season, the best time for a visit, the cliff often has a Nordwand character with mixed ice and rock at a high angle.

White Nile, Garbh Choire Mor, Braeriach (Climber, Rab Anderson)

Descents in winter can be tricky. This section of the amphitheatre often has a continuous cornice and finding a descent in poor weather can be difficult (it may be best to stay roped until the descent is located). The nearest descent is *via* the easy-angled spur and shelf which cut down under the west side of the cliff. The shelf is gained from a small promontory about 300 metres west of the top of Chokestone Gully (Map Ref 947 976). There is rarely a cornice at this point, though it may be hard to tell from above. Col Gully, from the col west of this descent, is more often corniced. The North-East Ridge of The Angel's Peak is a longer alternative but it is almost never corniced.

South-East Couloir 200m II/III   (1970)
This is the shallow couloir in the south-east corner of the corrie. The start is 50 metres left of The Shroud. It can be anything from a pure ice route to a snow basin. Finish on the left of a normally huge cornice.

In late season, this whole section of face may be very icy and climbable almost anywhere at the same standard. At least two other lines have been taken between the original route and The Shroud.

The Shroud 160m III   (1964)
This route follows the narrow gully parallel to and just left of Chokestone Gully. The foot of the gully proper, which can contain up to three ice pitches, is reached over ice-covered rocks.

The Flying Fox 130m IV,5   (1992)
A varied climb on the buttress left of Chokestone Gully. Start at the toe of the buttress.
1. 30m Climb a series of awkward walls and short slabs, always trending right, to reach a left-trending fault. This leads to a good stance.
2. 30m Continue along the fault to a smooth groove. Step left below it and climb steeply to the buttress crest. Slabby moves lead to easier ground.
3. and 4. 70m Continue up mixed ground on the crest, merging with the upper part of The Shroud.

Chokestone Gully 150m III   (1937)
The deep gash is straightforward for the first 60m, then it curves, narrows and steepens. Beyond this and above a snow amphitheatre is the great chokestone. Normally this provides a vertical ice pitch, its

Ebony Chimney, Coire Bhrochain, Braeriach (Climber, Grahame Nicoll) height depending on the build-up. If ice is lacking, it is possible to escape from the gully on the right below the chokestone. The cornice is usually easier on the right.

Bugaboo Rib 150m VS   (1958)
The buttress bounding the right flank of Chokestone Gully tapers to a vague rib above its lower steep section. The first two pitches of this route provide the only good rock in the corrie. Start between the central line and the gully.
1. 30m 4b Climb easy slabby rocks to a grass platform. A slanting crack on the steep wall ahead leads up right to a prominent block. Climb the crack for 6m, traverse round the block and under an overhang, then continue straight up to a large platform.
2. etc. 120m 4b Climb another crack leading up right to a landing place under an overhang (10m), then move round the exposed corner on the right and continue along a tapering shelf to a belay. Above, the ridge falls back and is an easy scramble to the top.
Winter: V,7   (1970)
Follow the summer route throughout, with technical climbing on the first two pitches, thereafter more relaxing.
Variation: **The Chimney Start** V,6
On the right side of Bugaboo Rib is a chimney system leading to the large platform (this is left of a larger depression). Climb the chimney (1 peg for aid) to finish up the easier upper part of the route.

The White Hotel 150m IV,4   (1987)
Climb the larger depression right of the Chimney Start to join and finish up Bugaboo Rib. It also serves as a direct start to Sasquatch.

Sasquatch 120m III   (1974)
Right of Chokestone Gully the cliff descends lower into the corrie. Start beyond these lower rocks at a horizontal ledge traversing left onto the face approximately 50 metres right of Bugaboo Rib. Use the ledge to gain and climb a shallow icy depression. Either continue direct to the top or trend left across another depression to finish at the top of Bugaboo Rib. This often provides the only reasonable break in a huge cornice.

The Waster 90m IV,3   (1987)
Right of Sasquatch are several left-trending lines which peter out into the easier-angled upper part of the cliff. The most obvious of these is

a corner immediately before a compact series of small ribs which terminate the cliff. This poorly protected route is based on this fault, starting up a steep right-slanting line.

The Wanderer 100m III   (1975)
This takes the fault between the first two ribs mentioned above, starting up a prominent gully with a steep right wall and a narrow rib on the left. With sufficient ice, the gully can be climbed directly, but a deviation to the left (crux) is more usual. Continue without difficulty to the cornice.

BRAERIACH

1296m (Map Ref 953 999)

The climbing on this monstrous mountain is best described by taking the corries in turn, from south to north. An Garbh Choire is the collective name of the great hollow forming the innermost recess of Braeriach, perhaps the most intriguing corrie in the massif on account of its size, remoteness, wilderness allied to beauty, and above all climate. Here are found the snowfields of midsummer - our nearest approach in this country to the neve of higher mountains.

   A large headland thrusting out from the plateau divides the corrie into two subsidiaries, each of great interest and character. These are Garbh Choire Mor and Garbh Choire Dhaidh; their cliffs are the least known in the massif.

GARBH CHOIRE MOR

The left-hand and larger subsidiary of An Garbh Choire has two sections; a lower corrie leading to an upper recessed pocket of buttresses tucked high under the plateau.

   In winter, huge cornices make the descent into the corrie from the plateau potentially the most dangerous in the Cairngorms. In very stormy weather it may be impossible to find a break in the cornice and a retreat back down the route of ascent may be the safest alternative (two abseils will be sufficient for many routes). The cornice edge may be invisible in thick weather and with an overhang of up to 10 metres it is easy to find oneself treading air (it is often worth keeping the rope on).

   The most likely choice is the headland between Garbh Choire Mor and Garbh Choire Dhaidh (usually the Garbh Choire Mor side). A surer alternative for returning to the bothy is the spur and shelf just beyond Col Gully and immediately right of the Corrie of the Chokestone Gully (Map Ref 947 976). At peak conditions both alternatives can be corniced but, at least one of them should be feasible.

In an emergency, an easy descent can be made south away from the cliffs to the head of Glen Geusachan, but this will be very arduous. In any case, a descent plan should be made before embarking on a route and certainly before emerging onto the plateau where any shelter will be lost.

In good visibility, Pinnacles Gully often has a break close in beside Pinnacles Buttress. This is a steep Grade I and may require an abseil. Great Gully is easy below the cornice, but can only be suggested in early season and still with an abseil, probably from its south side.

THE LOWER CORRIE

The rocks here are somewhat indefinite. There are three named features; **Col Gully**, the prominent scree rake going up to the Cairn Toul-Braeriach col (c.1125m); **West Buttress** on the immediate right of Col Gully; and **West Gully**, a long chute separating West Buttress from the buttresses of the upper corrie.

In winter much is wiped out, but the gullies give fair Grade I climbs, although usually well corniced. Col Gully is short and open; West Gully, longer, steeper and often heavily corniced, is the better climb. West Buttress gives a pleasant Grade II.

THE UPPER CORRIE

An obscure recessed corrie, yet enjoying a reputation largely due to its remoteness and its unique snow formations. The cliff has the classic buttress-gully formation; the buttresses are mainly narrow and compact. It bears a patina of lichen which apparently thrives on granite which is covered for long periods by snow and is responsible for the greenish hue of the buttresses, most pronounced when seen in contrast with the snowfields and gullies. Although the rock is mainly sound, extensive shattering occurs in places near the plateau.

Due primarily to its location, the upper corrie is unique in Britain for its annual accumulation of snow and as the site of our most permanent snow beds; in this century these have only disappeared in 1933 and 1959. At peak conditions, narrow gullies are transformed into open snow slopes and many rock features are wiped out. The main buttresses, due to the build-up at their base which can be up to 30m in a snowy year, are greatly diminished in height. For these reasons, identification of routes can be difficult, particularly in poor weather. From the right side of the flat area below the upper corrie (small moraine), normally where one would gear up, the cliff lies between 250 degrees magnetic (Great Gully) and 300 degrees magnetic (Phoenix Buttress).

The cornice, often without a flaw, reaches giant proportions and provides otherwise easy routes with problematic finishes. Climbers should be aware of possible failure at the cornice and choose their route accordingly. The cornices may still be unbroken in June. Another interesting feature is the formation of ice grottoes and tunnels below the plateau inside the cornice structure. This is caused by snow shrinkage during consolidation.

1 Crown Buttress 120m III   (1967)

The large mass separating the lower from the upper corrie is Crown Buttress. Its left flank is broken by a broad scree and grass terrace above and below which are steep walls. On its right flank (in the upper corrie proper), it forms a continuous arete from which vertical walls dip into Great Gully. The Crown, a flake of rock, can be seen against the sky at the top of the arete. Near the top of the buttress, a second arete appears just to the left; the great V-groove between the aretes is the line of the climb. Climb the edge overlooking Great Gully to a large block. Continue up steps to the base of the great V-groove. The groove is an icy chimney which gives an excellent steep pitch (35m, crux). Very Difficult in summer.

2 Great Gully 150m I

The gully on the right of Crown Buttress is the most defined gully in the corrie. In winter it is straightforward but very heavily corniced. Easy in summer.

She-Devil's Buttress is the broad buttress forming the right wall of Great Gully. Right of its crest are twin corners; the left one is taken by the original winter line of She-Devil's Buttress and the longer right one is Vulcan.

On its right side, right of Vulcan, is an impressive face with a line of overhangs just above mid-height. Tiara follows grooves on the right edge of the buttress and cuts in left immediately above the overhangs into a steep crack.

3 She-Devil's Buttress (Original Route) 120m V,6 *   (1993)
A mixed climb with two contrasting pitches. Start at the foot of the crest.
1. 50m Follow slabby grooves up the crest of the buttress to where it steepens.
2. 25m From the top of a spearhead of rock, step left onto a slab, then move up and right to a crack leading to a fine eyrie with a tabletop belay.
3. 45m Climb the vertical wall above, then move left into a shallow groove and continue up grooves on the crest to the top.
  Very Difficult in summer by the same line.

4 She-Devil's Buttress, Corner Line 120m IV,5 *   (1969)
A good route. Climb iced grooves and snow aretes on the edge overlooking Great Gully for 60m, then traverse right over a flake to enter awkwardly the leftmost of the twin corners. This gives a further 60m of sustained ice climbing to, hopefully, a snow prow breaching the cornice on the left at the top of the buttress. The route has also been started from Vulcan, crossing Virago, on an ice line which formed in late season.

5 Virago 125m V,6 *   (1993)
A mixed climb taking a line of grooves left of Vulcan. Start about 20 metres left of Vulcan, directly below three prominent grooves situated midway up the crag, to belay on a left-slanting shelf where the crag steepens.
1. 40m Climb a short groove to a ledge, then take a steep slightly left-trending groove through the wall above. From the small alcove at its top, move right and go steeply up to a belay at the foot of a steep corner with a good crack rising above. This is at the foot of the prominent grooves visible from below.
2. 35m Ignore the groove on the left and climb the crack straight above the belay past a small overlap. Step left into a steep flake groove and climb this with difficulty to belay in an overhung recess.
3. 50m Pull through the overhang and continue up the groove above to a small ledge overlooking Vulcan. Climb the smooth V-groove (crux) to easier ground which leads steeply back left and up to the plateau.

6 Vulcan 90m VS *   (1968)
The route takes the line of a very prominent V-corner, the rightmost of the twin corners on the front face of She-Devil's Buttress. Start in the bay right of the lowest rocks of She-Devil's Buttress below the groove.

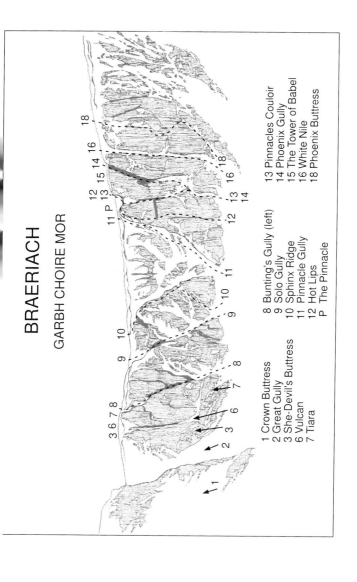

BRAERIACH

GARBH CHOIRE MOR

1 Crown Buttress
2 Great Gully
3 She-Devil's Buttress
6 Vulcan
7 Tiara

8 Bunting's Gully (left)
9 Solo Gully
10 Sphinx Ridge
11 Pinnacle Gully
12 Hot Lips
P The Pinnacle

13 Pinnacles Couloir
14 Phoenix Gully
15 The Tower of Babel
16 White Nile
18 Phoenix Buttress

Scramble up to a grassy recess and gain the bottom of the groove. Follow the groove all the way (three pitches of 4c). A little dirty in places.
Winter: V,4   (1975)
The prominent V-groove forms a series of ice pitches, the lower section being the crux. A first-rate route.

7 Tiara 80m VI,7   (1984)
A sustained climb in icy grooves and cracks. Just left of the crest besides Bunting's Gully is a long groove with an overhang at mid-height. Start up the groove and traverse 5m right about 6m below the overhang. Go up and slightly left to gain a smaller groove which starts at the right end of the overhang. Follow this over a steepening to the crest, then climb a 5m vertical wall to a belay (alternatively, split this pitch by going out right by a short groove onto the crest below the steepening). Descend 3m to the left and step delicately on to the upper slab in a very exposed position above the main overhangs. Climb a crack near the arete, then a groove a little left. Follow this to the crest, often a very sharp snow arete forming a break in the cornice (Vulcan in winter also finishes here). VS in summer; quality unknown.

8 Bunting's Gully
The first shallow gully right of Great Gully. On its right are vague twin ridges separated low down by a system of recessed corners but meeting some 30m below the plateau at a col common to both. The lower gully is easy to a fork at less than half-height; the cornice above this area is at its largest and frequently impossible. Both branches are Moderate and with poor rock.

Left Branch (Bunting's Gully Wall) 100m III   (1964)
The left fork runs up to an overhang. Go onto the right wall about 15m below the overhang, work up and right until near the crest on the right, then traverse left to an upper corner which leads to the cornice.

Right Branch (Snow Bunting) 100m II   (1966)
The right branch runs up to the col of the twin ridges and a finish common to these. A shallow gully runs up to a giant cornice.

The twin ridges to the right of Bunting's Gully are **Michaelmas Fare** on the left and the better defined **Egyptian Fantasy** on the right. Both are Very Difficult in summer. The recess between the ridges is **Gaunt Gully**, Grade II. At peak snow conditions, this section of the cliff largely banks out and the routes loose their identity. Michaelmas Fare is Grade III, directly following the crest overlooking Gaunt Gully. Egyptian Fantasy has also been climbed at a similar standard, although retreat was made from below an impossible cornice.

9 Solo Gully 100m I   (1964)
This gully, narrow at the bottom, is defined low down by Egyptian Fantasy on its left. For much of the winter the route is ludicrous, a straightforward snow slope leading to an impassable cornice. It does, however, provide a convenient descent for parties failing at nearby cornices. It is also fairly easy to traverse under the cornice to Sphinx Ridge.

10 Sphinx Ridge 100m Very Difficult   (1952)
Situated at the innermost point of the corrie above the snowfield, Sphinx Ridge rises rather shapely between Solo Gully on its left and, depending on the time of visit, either a wide section of slab or a great rock-fringed snow recess on its right. A classic route, but vegetated with some loose rock above the first pitch, and melting snow may leave the rock grimy in early summer. The frontal face is a nearly vertical triangle, on its left side is a slab which is defined on its left by a corner with overlaps. Start just right of this corner.
1. 35m Climb the slab rightwards to gain the crest. Go up either left or right on the wall above the gully to below the Sphinx. A direct start up the fine initial wall is Severe.
2. 25m Climb the corner on the left of the Sphinx and continue over a narrow ridge and col.
3. 30m Climb a short wall to a recessed corner, go up its right side until above the overlap, then traverse left to a platform. Go up the ridge above to the top of the pinnacle.
4. 15m Descend to the col and scramble to the top.
Winter: III *   (1966)
A very scenic route forming a sinuous snow crest in winter. Once the crest has been gained, either direct or by a small gully leading off Solo Gully, it is followed with one detour to the left. A superb double corniced arete leads to the main cornice.

To the right of Sphinx Ridge is a broad recess of indeterminate slabs and grass between it and Pinnacles Buttress. On each side of the recess are shallow gullies; the one under Sphinx Ridge is **Sphinx Gully**, Grade II; the one next to Pinnacles Buttress is Pinnacle Gully.

Both have been climbed in summer, as has a line between them, starting near Pinnacle Gully.

To the right of the recess is a close-set trio of steep buttresses separated by chimneys. The leftmost is Pinnacles Buttress, formed almost entirely of two pinnacles, the higher and smaller of which rises above a narrow col and stands out against the sky even when viewed from a distance. The lower pinnacle is very prominent from close below and has a crack-seamed north face with a line of overhangs. The original route, **Pinnacles Buttress** (Difficult, Grade III) climbs the left edge of the buttress to finish over the pinnacles. The lower section often banks out in winter.

11 Pinnacle Gully 150m I
The shallow gully forming the right side of the snow bay recess and immediately left of Pinnacles Buttress. It curves right and steepens behind the pinnacles, and there is often a break in the cornice.

12 Hot Lips 130m VS *   (1973)
On the north (right) side of Pinnacles Buttress is an intriguing crack-seamed face containing a band of roofs below which a ramp leads left to top right to finish in Pinnacles Couloir. A more direct line, close to the winter route, should be considered.

1. 40m Climb the ramp to large ledges near its end.
2. 35m 5a Traverse down and left, then go up cracks to an overhang 3m right of an open groove. Traverse left into the bottom of the groove, climb it and go left to a good ledge on the left arete (airy moves). Go right up a slab to near a large loose block.
3. 25m Move left up slabs to the top of the pinnacle.
4. 30m Continue to the plateau *via* the second pinnacle (loose).

Winter: VI,7 *   (1993)
A winter ascent but with a more direct first pitch; a fine sustained route. From halfway up the initial ramp, a short traverse left led into cracks leading to the left side of the open groove of the summer line, which was followed to the top. Icy conditions limited the protection but perhaps eased the difficulty.

13 Pinnacles Couloir 120m III   (1971)
This is the obvious couloir leading to the col on Pinnacles Buttress. A left-rising traverse from below The Tower of Babel leads across Phoenix Gully to the foot of the couloir. Finish by a steep snow or mixed arete to the plateau.

14 Phoenix Gully 100m IV,3 **   (1967)
A classic climb amidst fine surroundings, this is the steep icy gully
between Pinnacles Buttress and The Tower of Babel. The cornice may
be problematic. Very Difficult in summer.

15 The Tower of Babel 120m HVS *   (1969)
The central compact buttress of the Pinnacles trio provides perhaps
the best climb in the corrie, low in its grade. It consists of a small
overhanging south-west face overlooking Phoenix Gully on the left, and
a large south-east face containing the route. Start just right of the lowest
rocks and at the bottom of a shallow gully descending diagonally from
the top of the first pitch of Phoenix Gully (this is Pinnacles Couloir in
winter).
1. 20m 4b Climb easy rocks, then pull up right onto a steep wall. After
5m, climb a crack on the left and traverse left to the edge of the buttress.
2. 30m 5a Climb a good crack, move over an overlap using footholds
on the left edge of the buttress, follow a fine slab a short way, then work
right to a crack. Climb this and a steep corner to below a short
overhanging crack.
3. 25m 4b Climb the crack, then go up an easier natural line of cracks.
After 15m the buttress becomes more broken on the right, but it is still
continuous on the left. Follow a diagonal crack left to a perch on the
crest below the final short rise of the buttress.
4. 45m 4c After 5m take a ledge on the left and so to the top.
Alternatively, a little below the ledge traverse right and pull onto a slab
which gives a few thin moves.
Winter: VI,7 **   (1987)
Follow the summer line except gain the main corner-crack line (pitch
2) a little lower. On pitch 4, use a ledge system on the left (short descent
needed).

16 White Nile 120m V,5 **   (1977)
A continuous run of very steep ice between The Tower of Babel and
the rightmost buttress, Phoenix Buttress. The route is obvious apart
from a slight detour at two-thirds height where one of the many ice
walls encountered can be avoided by a groove running diagonally
left to an overlap, above which an iced slab allows a traverse back
right. White Nile is probably the best ice route in the corrie, but it is
not often in condition; the best chance is late season, after melt-
freeze from above.

17 Phoenix Edge 120m VS   (1979)
Phoenix Buttress is the right-hand of the Pinnacles trio. It has a narrow, leaning left wall overlooking White Nile. The route follows the defined crest between this leaning wall and easier ground on the right. Reasonable climbing but a little artificial. Start about 30m up from the lowest rocks where the true crest starts. The normal buttress route (Very Difficult) also starts here.
1. 45m 4b Climb a corner and continue up slabs and grooves close to the edge to a large platform.
2. 20m 4b Climb a slabby wall immediately left of a perched block. Continue up left until a short groove leads to a point above piled blocks.
3. 55m Climb a corner and slabs to easy ground.
Winter: V,6   (1991)
This is based on the summer route, but the exact line and grade varies with conditions. A short chimney right of the initial corner leads to a left-trending line to the summer belay. The right edge of the slabby wall was climbed, including the mantelshelf onto the perched block, followed by a return left to finish up the summer route.

18 Phoenix Buttress 150m III   (1971)
This is a good but vegetated line in summer (Very Difficult), so it should provide an excellent winter climb. Start at the base of the defined crest of the buttress. Work up and right *via* grooves for 50m to a steep nose. Traverse left round this and climb the groove above the piled blocks beneath a steep wall. Step right and go up a short steep corner to a large slab. Move up and right into a groove which is followed to the plateau.

19 Forked Lightning Route 100m III   (1974)
On the right side of Phoenix Buttress, at the head of a large snow bay, are two ice lines linked by a horizontal traverse along snow. These form a forked lightning shape in late season when seen from the bothy.

On the right side of the upper corrie is a gully, Grade II in early season but normally Grade I. Left of it, and right of a wide broken buttress, a shallow ridge provides the line of **Sidetracked**, Grade III; the route soon banks out.

GARBH CHOIRE DHAIDH

Garbh Choire Dhaidh (pronounced Yay, rhyming with "say") is the right-hand subsidiary of An Garbh Choire. Its cliffs are higher but more slabby than those of Garbh Choire Mor. What it lacks in steepness, however, is more than offset by the clean rock and picturesque situation. It is open walled, south-facing and sun-catching; from the plateau rim the young River Dee falls 200m from its source to the corrie floor. After running a subterranean course among huge boulders, it reappears flowing over a charming turf meadow on which it widens into attractive pools.

To the left of the Dee Cascade, the corrie wall is continuously steep but vegetated and the rocks lack mass and character. In winter this is often transformed into an open snow slope topped by a huge cornice.

Dee Waterfall II   (1810)
This early scramble was probably made up the right side of the cascade over grassy slopes and rock outcrops. In early winter it gives a pleasant route to the plateau when ice is present.

THE MAIN FACE
The left side is a high-angled wall of polished, exfoliated slabs which angle into an impressive corner-chimney in the centre, The Great Rift. This fault is not prominent from the normal approach by the right side of the corrie but is well seen from further left. Unfortunately, these slabs are usually streaming with water and the rock should be treated with suspicion as the two earliest routes here have suffered major rockfall.

The right side between The Great Rift and The Chimney Pot, a deep gully sunk in an angle formed by the detached Pisa buttress on the extreme right, is divided into ribs and grooves and gives some fine routes, perhaps the best rock climbing on Braeriach.

In winter the cliff is unreliable because of its southerly aspect. Early in the season the twin icefalls of The Culvert and The Great Rift give fine climbs. Later on the sun plays havoc with the ice and the face may be totally clear by mid-February. The easier routes however, may be in condition for longer but cloudy weather is still recommended.

Winter descents are easier than those into Garbh Choire Mor. The slope between this corrie and Coire Bhrochain is of moderate angle and rarely has a cornice. Care must be taken to bypass the cornice which extends well to the east of the cliff.

1 Billabong 140m III   (1969)
The obvious short steep icefall on the left of the main face is usually in
condition. Finish more easily up the ridge slanting rightwards, or
escape left to easy snow.

In summer, the extreme left of the main face has a rockfall scar which
used to be the crux diedre of the route (Hard Severe). The route now
looks dangerous and of uncertain grade.

2 Digeridoo 130m HVS   (1985)
The line of corners left of The Culvert is slow to dry. Start up the first
green slab left of The Culvert.
1. 45m 5a Climb a shallow crack in the centre of the green slab. Go
easily up right to gain a corner and follow it to a belay.
2. 20m 4c Continue up the corner to a wedge of dangerous blocks
below a vegetated groove. Traverse right below the blocks into a
subsidiary corner and climb it to a ledge on the right.
3. 50m 4b Return left immediately to the main corner and climb
pleasant knobbly slabs trending slightly right at the top.
4. 15m Follow a vague ridge to the top.
Winter: VII,6   (1991)
A good line but poorly protected. The green slab banks out and the line
is better located as the central of three left-facing, left-slanting corners.
Gain this and follow it past the wedge of blocks and a steep vegetated
section, a distinctive feature of the route. Continue up the corner and
cracks above, then move left into a parallel crack line and go up this to
a small bay. Climb the corner at its back, then go right by short slabby
walls. Continue rightwards up a vague rib, then climb easily to the top.
Tension was used to reach a belay in a corner on the right after the
steep section, but belaying at the wedge of blocks should make this
avoidable.

3 The Culvert 125m V,4 **   (1981)
A stepped ramp system, starting close on the left of The Great Rift,
forms an icefall parallel to The Great Rift, and probably coming into
condition before the Rift at the start of the winter. It gives four pitches
of steep ice, reminiscent of the better routes on Hell's Lum Crag.

4 The Great Rift 140m Very Difficult   (1954)
When reasonably dry, the striking corner-chimney in the centre of the
face gives one of the best chimney pitches in the massif. The initial

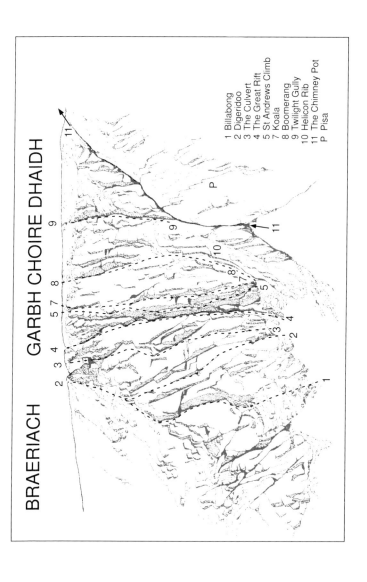

BRAERIACH   GARBH CHOIRE DHAIDH

1 Billabong
2 Digeridoo
3 The Culvert
4 The Great Rift
5 St Andrews Climb
7 Koala
8 Boomerang
9 Twilight Gully
10 Helicon Rib
11 The Chimney Pot
P Pisa

smooth pitch is avoided by a start on the right of the waterslide. Climb two consecutive clean ribs (45m) to a prominent inset corner which leads left into the Rift below a cave. Leave the cave directly or by slabs on the left and enter another and bigger cave with a great overhanging roof. Climb the slabs on the left, then return right and overcome the roof by a short steep wall (crux). The Rift now opens and becomes easier but with short interesting pitches.

Winter: V,4 *   (1965)
Sustained and very icy, this excellent climb is recommended early in the season when the sun is still weak.

5 St. Andrews Climb 130m Severe *   (1957)
The first of three fine, quick-drying climbs on the ridges bounding The Great Rift on the right. It follows a corner system on the wall immediately right of the Rift. Scramble up the green lower rocks to below a spindle-shaped rock mass.

1. 30m Climb the corner on the right of this feature and at its top step right and go up to a stance.
2. 30m   Climb the right-hand corner until the main corner can be regained and followed to a fine platform.
3. 25m Above is a corner with an overhang; climb the short wall just on its right (crux), then go up the edge.
4. 45m A steep slabby wall tops this section of cliff. Finish up its left edge, then scramble to the top.

Winter: V,6   (1986)
Climb the summer route, except follow the main corner throughout and avoid the steep slabby wall at the top by a chimney-groove on its left.

6 Kookaburra 130m Hard Severe *   (1963)
The prominent arete on the immediate right of St. Andrews Climb includes a superb, improbable pitch up the very crest overlooking St. Andrews Climb and the Rift. Climb awkward slabby rocks to the base of the arete (if wet, start up St. Andrews Climb and traverse right to the arete). Follow the exposed arete as closely as possible to a ledge system. Finish up the left edge of the slabby walls above, as for St. Andrews Climb.

7 Koala 130m VS *   (1967)
A corner system 10 metres right of Kookaburra ends in overhangs. Climb to the base of the corner and follow it in two excellent pitches to

break right through a nest of overhangs (4c) onto more broken ground. Above, finish up the centre of the steep slabby wall.
Winter: VI,6   (1987)
Take the summer line, except on pitch 2, climb a groove on the right.

To the right of Koala is a prominent V-chimney groove. This is **Kangaroo**, Severe and vegetated; V,6 in winter.

8 Boomerang 150m III   (1962)
A prominent rib low down bounds Chimney Pot on the left. This is Helicon Rib. On the left of the open gully (Twilight Gully) which separates Helicon Rib from the main cliff is a small arete. Boomerang starts in the groove behind this and curves left. In lean icy conditions it contains up to three long ice pitches when it will be Grade IV. Very Difficult and vegetated in summer.

9 Twilight Gully 150m II **   (1971)
The open bow-shaped gully just left of Helicon Rib is frequently a snow chute capped by a huge cornice. In leaner conditions, it can be an excellent long runnel of ice.

10 Helicon Rib 130m Difficult   (1949)
The prominent rib forming the left wall of The Chimney Pot has a lower section which forms a narrow crest of good rock. Above this, and beyond a sneck, the rock deteriorates and becomes very shattered.
Winter: III   (1964)
Follow the summer route.

11 The Chimney Pot 140m II *   (1959)
This chimney-gully should not be mistaken for The Great Rift. It is hidden from most viewpoints by the rocks of Pisa. There is usually one ice pitch at the great chokestone. Difficult in summer, mostly scree, but it has a very wet through route under the great chokestone.

The long buttress on the right of The Chimney Pot is **Pisa** (Difficult, Grade II). It is scrappy in both seasons but provides an entertaining summer descent from the climbs around The Great Rift. Descend Pisa to a prominent block (cairn) just above the level of the sneck on Helicon Rib, then traverse unlikely ledges into The Chimney Pot and descend the crest of Helicon Rib.

COIRE BHROCHAIN

Coire Bhrochain, on whose cliff edge the summit of Braeriach stands, is one of the finest in the Cairngorms for altitude, scenery and pure corrie form. The cliffs face south and provide pleasant routes on rough and clean granite. The corrie is, however, very remote and not in the modern idiom; the routes are natural mountaineering lines in the lower grades and neglected nowadays.

In winter the features of the Black and Braeriach Pinnacles lend beauty and grandeur to the corrie, but the cliff lacks the classic ice lines and again is rarely visited. In thick weather, the best winter descent is down the slope between this corrie and Garbh Choire Dhaidh; rarely corniced.

The cliff is divided by two pronounced breaks into three broad masses called West, Central and East Buttresses. On the left is West Buttress separated from Central Buttress by West Gully, a broad scree shoot fanning out widely at its base. Central Buttress is cut off from East Buttress by East Gully, narrow for most of its height but funnelling out at the plateau.

WEST BUTTRESS

The main mass above its easy lower rocks is built of parallel ribs with intervening slabby corners opening out into funnels of poor quality rock. The most striking feature is a great square summit tower at the top left of the face and to the right of an open chimney. There are two smaller buttresses high up and further left. Two obvious ramps slope up right in the lower half of the buttress. These provide the starts to Direct Route and Vanishing Shelf. On the right of the main mass and separated from it by The Great Couloir is Domed Ridge which flanks Lower West Gully. Branching from West Gully and striking up behind Domed Ridge to the plateau is Campion Gully. Between Campion and Upper West Gully is Azalea Rib, a smaller subsidiary of Domed Ridge.

1 Pioneers' Recess Route 200m II   (1969)

This route goes up the open chimney and recess on the left of the main mass, between the square tower and the detached buttress next left, which tapers to a spectacular hooked feature called The Fang (Very Difficult). Iced slabs and steep open snow slopes lead to the foot of the icy chimney. Exit steeply on the left from the recess above. Grade III in lean conditions; Moderate in summer.

BRAERIACH COIRE BHROCHAIN

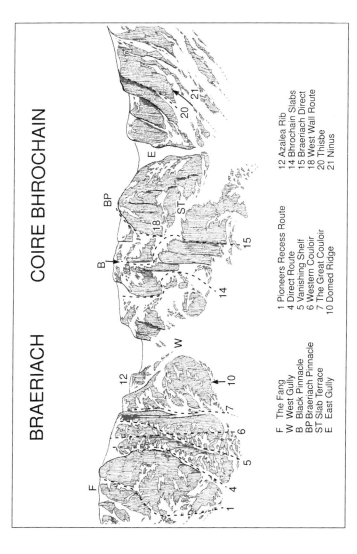

F   The Fang
W   West Gully
B   Black Pinnacle
BP Braeriach Pinnacle
ST Slab Terrace
E   East Gully

1   Pioneers Recess Route
4   Direct Route
5   Vanishing Shelf
6   Western Couloir
7   The Great Couloir
10 Domed Ridge

12 Azalea Rib
14 Bhrochain Slabs
15 Braeriach Direct
18 West Wall Route
20 Thisbe
21 Ninus

2 Fang Face 200m V,7   (1992)
An atmospheric route climbing directly up the crest of the buttress left
of Vanishing Point. Start left of Direct Route and climb a right-facing
corner, then move right to climb a shallow trough-groove system about
7m left of Vanishing Point's corner system. When this runs out, follow
cracks and grooves on the left side of the crest to easy ground below
the Tower. Cross the gully on the left (Pioneer's Recess Route) and
climb The Fang by the cracked facing ridge. Descend the far side on
large flakes to a narrow col, then follow the easy crest to the cornice.

3 Vanishing Point 200m IV,4   (1988)
A fine route which starts at the foot of the ramp of Direct Route and
climbs the obvious right-facing corner system trending slightly right.
Continue straight up to below the final tower, then move right to finish
up the chimney-grooves of the Direct.

4 Direct Route 200m IV,4 *   (1968)
A fine route following the most prominent of the grooves on the main
mass somewhat right of centre. Start up the left-hand of the two obvious
ramps, the right-hand one being Vanishing Shelf. Follow the ramp up
right to a short chimney. Much variation is possible in the middle and
upper sections. Finish by the rightmost of the twin chimneys on the right
flank of the Tower, then take the rib on its right. The summer route
approximates to this line (Severe).

5 Vanishing Shelf 200m III   (1959)
The next prominent shelf, a counterpart to Direct Route, ends at a high
balcony overlooking the pitch in the Great Couloir. Follow the shelf to
the balcony at its far end. Go out left on a ledge and make a long
traverse up and left to a scoop which leads to a huge cornice. Difficult
in summer.

6 Western Couloir 200m III   (1970)
This is the shallow couloir between the upper couloir of Vanishing Shelf
and Direct Route. Climb the lower slabs directly, crossing Vanishing
Shelf, and follow the couloir to a possibly gigantic cornice.

7 The Great Couloir 200m III **   (1957)
The long defined gully separating the main mass from Domed Ridge.

Above mid-height, it bends rightwards round a subsidiary rib on the main mass. Straight ahead in the angle between the rib and the left wall is a prominent deep chimney forming a left branch; this is Ebony Chimney.

The Great Couloir is named for its character in winter when it forms a most beautiful chute, steep in its upper part and heavily corniced. A superb route in thin conditions, when the big chokestone is not built over and presents a hard ice pitch. Very Difficult in summer.

8 Ebony Chimney 80m Severe (1967)

An entertaining climb in dry weather, well worth groping through the initial 5m of overhanging slime. Surmount the first big chokestone and continue up the fine chimney above until the way is blocked by another enormous chokestone, passed by traversing out right. Above, enter another magnificent through route, emerging higher up beneath great roofs. Go right along a ledge and climb a wall and corner to a stance on the rib on the right. Move up the crest, then go right into a steep groove overlooking The Great Couloir and follow this groove to easier ground.

Winter: VI,6 *** (1982)

One of the best short climbs in the Cairngorms, very steep and sustained yet full of variety. Follow the summer route throughout; the through route does not fill up although a little excavation may be required to gain entrance. The chimney is normally very icy and may be poorly protected.

9 Ivory Tower 65m HVS (1984)

The rib between Ebony Chimney and The Great Couloir is guarded by a girdling overhang thwarting a direct ascent. Start from a belay on the right of The Great Couloir.

1. 30m 5b Climb rocks on the right to gain the top of a large chokestone (as for The Couloir). Traverse left onto the wall at a point below a prominent bulging crack. Climb this and another crack which leads to ledges on the crest.

2. 20m 4c Move round right and traverse horizontally right to gain and climb a corner to pale rocks. Continue until it is possible to move back left across the wall and regain the crest.

3. 15m 5a Ebony Chimney crosses the rib at this point. Climb directly up the wall on the crest to a platform. Easy rocks now lead to the top.

10 Domed Ridge 200m III   (1955)
The broad ridge between The Great Couloir and West Gully. A tower at mid-height is the crux; easier on the right. After a crest, avoid the final dome on the right. Moderate in summer.

11 Campion Gully 130m II   (1954)
This is a left branch of West Gully, striking up behind Domed Ridge to the plateau. Difficult in summer.

12 Azalea Rib 150m I *
This ridge forms the upper left wall of West Gully. Start just above Campion Gully and climb a snow trough, then a shelf on the right to a narrowing. A short blocky corner leads to the crest on the left, then follow this over a pinnacle to the steep upper wall. Avoid this by a traverse left and a short chokestone chimney.

13 West Gully 150m I *
This wide snow corridor is steeper at the top and ringed by a big cornice which is usually complete, but smaller at the top right. It provides a good descent route if the cornice can be passed (often by abseil from the corner nearest Braeriach summit). Moderate in summer, with steep earth and rubble at the top.

CENTRAL BUTTRESS
This has a much more diversified structure than West Buttress, with several distinctive features. Centrally placed and cut-off from the mountain on all sides is Black Pinnacle, a well known feature, being so visible from the plateau. On the left of Black Pinnacle and almost extending to West Gully is a great recessed area of slabby ground, the Bhrochain Slabs.

On the right of Black Pinnacle and extending to East Gully is Braeriach Pinnacle, in reality a big individual buttress whose top is almost level with the plateau. The Slab Terrace, containing a large low-angled slab leading to an easy grassy gangway, leads up left from the foot of Braeriach Pinnacle to Central Buttress Gully, a broad hidden chute between the Pinnacles, and beyond to the start of the routes on Black Pinnacle.

14 Bhrochain Slabs 200m Very Difficult   (1944)
Pleasant climbing, but a little scrappy. On the left of Black Pinnacle and from the rocks directly below it (Braeriach Direct), a continuous sheer

wall drops to Bhrochain Slabs forming a vast corner, the line of the climb. The route is open to variation at the same standard. Start about 50m up and left of the lowest rocks of Central Buttress. Go straight up for about 20m, then trend right to a steep slab near the main corner split by several cracks (40m). Climb the rightmost crack, which slopes to the right (25m). Climb an easy-angled slab up left, then another slab using the right-hand of twin cracks, to reach a platform (at this point North-West Chimney crosses. It runs up to the saddle of Black Pinnacle; Moderate). Go up the rocks ahead until forced to make a short descent and traverse left along an exposed slab. Climb a rib on the slab, then go left again to turn a corner into the upper section of the climb. Either follow a slabby groove, then the rocks on its right (easy), or climb straight up the slab past a small curving corner.

Winter: III   (1960)

The route tends to bank out to Grade II, particularly late in the season, but it follows a good line.

15 Braeriach Direct 250m Severe   (1956)

A direct mountaineering route from the lowest rocks to Black Pinnacle and the plateau, which is reached a short distance east of Braeriach's summit. It offers good situations, but not quality climbing. The line is open to variation but keep to clean rock. From a frontal view, the vertical left wall of Black Pinnacle stands out from the cliff like a gnomon of a gigantic sundial, the dial plate being a great 80m slab isolated by sheer walls plunging to Bhrochain Slabs. The route approximates to this crest above Bhrochain Slabs. Start just left of the lowest rocks. Climb easy pink slabs to a long grass ledge and go to its left end (30m). Work out left to a block platform on the crest overlooking Bhrochain Slabs (30m). Move down and round a little crest on the right to climb an awkward wall (crux), then continue up slabs and blocks to Slab Terrace (30m). From immediately below the sharp edge of Black Pinnacle, traverse easily left to Sundial Slab. Start in the corner, them move to the left edge and gain a platform behind the pinnacle. Climb to the summit from here and return back to the neck. Continue to the plateau by the smooth slab ahead using a fault leading right.

From the neck, one can scramble down Central Buttress Gully on the right to the start of West Wall Route.

Winter: IV,3 *   (1983)

The scenery is even better in winter. Climb the lower tier to Slab Terrace by a fine icefall (90m), about 25 metres right of the summer line. Sundial Slab corner is spectacular but straightforward in good conditions.

16 Midwinter 90m IV,4   (1987)
The chimney-groove system between Braeriach Direct summer and
winter lines, finishing on Slab Terrace, provides the best start to
Braeriach Direct under powder. Climb a wide chimney 10 metres right
of Braeriach Direct to its end, then follow left-trending cracks to a belay.
A delicate traverse right leads to a steep groove which ends at the
terrace.

Two short winter climbs have been made on the small face below
Slab Terrace and right of Braeriach Direct. These are a short chimney
(Grade IV), and a groove to its left (Grade V).

17 The Black Pinnacle 150m Moderate *   (1911)
Recommended as an expedition going by Slab Terrace to its end below
the easy first pitch of Central Buttress Gully, which stands between
Black Pinnacle on the left and Braeriach Pinnacle on the right. This
pitch leads to an amphitheatre where the gully forks. The true gully runs
up behind Braeriach Pinnacle; the more open left branch leads to the
neck of Black Pinnacle. A short easy chimney leads to the serrated
crest and the outer tooth of the pinnacle.
Winter: II **   (1949)
Follow the ordinary route *via* Central Buttress Gully Left Branch to the
neck, or (as on the first ascent), climb the slabs on the left of the gully,
then traverse left to a point between the hillward prongs of the pinnacle.
Gain the pinnacle summit from the neck and return. Snow leads to the
cornice, often large. This final slope collects windslab and is prone to
avalanche.

There are two alternative summer routes from Slab Terrace to the
pinnacle summit; **Slab Route** (Moderate, the line of the first winter
ascent of the Pinnacle) and **Direct Route** (Difficult) which follows a
corner just right of roof tile overhangs and cuts back left to the crest
(this has the best rock of all three possibilities).
The true (right) branch of **Central Buttress Gully** gives an interesting winter climb through grand scenery, Grade I. In summer it is
Moderate, but a better summer line (though neither is good) is **Central
Chimney** (Moderate), which cleaves the amphitheatre wall between
the left and true branches.
Braeriach Pinnacle is the biggest feature of Central Buttress, lying
between Central Buttress Gully and East Gully above Slab Terrace. Its
time-honoured name is rather misleading, for only from the plateau

does it show any trace of pinnacle form. In reality, it is a broad-based buttress whose rocks slope up from right to left, ending in a ridge formed by an undercut wall overhanging upper Central Buttress Gully. This ridge is West Wall Route.

The frontal face is big but lacks defined lines; the routes are open to variation. The old established routes are **Original Route** on the left (Difficult); **The Lampie** (IV,5) is a direct winter version. **South Face** (Difficult, Grade II) is in the centre and **Eastern Route** (Moderate, Grade II) lies on the edge of East Gully.

18 West Wall Route 100m Mild Severe *   (1942)
A good route, steep and exposed, but some of the rock is flaky. Start just above the pitch in Central Buttress Gully and traverse right to a small platform on the edge of the buttress. Climb on the right of the edge to gain a second platform, smaller and 15m above the first. Continue directly up the arete or the steep wall just to the right (20m). Follow a quartz vein straight up the exposed edge overlooking the gully until it is possible to traverse right into a groove which leads back to the crest at a broad platform. The angle now eases and it is a pleasant scramble along an airy ridge to the top of the pinnacle.
Winter: IV,5   (1984)
Follow the summer route.

19 East Gully 150m I   (1901)
A straight-cut narrow chute, with no pitches; a possible descent route in good conditions. The wide upper funnel is usually well corniced but with an easy exit on the right. Moderate in summer.

EAST BUTTRESS
This is composed of four more individual buttresses set side by side and divided by three gullies. The rock is rough, but in many places it is very loose and none of the routes can be recommended in summer.

Bordering East Gully is **Near East Buttress** (Moderate, Grade II), and on its right is **Tigris Chimney** (Grade II), a chimney which opens out into a shallow snow scoop. To the right of Tigris Chimney is **Babylon Rib** (Moderate, Grade II), which is a ridge in two parts, a narrow wedge-shaped lower section and, above a large platform, a narrow arete to the plateau. The next gully is **Pyramus** (Moderate, Grade I); a pointed rib at the foot furnishes the gully with two branches which join 60m up. On the right is **The Lion** (Difficult, Grade II), an attractive ridge with steep walls falling into Thisbe on the right.

20 Thisbe 110m III *   (1955)
A fine but short gully climb, well defined by high walls and with four
varied ice pitches early in the season. Later on, some of the pitches
may bank out. In summer it is also a good gully climb, Difficult.

The steep buttress on the extreme right of the corrie, forming the
right wall of Thisbe, is Ninus (Difficult). Two routes, meeting at less than
mid-height, have been made. The winter version of Ninus starts on the
left at the foot of Thisbe.

21 Ninus 150 III   (1970)
A good buttress climb. Start at the foot of Thisbe and climb up and right
to gain an obvious snow ramp. Continue right to a depression and follow
this to a snow basin. Traverse left and climb the rib in pitches to the
plateau.

COIRE AN LOCHAIN
This is the rightmost of the trio of corries which give the north side of
Braeriach its fine character when seen from Speyside. It is the most
interesting scenically of the three and the only one having rock for
climbing.
The loch from which it derives its name is one of the finest specimens
of mountain loch in the Cairngorms and the largest sheet of water at
such an elevation (998m) in the country. The loch is girt by slabs and
the best defined climb is on the right side where a pinnacled ridge rises
on the right of a narrow gully. This is **Derelict Ridge** (Difficult, Grade
III), keeping to the steep acute edge overlooking the gully. The gully
itself is Grade I, short but well defined.

The Icefall 150m II   (1989)
In early season the icefall at the back of the corrie gives an excellent
route of continuous ice, close to Grade III, but it banks out completely
in mid season. It is well seen from Speyside and is usually approached
via Gleann Einich.

Coire Ruadh, the central of the three corries, gives fair snow climbing
and the narrow ridges bounding it on either side are interesting winter
routes to the plateau. That on the left, forming the boundary with Coire
Beanaidh, leads directly to the summit of Braeriach and is the better
of the two.

SRON NA LAIRIGE
(Map Ref 964 006)

These crags on the northern top of Braeriach overlook the Lairig Ghru and although they add to the appearance of this famous pass, they give little in the way of good climbing. At the north end of the broken and indistinct section of steeper ground there are several ribs which give generally undistinguished climbing. There is, however, a more reasonable buttress.

Lairig Ridge 135m Difficult   (1950)
The best feature of the cliff is a fine towered ridge at the southern end of this section. It has a 30m slabby wall at its base. Climb the wall by its right edge, avoid an overhang on the left, then go up to easy ground. Scramble to the ridge proper and start up this on the right by walls, then take slabs to a short chimney which leads to the crest. Follow this direct over towers to the top.
Winter: III   (1985)
Follow the summer route.

Sinclair's Last Stand 150m III   (1992)
This route takes the central grooves on the face immediately right of Lairig Ridge. Start about 30m up from the lowest rocks at an ice smear.
1. 50m Climb the smear and the groove to below a short wall.
2. 40m Turn the wall on the left, then go up slightly right and climb the next groove.
3. 20m The next groove is very thin, so traverse left to a big flake on the edge and climb the crest on the ridge.
4. 40m Continue up the crest to the top.

'Gormless 120m II/III   (1980s)
The furthest right of the faults to the right of the last route starts off as open ramps, then develops into more defined grooves. Where these fork, trend right to finish near the top of the ridge.

CREAG AN LETH-CHOIN
(Map Ref 968 033)

Also known as Lurcher's Crag, this broken rambling cliff lies on the flank of the Lairig Ghru below the summit of the same name. These routes are included in this chapter for convenience, being quite close to the approach to Braeriach from the north. The crag is divided into three sections (North, Central and South) by North and South Gullies, scrambles in summer. The Central Section lies directly below the summit of Creag an Leth-Choin but the rocks are better defined in the Southern Section.

In summer, the ribs give climbing of about Moderate standard and scrambling on reasonably sound rock. In winter, various routes besides those described can be worked out, depending on conditions. Because of the cliff's westerly aspect, conditions here can be very different from other crags in the area and can occasionally give the best climbing around. At times, great quantities of ice can accumulate, making all the climbs long but not too steep ice routes. A large number of other ice pitches and bulges can be found the whole length of the cliff.

The crag can be approached in a number of ways. From the north, either follow the track leading into the Lairig Ghru or follow the path from the Sugar Bowl car park (Map Ref 986 073) through the Chalamain Gap, then contour the slopes to the crag. An alternative is from the Coire Cas car park by traversing the hillside and contouring Creag an Leth-Choin before descending to the crag, or by descending from the col at the head of Lurcher's meadow.

North Gully 240m III   (1965)
The big sprawling gully at the highest section of the most northerly part of cliff usually has two big but not too difficult ice pitches.

Central Gully 300m III *   (1970)
The most obvious gully in the middle of the cliff has several ice pitches in the bottom half. Either the left or right branches can be followed to the top.

Window Gully 220m III   (1972)
Midway between North and South Gullies is a large icefall halfway up the face. Climb quite steeply for 75m to an overhanging wall, from which the ice falls in a screen. Go left between the ice and the rock, cut a

window and follow steep ice to easier ground. If the front face is climbed on the outside the climb is harder. Continue up the gully to the top.

Irish Wolfhound 75m IV,6   (1994)
Roughly 150 metres north of Deerhound Ridge is a high rocky amphitheatre with a steep chimney/gully on its back wall. Climb the wall just left of the chimney and finish up the obvious groove.

Deerhound Ridge 180m III   (1994)
At the southern end of the cliff is one ridge which descends much lower than the rest of the surrounding crags. There is one squat buttress south of this. Climb the ridge by a zigzag line in its lower part, then by the left side to reach an easy col. A groove on the left side now gives the crux, then follow the blocky crest to the top.

The South-West Cairngorms

The first part of this chapter describes the remote and unfrequented climbing possibilities on the mountains on both sides of the southern part of the Lairig Ghru. The easiest approach is from Braemar, and Corrour Bothy serves as a convenient base. In the second half of the chapter climbs on the Gleann Einich face of Sgor Gaoith and Sgoran Dubh are described, followed by routes in Glen Feshie. These climbs are very much off the beaten track of Cairngorm climbing and are nowadays quite unfrequented.

BEINN BHROTAIN

1157m (Map Ref 954 923)

This massive and remote mountain presents some climbing on its steep scarp faces some distance from the actual summit. Towards the River Dee the mountain presents a continuously steep slope, but little in the way of continuous rock. There are three sections of cliff.

The southern section is marked at its right end by a wide and easy-angled grass and scree chute. A little to the left is a defined gully (**Green Gully**, Moderate, Grade I) which offers a direct route from Derry Lodge to the summit of the mountain. Near the centre of this section is a recess with steep rocks on its left and slabs either side. The left-hand slabs are quite short and interspersed with patches of vegetation. They contain several dykes (narrow bands of different rock) which rise diagonally left across smooth slabs and two of which, despite appearances, give amusing and unusual climbs. Both are hardest at the start and unprotected without pegs (peg runners were used on Brodan's Dyke).

Brodan's Dyke 90m VS   (1983)
This follows the narrow leftmost dyke. Start at the foot of the slabs.
1. 30m 4c Climb twin dykes up left over a bulge. Continue on the main upper band to the top of a heather slope below a small overlap.
2. 35m Climb slightly right to heather, then continue up the next section of the band to ledges with a belay up on the right.
3. 25m From the left end of the ledges, follow the band up round and across a grassy fault to finish up waterwashed slabs with an exit left.

Clonedyke 65m HVS   (1984)
The rightmost dyke, which is immediately right of a wider dyke. Start
by an awkward scramble to a poor belay just below and left of the start
of the dyke (on the wider dyke).
1. 45m 5a Climb straight up the slab to the base of the thin dyke. Follow
this to a long grass ledge - good small wires just to the left.
2. 20m 4b Continue up the dyke. Exit on the left, *via* a further 30m of
scrambling.

The central section is a large area of glaciated slabs containing a
conspicuous inverted-V overlap. Unfortunately the slabs are penetrated at mid-height by great swards of vegetation. These slabs have
been climbed at the highest point of continuous rock (in the centre) to
give a 300m Very Difficult route of reasonable quality; there are good
situations at the start and finish but it is easy-angled in the middle.
The northern section has nothing to offer the climber. There is a
short gully high up on the nose between the Dee Valley and Glen
Geusachan, and heavily vegetated patches of slab on either side.

COIRE CATH NAM FIONN
(Map Ref 951 933)

This corrie forms the north-west face of Beinn Bhrotain and is one of
the most secluded spots in the Cairngorms. High on the left at the
entrance is Fingal's Buttress, composed of steep slabby rock on its left
and centre; on the right it throws down ribs into a scree-filled amphitheatre. From the corrie floor a crack can be seen rising in three short
sections up the edge where the ribs and slabs meet. This is **Tiered
Cracks** (100m, Very Difficult; Grade IV,5 in winter).
The rest of the face to the Beinn Bhrotain–Monadh Mor col is
vegetated buttresses with two defined gullies which give good Grade
I climbs. **A Gully** is the left-hand and steeper; **B Gully** is on the right.

CARN CLOICH-MHUILINN
942m (Map Ref 968 907)

On the north slopes of this top of Beinn Bhrotain is a band of slabs
about 60m high. These are climbable in several places at about Severe.
A few short problems are possible but don't merit a special visit.

THE DEVIL'S POINT
1004m (Map Ref 976 952)

This striking headland contributes in no small measure to the great character of the Lairig Ghru. In spite of its fierce appearance, it is most disappointing to the climber. Much apparently attractive ground is in fact unstable vegetation and loose rock. The whole face may be wandered over, save at the northerly belt of slabs topped by its huge overhangs. Even these are less steep than they look. Passing the right-hand end of the overhangs is the poor quality **Corrour Slabs** (Difficult, Grade II).

In winter the mountain improves, and after heavy snow it provides a magnificent spectacle. However, the natural lines are insufficiently steep to give anything other than Grade I climbs, though these are good. The four best defined lines are:

(a) The open chimney below the south end of the huge overhangs, continuing past the overhangs to steep slopes and ribs above.

(b) **South-East Gully**, an open depression striking up to the summit at the south end of the Dee face.

(c) **South-West Gully** lies just inside Glen Geusachan and has steeper rocks on its left edge (**South-West Arete**, Difficult).

(d) **Geusachan Gully** is the large gully well to the left of South-West Gully. It is more defined than the others and cuts back diagonally to the summit.

The mountain continues west into Glen Geusachan as a great wall of slab, of minimal interest to the climber. The only feature hereabouts is the Devil's Cave, perched in the midst of the slabs, two-thirds of the way up the face in a steep wall facing the glen. It is hidden from the Dee approach and is reached by turf ledges from the west. The first recorded visit was in 1929 and since then visits have been rare, although it has been slept in by seekers after the unusual.

CARN A' MHAIM
1037m (Map Ref 994 952)

High up on the face opposite Corrour bothy are short ribs and slabs offering problems up to 30m long. Further north is the Palette (Map Ref 986 966), an unmistakable patch of slab, aptly named from its shape and colour.

The left side of the Palette is barred high up by a big overlap penetrated only by Gadd's Route at a prominent nose. At its right end it becomes more broken and here Medium Rare goes through. On the right side of the Palette and lower down is a smaller overlap system which forms an inverted-V. Tickled Pink goes through the left arm of the V and Pink Dwarf takes the apex. The characteristic feature of the Palette is a set of parallel pink streaks low down. These provide the three right-hand routes with excellent crux pitches of unprotected padding. Unfortunately most of the slab is less smooth and the routes have long easy sections.

Gadd's Route 150m E1   (1955)
There is a very prominent white corner created by rockfall.
1. 5a Go up the slabs to the foot of the corner and climb the right-hand rib using grassy cracks.
2. 4c Continue directly up slabs and climb an overlap to a prominent cracked nose at a weakness in the big overlap.
3. 5c Surmount this by the short overhanging corner (old ring peg) on the right.
4. Continue up slightly right to a heather patch and climb the final overlap to gain the easy upper slabs, where it is convenient to traverse off right.

Medium Rare 115m E1   (1984)
Right of the white corner is a fine sheet of slab with several water-washed pink streaks. This route takes a very straight line including the left-hand pair of streaks. The bottom of the slab has a prominent crescent-shaped overlap; start below its left end.
1. 25m Climb up past the left end of the overlap and go rightwards to below the left-hand pair of streaks.
2. 45m 5b Climb either streak (the right is slightly easier), then go straight up slabs to the left end of a small overlap.
3. 45m Climb a shallow right-facing corner (just left of a steep slab and in line with the lower streak), then go right under a small overlap, back left and climb slabs to a system of short corners at the right end of the big overlap. Slant left up the left-hand corner, then go right across a slab to easier slabs and finish up these.

Tickled Pink 105m HVS   (1981)
This route takes the less steep right-hand streak above the right end of the crescent-shaped overlap, starting right of it.

1. 20m   Climb slabs to pass the right end of the crescent-shaped overlap and continue up slabs on the left to belay left of a long grass ledge, below and left of the pink streak.
2. 45m 4c   Go up to the overlap, cross it left of the pink streak, then traverse right along the lip under a minor overlap to gain and climb the streak past a hole. Continue straight up the slab above to a small overlap.
3. 40m 4c   Go over the overlap and climb a slab to the left-hand of two short overhanging cracks in the next bigger overlap (the left arm of the inverted-V overlap). Climb the crack, continue up right and go up slabs to easier ground.

Pink Dwarf 95m VS   (1981)
1. 55m 4a   Climb the widest pink streak towards the right end of the slabs. This leads directly to the small overlap near Tickled Pink.
2. 40m 4b   Move right and climb a slab to the top of the inverted-V overlap. Pull out right from a short corner at the very apex of the V, then go left and right up easy slabs.

On the east side of Carn a' Mhaim, the sections of slab overlooking Glen Luibeg are of little interest other than for making sporting lines to the summit from Derry Lodge. Various routes up to Very Difficult have been made from 1940 onwards, including a line from bottom right to top left and a direct line. The best route to the summit in winter from this direction lies up the little tapering gully in the recess between the slabs (**Silver Chimney**, 100m, Grade I). The slabs left of Silver Chimney have also been climbed in winter.

GLEANN EINICH

On the western slopes of Gleann Einich, the peaks of Sgoran Dubh Mor and Sgor Gaoith throw down five great buttresses along a 3km stretch of the glen and shore of Loch Einich. Each buttress is roughly triangular in shape and cut by a complex of gullies and chimneys into a series of discontinuous aretes which merge near the top into low-angled ridges leading towards the summits above. Distinctive, funnel-shaped hanging corries separate the buttresses.

The five buttresses (really six, but the first two are considered as one) are numbered from 1 to 5 going from north to south (right to left) and are generally of poor and broken rock. Apart from a burst of enthusiasm at the turn of the century, these crags have never enjoyed much popularity; access is long, the rock climbs range from uninspiring to dangerous, they tend to be discontinuous and there are much better climbs virtually everywhere else. However, some winter routes are worthwhile and there has been a vague return of interest probably linked to the diminishing potential for new routes on the more accessible crags. Unfortunately, with a cliff base at 650m, good winter conditions are not all that common here.

Approaches
From Aviemore, take the ski road to Coylumbridge or Whitewell (see Braeriach access), then the track to Loch Einich (13km). Take the path along the west side of the loch to reach the buttresses. Using a bicycle or skiing is probably the best way to do this in a reasonable length of day. Beware of crossing the terrible peat bogs of Gleann Einich below the loch.

   Alternatively, from Achlean at the head of the public road in Glen Feshie, ascend over Carn Ban Mor, descend steep ground to the south of the buttresses, then traverse to the climbs

NO.1 BUTTRESS

This is really two buttresses, the northern and the southern sections being separated by **The Willow Spout** (Grade I); the left fork is the more interesting. The northern section consists of a series of ribs of about Very Difficult in standard, with Roberts' Ridge forming the right side of The Willow Spout.

   The southern section has a distinctive 45m wall of steep rock at one-third height, the Northern Rampart, which separates the lower and upper rocks and does provide some more interesting pitches.

Roberts' Ridge   150m   IV,6   (1987)
The steep well defined ridge overlooking The Willow Spout ends in a knife-edge leading to a little pinnacle called The Anvil. Start close to the gully and climb to the remains of a tree and a chimney. Climb the chimney, then zigzag up to the top of the steeper section. Continue to a steep crack in the upper wall, climb this and carry on to the top of The Anvil. Descend by abseil and continue up the ridge.

   In summer the route is Severe and well worth doing. Avoid the rockfall area on pitch 2 by a groove on its left, then traverse right. The upper wall is a fine pitch.

NO.2 BUTTRESS

This and No.3 Buttress constitute the largest mass of rock and are separated by Fan Corrie which drains down into the narrow 2/3 Gully. This buttress consists of a number of ribs which converge near a col high up. About halfway along, a Y-shaped scree shoot, **Decoy Rib** (Grade III), gives indefinite climbing up the left side of the rightmost rock mass.

Rose Ridge 260m IV,5   (1986)
This lies directly above a long thin runnel and is marked by a conspicuous wall which forms the north flank high up. Follow the crest of the ridge. The first five pitches are sustained but escapable and lead to 100m of easier ground below the col.

Bachelor's Chimney 140m IV,5   (1990)
The deep chimney high on the buttress 50 metres left of Rose Ridge involves three pitches; the first up steep slopes to a through-route, the second climbs a steep wall by a groove on the right and the last leads to a cave which is negotiated by another through-route. Finish up mixed ground.

FAN CORRIE

The upper corrie between No.2 and No.3 Buttress harbours two large buttresses and many ribs. The right-hand of these is Diamond Buttress which can be approached up 2/3 Gully.

Diamond Buttress 120m III,4   (1986)
The lower and upper parts of the ridge are straightforward but are separated by a steeper wall which is climbed by a V-groove directly above a pointed block.

NO.3 BUTTRESS

This takes the form of a steep wall rising above smooth slabs on the left and heather slopes on the right. The prominent though ill-defined Diagonal Rake runs up from right to left across the wall which is divided vertically by several chimneys.

Tristar Chimney 160m III,4   (1986)
Start just right of the foot of Diagonal Rake. Climb a short ice pitch to gain the main fault and follow this over two chokestones to the top.

Cripple's Cleft 120m III,4   (1987)
A thin crack with several chokestones starts more than halfway up the
Diagonal Rake. Approach *via* the rake and climb the fault to its top, then
continue by 300m of exhilarating ridge to the plateau.

NO.4 BUTTRESS

This presents a considerable frontage to the loch but is rather broken
and offers little in the way of continuous climbing. Also on this buttress,
but at right angles to it, is an array of ridges. Higher up, three distinctive
ribs taper and converge. They face out across the glen and are
bounded by the tiny tributaries of the burn on the immediate left of No.4
Buttress.

Einich Rib 100m IV,5   (1988)
The central and most attractive of the ribs. Start at the centre up a little
semi-detached arete, then go straight up to finish up a short easy upper
arete.

NO.5 BUTTRESS

The last buttress is characterised by a striking pinnacle above mid-
height (A' Chailleach – the Old Woman). The right-hand edge leading
to the pinnacle is taken by Pinnacle Ridge. The deep No.5 Buttress
Gully (Grade II), cuts the right-hand wall of the buttress; further left is
the more impressive chimney-gully line of The Slash. Between these
two faults is **The Auld Wifie** (230m, IV,6), which takes a line on the
ridge to the left of a short gully and leads onto Pinnacle Ridge up which
it finishes. Right of The Slash is **Resurrection** (VS) which climbs the
slabs *via* a short chimney, rowan sapling and cracks.

The Slash 200m V,6 *   (1987)
The obvious fault on the left of the buttress gives interesting climbing
through superb scenery.
1. 40m Climb the gully over three short ice pitches.
2. 45m Climb a constricted chimney-groove, then follow the gully over
a chokestone to below a large chokestone.
3. 30m The chokestone leads to easy snow below steep ice.
4. 45m Climb the ice pitch in the corner-chimney on the right side to
easy snow.
5. 40m Follow the gully over a short ice pitch, then take the easy upper
fault to gain the ridge near the top.

A' PHOCAID

This lies between No.5 Buttress and Coire Odhar. In the left of the corrie lies a deep easy gully. About 50 metres right of the gully are two parallel faults, about 100m in length, which are separated by a narrow ridge. **The Sporran** (Grade III) takes the left-hand fault. The right-hand fault is taken by **Pick Pocket** (Grade III) and is gained by easy iced slabs and a long ice groove.

GLEN FESHIE

The final part of this guide describes the tranquil but fairly easily accessible climbing in Glen Feshie. It is, perhaps, a place to explore when the hustle of the Northern Corries becomes overpowering.

COIRE GARBHLACH
(Map Ref 879 945)

This corrie has been long regarded as obscure and of scenic interest only, as it lies well away from the main climbing areas on the western border of An Moine Mhor, the vast gently sloping tableland above Glen Feshie. Access is by public road to Achlean on the east bank of Glen Feshie. There is hostel accommodation in Glen Feshie and a fine bothy at Ruigh-aiteachain (Map Ref 847 297).

Coire Garbhlach itself is a narrow trenched valley, rather than a true corrie, with a steep wall composed in the main of grassy rakes with vegetated, fragmentary buttresses. Just short of where Coire Garbhlach opens out into Fionnar Choire, there are some rocks on the northern side, characterised by a prominent cave. Hermit's Ridge takes the rib on the left of this cave.

Hermit's Ridge 100m Very Difficult   (1932)
The lower difficulties can be avoided; higher up a small tower can be climbed direct or avoided on the left. Beyond a col is a wall which can be climbed direct (Severe) or turned on the right by a chimney which leads back to the crest. Follow this to the top.
Winter: IV,4   (1968)
Follow the summer line.

Further up the corrie on the south side is a line of broken buttresses and ramps which do not extend to the plateau. Several winter routes can be found here, up to about Grade III, and the ice formation is fairly reliable although the climbs are very open to variation and escape. **Garbh Ridge** (IV,4) takes the crest of the second ridge from the top of the smooth wall of the upper corrie (it is just left of a buttress topped with two towers). It is easy apart from the traverse across a steep wall separating the lower ridge from the upper. More ice climbing may be found in the area of the waterfall formed by the southerly tributary of the Allt Garbhlach where it cascades over the plateau edge.

UPPER GLEN FESHIE

Upper Glen Feshie is framed between two crags. On the right (south-west) is Creag na Caillich (Map Ref 853 903), and facing it on the left is Creag na Gaibhre. At the right end of Creag na Caillich is a prominent buttress with a large crack at mid-height and flanked on the right by a gully.

Coylum Crack 300m III,4   (1977)
Climb the gully to the base of the buttress, reach the crack and from it traverse diagonally left to a shoulder. A runnel then leads to the top.

On Creag na Gaibhre the rocks are high up and divided by a waterfall. On the hillside to the right are two chasms, the more prominent is Grade II. The icefall is divided by a prominent rib which separates the following routes. Both routes are best approached by starting from well to the right to gain a narrow gully behind a small buttress.

Cascade Cave 80m IV,4   (1977)
At the base of the waterfall is a large cave. Approach by the narrow gully and gain the icefall. Climb this to the overhang, take the left fork, then go diagonally to a shoulder and climb a chimney to the top.

Eastenders 90m IV,4   (1986)
The right-hand icefall. Climb the narrow gully for 10m to where the icefall splits. Climb the right-hand icefall in two pitches to broken ground.

Graded List of Summer Climbs

This list includes all the summer rock routes from VS upwards in both this and the companion volume to the southern part of the Cairngorms.

E7
Aphrodite
Realm of the Senses
L'Elisir d'Amore

E6
Fer de Lance
Web of Weird
Improbability Drive
Cannibal
The Shetlander
The Existentialist

E5
Flodden
Slartibartfast
Run of the Arrow
Groanmaker
Perilous Journey
Ascent of Man
Naked Ape
Thor

E4
Cupid's Bow
The Israelite
Sans Fer
Dragon Slayer
Voyage of the Beagle
The Quickening
The Skater
Iron in the Soul
Missing Link
The Bedouin
Range War
Stone Bastion
Bombadillo
The Spire
The Hurting
The Snake

Chariots of Fire
An Saobh-chreideach
Billy Nomates

E3
Crazy Sorrow
The Giant
Eye of Allah
Flakes of Fear
Jezebel
Scarlet Fever
The Wicker Man
Idol Threat
The Outlands
Heart of Gold
Two's Company
Infidel
Slithy Tove
DD's Recurring Dreams
The Gathering
Death's Head Route
Vampire Direct
Henchman
King Crimson
The Harp
Cougar
Pointlace
Black Spout Wall
Bete Noir
In the Pink
The Empty Quarter
The Deluge

E2
Haystack
Friends Essential
Arc of a Diver
Scythe
The Sharp End
Crimson Cringe

Zircon
Alice Springs
Masque
Culloden
Twisted Sister
The Crow
Chimera
The Demon
Rib Tickler
Gulliver
Nevermore
Drainpipe Crack
Sous les Toits
Steeple
Talking Drums
The Pin
Snipers
The Sword of Damocles
The Sacrament
Cayman
North-East Cruiser
Falseface
The Prowl
Vampire
Post Mortem
Edgewood
Evil Spirits
Solitaire
Babes in the Wood
Fraud Squad
Goliath Eliminate
Tough-Brown Integral
Drop Out
The Vault

E1
Stiletto
Perestroika
Rolling Thunder
Dirge
Optical Illusion
Dubh Loch Monster
Mort
Three Step
Vixen
Tickler

Gadd's Route
Scalpel Direct
Desolation Crack
Chindit Direct
Falkenhorst
Raptor
High Step
Lonesome Pine
Weevil's Way
Dragonfly
Waterkelpie Wall
The Grinder
Yin and Yang
The Vicar
Chocolate Girl
Fox Moth
Twister
Independence
King Rat
Medium Rare
Rockover
The Stretcher
Mantichore
The Needle
Poison Dwarf
The Primate
The Nihilist
Pantheist
Sapphire
Prince of Darkness
Damien
The Blue Max
The Exorcist

HVS
The Devils Alternative
Katsalana
Ivory Tower
The Chancel
Mirage variations
Time Traveller
Bellows
Slochd Wall
Dark Horse
Umslopogaas
Magic Crack

Talisman direct start
Sand-Pyper Direct
Epitome
The Sting
Cutlass
The Bishop
Beelzebub
Barndance
Never Mind
Daddy Longlegs
War and Peace
Amethyst Pillar
Quickstep
Limbo Dance
Consolation Groove
Joker's Buttress
Snakebite
The Catwalk
Clonedyke
Tickled Pink
Ventriloquist
The Omen
Second Sight
Hood Route
Pushover
Crypt
Contra-flow
Predator
The Scent
Sgian Dubh
Goliath
Damnation
The Chute
Digeridoo
Abdel Wahab
Dogleg
Fool's Rib
A Likely Story
Windchill
Next to Last
Streaker's Root
The Gowk
The Tower of Babel
Devil Dancer
Salamander
Sheath

Cyclops
The Inquisition
Dinosaur/Pink Elephant

VS
Pinnacle Grooves
The Strumpet
The Citadel
No Blue Skies
Bastille
Gibber
Devil Dancer
Good Intentions
The Link (direct)
Trunk Line
Come Dancing
Homebrew
Brodan's Dyke
Hot Toddy
Tough-Guy
Hot Lips
The Last Oasis
Helter Skelter
Postern Direct
Windchill
Longbow Direct
The Chebec
Monarch of the Glen
Koala
The Mousetrap
Ghost Crack
Mack's Dilemma
The Dagger
The Gnat
Scabbard
Bloodhound Buttress
Vertigo Wall
Black Mamba
Lion of Judah
Pythagoras
Fingers Ridge Direct
Shotgun
Delicatessen
Vulcan
Doctor Janis
Prore

Sermon
Big De'il
Whispers
Glasnost
The Hin'most
The Clean Sweep
Nomad's Crack
Tough-Brown Ridge Direct
Parallel Gully B
The Last Tango
Hell's Bells
Jewell-Kammer Route
Sundance
Indolence
Djibangi
Tearaway
Carmine Groove
Salvation
Apres Moi
Speakeasy

Sawfly
Angel's Edgeway
The Carpet
Mariella
The Underworld
Ali Baba
Hackingbush's Horror
Fall-out Corner
Sabre
Pinnacle Face
The Fly
Bugaboo Rib
Hellfire Corner
The Only Game in Town
Hourglass Buttress
Phoenix Edge
Firewater
Styx
Pink Dwarf
Lamina

List of First Ascents

COIRE AN T-SNEACHDA

S	1904	1 Apr	Pygmy Ridge	H.Raeburn, W.A.Gordon, G.H.Almond, A.Roth
W	1904	1 Apr	Central Gully	T.E.Goodeve, A.W.Russell, A.E.Robertson
W	1935	24 Mar	Aladdin's Couloir	A.Henderson, E.M.Davidson
S	1936	Apr	Original Route	A.Henderson, E.M.Davidson, J.Geddes, A.Gray
W	1939	Easter	Jacob's Ladder	A.Henderson, F.Mitchell
W	1946	Easter	Aladdin's Mirror	EUMC party
W	1946	Easter	The Runnel	EUMC party
W	1946	Easter	Crotched Gully	EUMC party
S	1952	12 Aug	Fiacaill Buttress	W.Rae, J.Hansbury
S	1953	9 Aug	The Lamp Direct	R.Naylor, M.W.Parkin
S	1954	Sep	Fingers Ridge	D.J.Bennet
S	1957	Apr	Western Rib	D.J.Bennet
W	1958	17 Jan	Fiacaill Couloir	T.W.Patey

The start of a fine series of solo new routes.

W	1959	Feb	Spiral Gully	T.W.Patey
W	1959	Feb	Patey's Route	T.W.Patey

First recorded under Original Route but renamed to avoid confusion.

W	1965		The Haston Line	D.Haston and party.

Never properly recorded before.

W	1967	Feb	Broken Gully	T.W.Patey, J.McArtney, J.Cleare
S	1967	24 Jun	Broken Pillar	K.Schwartz
W	1969	4 Jan	Invernookie	K.Spence, J.Porteous
W	1969	19 Jan	Fingers Ridge	J.R.Dempster, J.I.Wallace
S	1969	Summer	Fiacaill Buttress Direct	G.Shields and party
S	1969	10 Aug	Damnation	D.Sharp, B.Taplin

1 peg for aid, FFA unknown

S	1969	2 Sep	Goodgame	D.Sharp, B.Taplin

Like the catch-phrase, now lost in the mists of time.

W	1972	Winter	Western Rib	W.March, R.Mansfield
W	1972	12 Feb	Doctor's Choice	W.March, N.Dilley
W	1972	13 Feb	Original Route	W.March, B.Manson
W	1973	Winter	Fiacaill Buttress	G.Adam, W.March

Possibly climbed in mid-1960s by D.Duncan and partner.

W	1978	18 Mar	Fluted Buttress Direct	A.Fyffe, S.Crymble
W	1979	19 Feb	Belhaven	A.Fyffe, K.Geddes
W	1979	1 Mar	Rampant	A.Fyffe, T.Walker
W	1980	8 Nov	Cruising	K.Spence, R.Anderson

| W 1981 | Winter | Terms of Endearment | A.Liddell and party |
| S 1981 | 16 May | Magic Crack | G.S.Strange, M.Ross, J.Wyness, D.Dinwoodie |

An excellent find, the best rock pitch in the corrie. The present start: A.Fyffe, M.Bagness, Jul 1984.

W 1982	14 Mar	The Genie	D.Sanderson, J.Tomasi
S 1984	9 Jul	Fingers Ridge Direct	A.Fyffe, M.Bagness
W 1985	19 Nov	The Prodigal Principal	G.Reid, J.Lyall

Top pitch climbed previously by M.Diggens and party.

W 1985	20 Nov	Damnation	J.Grosset, M.Sclater
W 1985	7 Dec	White Magic	A.Cunningham, A.Nisbet
W 1985	13 Feb	Wavelength	A.Fyffe, D.Bowen
W 1986	2 Jan	The Seam	J.Grosset, J.Lyall
W 1986	18 Jan	Doctor Janis	J.Grosset, J.Lyall

The top pitch only, superceded by the direct version.

| W 1986 | 23 Jan | The Message | A.Cunningham, W.Todd |

The first important route on an unaccountably neglected piece of rock although Patey did a climb on the right flank and a line which appears to be similar to The Hybrid but escaping left at the top.

W 1986	31 Jan	Jailbreak	A.Fyffe, A.Liddell
W 1986	5 Mar	Honour among Thieves	A.Fyffe, H.Redfern, A.Johnson
S 1986	30 Jun	Ali Baba	A.Fyffe, T.Walker
S 1986	30 Jun	Babes in the Wood	T.Walker, A.Fyffe
W 1987	Feb	The Melting Pot	A.Cunningham, A.Nisbet
W 1987	9 Feb	Short Circuit	S.Monks, G.Reid, A.Fyffe
W 1987	4 Apr	Doctor Janis Direct	J.Grosset, J.Lyall, A.Nolan
W 1987	13 Dec	Seam-stress	J.Grosset, M.Sclater, J.Lyall
W 1987	15 Dec	Slaterless	J.Grosset, R.Wild
W 1988	Jan	The Lamp	A.Liddell and party
W 1988	Jan	Rampant Direct Start	G.Reid, J.Hepburn
W 1988	4 Mar	Polar Crossing	A.Fyffe, J.Hepburn
W 1988	30 Oct	Sax Appeal	R.Anderson, C.Greave
W 1988	26 Nov	Pot of Gold	J.Lyall, S.Spalding
W 1989	25 Mar	The Honey Pot	J.Lyall, M.Sclater
S 1989	18 Jul	Wachacha	S.Aisthorpe, J.Lyall
S 1989	18 Jul	Mariella	S.Aisthorpe, J.Lyall
S 1989	19 Jul	Salvation	S.Aisthorpe, J.Lyall
W 1989	27 Dec	Salvation	J.Lyall, A.Nishbet
S 1990	4 Jan	The Stirling Bomber	A.Cunningham, A.Fyffe

So called because of the huge flake which fell out of the top of the chimney.

W 1990	6 Jan	Wachacha	J.Lyall, A.Nisbet
W 1990	Feb	Houdini	A.Cunningham, A.Fyffe
W 1990	16 Feb	Smokestack Lightnin'	A.Cunningham, A.Fyffe
S 1990	14 May	Watch Out	G.Ettle

Back rope soloed.

S 1990	23 Jul	Edgewood	D.Etherington, A.Nisbet
S 1990	26 Jul	Doctor Janis Direct	A.Nisbet, J.Lyall

Nisbet begins his campaign of summer ascents of winter routes.

S 1990	31 Jul	North-East Cruiser	D.Etherington, A.Nisbet
W 1990	3 Nov	Watch Out	G.Ettle, J.Fitzpatrick

FFA: G.Ettle, J.Findlay Mar 1995

W 1990	Nov	The Opening Break	A.Cunningham, A.Fyffe
W 1990	20 Dec	No Blue Skies	A.Fyffe, L.Healy
W 1990	20 Dec	Fingers Ridge Direct	A.Nisbet, J.Lyall
W 1990	21 Dec	Droidless	C.Forrest, G.Ettle
W 1991	6 Jan	Mariella	C.Forrest, G.Ettle, A.Nisbet
W 1991	7 Jan	Brief Encounter	J.Lyall, M.Sclater
W 1991	10 Jan	The Firefighter	G.Ettle, D.Jarvis
W 1991	15 Jan	Topless	J.Lyall, R.Wild
W 1991	15 Jan	The Paramedic	G.Ettle, D.Jarvis
W 1991	13 Feb	Burning and Looting	A.Cunningham, A.Fyffe

Only the top pitch was new as it started up Rampant Direct Start.

W 1991	16 Feb	The Flying Doctors	G.Ettle, J.Lyall, S.Cameron
W 1991	15 Nov	The Messenger	G.Ettle, C.Campbell
S 1991	Aug	The Hurting	R.Mansfield, S.Blagbrough, N.Ritchie
W 1992	Jan	White Dwarf	G.Ettle, J.Lyall
W 1992	10 Jan	Vortex	G.Ettle, J.Lyall
W 1992	13 Jan	Trampled Underfoot	G.Ettle, J.Lyall
W 1992	10 Mar	Escapologist	G.Ettle, J.Lyall
W 1992	30 Mar	Piccolo	S.Aisthorpe, J.Lyall
W 1992	21 Nov	Kuryakin's Corner	N.Main, J.Preston
W 1993	26 Jan	The Third Wish	G.Ettle, J.Finlay
W 1993	31 Mar	Spiral Gully Variation Finishes	G.Ettle, J.Lyall
S 1993	24 Jul	Trunk Line	J.Lyall, N.Forwood
W 1993	30 Dec	Yukon Jack	M.Sinclair, C.Schiller
W 1994	24 Jan	The Three Decrees	S.Aisthorpe, M.Hind, J.Lyall
S 1994	7 Jul	No Blue Skies	A.Nisbet, G.Nisbet
S 1994	7 Jul	Fiacaill Buttress Direct	A.Nisbet, G.Nisbet
S 1994	13 Jul	Jailhouse Rock	A.Nisbet, G.Nisbet
W 1994	8 Dec	Saturation Point	J.Lyall, A.Nisbet

COIRE AN LOCHAIN

S 1931	Jul	Central Crack Route	A.Harrison, L.St.C.Bartholemew

Named from the crack in the Great Slab that the route originally started up.

S 1933	23 Aug	Ewen Buttress	J.Ewen, E.M.Davidson

Named after MMC member who was killed in the Alps.

W 1934	14 Apr	Right Branch Y Gully	R.F.Stobbart, T.Stobbart, Harbinson

W 1935	24 Mar	The Couloir	E.M.Davidson, A.Henderson

In descent

W 1935	13 Apr	The Vent	E.M.Davidson, R.F.Stobbart, Macbain, J.Geddes
S 1945	17 Jul	Savage Slit	R.B.Frere, J.D.Walker
S 1948	30 Oct	The Vent	F.F.Cunningham, A.G.MacKenzie
S 1949	May	Western Route	C.Ross, J.Brewster, D.Banks
S 1949	4 Sep	Vent Rib and Traverse	H.Watt, W.A.Russell
W 1952	16 Nov	Left Branch Y Gully	T.W.Patey, G.Nicol, A.Wedderburn
W 1957	21 Apr	Savage Slit	G.Adams, J.White, F.Henderson

1 peg for aid but a technical route for its time. FFA unknown

W 1958	2 Feb	Central Crack Route	T.W.Patey

First of a number of fine solo first ascents.

W 1959	Feb	Ewen Buttress	T.W.Patey, V.N.Stevenson
W 1959	Feb	The Milky Way	T.W.Patey, V.N.Stevenson, I.W.Armitage
W 1959	Feb	Western Route	T.W.Patey

A very impressive solo effort.

S 1963	31 Oct	Gaffer's Groove	T.W.Patey, D.Whillans

Climbed in heavy rain.

S 1964	17 May	Fall-out Corner	T.W.Patey, R.Ford, M.Stewart

1 peg for aid, FFA unknown

S 1964	7 Aug	Crow's Nest Crack	R.B.D.Stewart, D.Lynn, D.C.Easson
S 1968	31 Aug	War and Peace	G.Shields, W.Gorman

2 pegs plus several nuts for aid. FFA: A.Nisbet, B.Davison, 1983

S 1968		Nocando Crack	G.Shields

Second did not follow

S 1968		Ventricle	J.Cunningham, G.Shields

Nuts for aid on pitch 1 and 1 peg for aid on pitch 2. FFA unknown

S 1968		Procrastination	J.Cunningham, G.Shields
S 1968	25 Jul	The Vicar	G.Shields, S.Wilkinson

Pegs and tension for aid. FFA: A.Nisbet, B.Davison, 29 Aug 1983

S 1968	21 Aug	Bulgy	G.Shields, R.Doig

1 nut for aid. FFA unknown

S 1968	25 Aug	Daddy Longlegs	G.Shields, B.Hall

5 pegs and 6 nuts for aid. FFA: A.Nisbet, B.Davison, 29 Aug 1983

W 1968	24 Dec	Chute Route	M.Harris, D.Scott, R.Shaw
S 1969		Puffer	J.Cunningham and party
S 1969	5 Jul	Prore	G.Bradshaw, B.Taplin
S 1969	23 Jul	Grumbling Grooves	G.Shields, S.Wilkinson
S 1969	8 Aug	Auricle	J.Cunningham, W.March
S 1969	8 Aug	Never Mind	J.Cunningham, W.March

"Make a controlled slide down the edge to gain a foothold." 2 pegs for aid and a tension traverse which still remains.

S 1969	11 Sep	Oesophagus	B.Taplin, D.Taplin

W 1969	31 Dec	Iron Butterfly	S.Docherty, B.Gorman
W 1969		Ventilator	D.S.B.Wright and party

Previously wrongly attributed to D.J.Bennet, A.Sommerville who recorded the route prior to the above party.

S 1970	19 Sep	Vagrant	M.Geddes, H.M.Gillespie
W 1971	9 Apr	Oesophagus	W.March and party
W 1971	30 Dec	Andromeda	R.D.Barton, J.C.Higham
W 1975	Feb	Glottal Stop	J.Cunningham, R.Baillie

Climbed under heavy snow and now of uncertain location.

W 1975	Feb	Gaffer's Groove, Winter Variation	J.Cunningham, A.Fyffe
S 1976	Jun	Transformer	A.Fyffe, R.D.Barton
W 1979	28 Dec	Procrastination	M.Fowler, A.Henderson
S 1981	Jul	The Overseer	D.Lawrence, A.Nisbet
S 1983	24 Aug	The Demon	B. Davison, A.Nisbet
W 1983	10 Dec	The Overseer	A.Nisbet, E.Clark
W 1983	11 Dec	Sidewinder	A.Nisbet, E.Clark
W 1983	17 Dec	Grumbling Grooves	S.Allan, A.Nisbet
W 1983	18 Dec	Crow's Nest Crack	S.Kennedy, C.McLeod
W 1983	18 Dec	Sidewinder Direct	S.Allan, A.Nisbet
W 1984	29 Nov	Auricle	C.MacLean, A.Nisbet
W 1984	27 Dec	Ventricle	C.MacLean, A.Nisbet
W 1985	7 Dec	Astroturfer	J.MacKeever, I.Dawson
W 1985	9 Dec	Fall-out Corner	A.Cunningham, A.Nisbet
W 1985	31 Dec	The Andromeda Strain	J.MacKeever, I.Dawson
W 1986	20 Jan	Torquing Heads	W.Todd, A.Cunningham
W 1986	3 Feb	Demolition Man	I.Rae, J.Kerr
W 1986	13 Mar	The Migrant	A.Cunningham, A.Nisbet
W 1988	13 Nov	Torque of the Devil	R.Anderson, C.Greaves
W 1988	19 Nov	The Hoarmaster	R.Anderson, G.Nicoll, R.Milne
W 1988	26 Nov	Hooker's Corner	R.Anderson, C.Greaves
W 1988	27 Nov	Bulgy	A.Nisbet, J.Preston
W 1989	26 Nov	The Deviant	R.Anderson, C.Anderson, T.Prentice
W 1989	1 Dec	The Head-hunter	A.Fyffe, R.Mansfield
W 1989	2 Dec	Deep Throat	R.Anderson, T.Prentice, R.Milne
W 1989	3 Dec	Tracheotomy	R.Anderson, T.Prentice, R.Milne
S 1990	18 Jul	Deep Throat	A.Nisbet, H.Meldrum, N.Ritchie
S 1990	2 Aug	Ventriloquist	J.Lyall, B.Kellet
W 1990	1 Dec	Western Slant	R.Anderson, C.Anderson
W 1990	19 Dec	Conundrum	J.Lyall, A.Nisbet
W 1990	21 Dec	Ventriloquist	J.Lyall, A.Nisbet
W 1992	12 Jan	The Crack	R.Anderson, R.Milne
W 1992	26 Jan	Snow Bunting	R.Anderson, G.Ettle
W 1992	Jan	The Inquisition	R.Anderson, G.Ettle, R.Milne
W 1992	Jan	The Executioner	R.Anderson, G.Ettle

W 1992	19 Feb	War and Peace	B.Davison, A.Nisbet
W 1992	21 Mar	Vent Rib Direct	A.Nisbet, G.Ollerhead
W 1992	23 Mar	Empty Space	G.Ettle, J.Lyall, J.Findlay
S 1992	20 Jun	The Inquisition	J.Lyall, D.Bulmer
W 1992	14 Nov	Prore	G.Ettle, R.Milne
W 1992	20 Nov	Overseer Direct	A.Nisbet, N.Main
W 1992	2 Dec	Torquing West	A.Nisbet, J.Preston
W 1992	9 Dec	Nocando Crack	A.Nisbet, J.Preston

Several pegs and nuts for aid on pitch 3.

W 1992	20 Dec	The Vicar	G.Ettle, A.Nisbet
W 1993	17 Oct	Aqualung	G.Ettle, J.Preston
W 1993	13 Nov	Occidental Discovery	G.Ettle, B.Goodlad
W 1993	31 Dec	New Age Traveller	A.Nisbet, J.Preston
W 1994	20 April	Inventive	A.Fyffe, J.Hepburn
S 1994	6 Jul	Hoarmaster	A.Nisbet, G.Nisbet
W 1995	13 Feb	Coronary By-pass	A.Fyffe, J.Hepburn
W 1995	14 Feb	Appetite for Destruction	A.Fyffe, J.Hepburn

STACAN DUBHA

S 1954	1 Aug	Ribbon Ridge	T.W.Patey, A.Watson
S 1957	7 Apr	The Shuttle	G.Adams, R.H.Sellars
S 1969	20 Aug	Zigzag	B.Taplin, D.Taplin

CARN ETCHACHAN

S 1904	Jul	Castlegates Gully	H.Stewart, A.B.Duncan
W 1914	Easter	Castlegates Gully	J.McCoss, W.B.Meff, R.Clarke, W.Shepherd
S 1952	24 May	Castle Gully	H.S.M.Bates, K.A.Grassick, A.G.Nicol
S 1952	Aug	False Scorpion	K.A.Grassick, H.S.M.Bates, A.Q.Gardiner, A.Farquharson
W 1952	6 Dec	Scorpion	T.W.Patey, J.M.Taylor, K.A.Grassick, A.G.Nicol

A remarkable first winter ascent on a big cliff.

S 1953	10 May	Scorpion	H.S.M.Bates, T.Shaw
S 1954	10 Aug	The Battlements	T.W.Patey, W.D.Brooker

The start of Patey's exploration of the rock potential of this cliff.

S 1954	25 Sep	Boa	T.W.Patey, F.R.Malcolm, A.Thom
S 1954	2 Oct	Equinox	T.W.Patey, L.S.Lovat
S 1954	2 Oct	Python	T.W.Patey, L.S.Lovat
S 1955	29 Jul	Crevasse Route	T.W.Patey, M.Smith, A.Duguid

Variation by P.MacDonald, G.Johnstone, Sep 1967

S 1955	29 Jul	Eastern Approach Route	T.W.Patey
S 1955	7 Aug	Pagan Slit	G.Adams, R.W.P.Barclay
S 1955	13 Aug	The Guillotine	T.W.Patey, A.Duguid
S 1956	12 Aug	Nom-de-Plume	R.W.P.Barclay, R.H.Sellars
W 1957	10 Feb	Route Major	T.W.Patey, M.Smith
W 1964	5 Jan	Castle Gully	K.A.Grassick, D.Burnett
W 1970	Mar	False Scorpion	W.March, O.Ludlow
W 1975	14 Mar	Sideslip	A.Fyffe, R.O'Donovan

Corresponds in part to an early route, Revelation Arete, which fell down.

W 1977	5 Mar	Attic Rib	R.J.Archbold, D.M.Nichols
S 1977	29 May	Red Guard	R.J.Archbold, N.D.Keir

Lower chimney had probably been climbed before.

W 1978	5 Mar	The Sword	J.C.Higham, D.Wright

The start often climbed by mistake for the beginning of Scorpion.

W 1978	24 Mar	Red Guard	N.D.Keir, M.Freeman

Tension traverse and 3 pegs for aid on the summer line. Keir's first big route wearing "trampons" – tricouni plates. The "dirty continuation groove", first climbed by G.Smith and R.D.Barton, is now the usual winter line.

S 1978	11 Jul	Time Traveller	A.Fyffe, D.Morris

Renewal of interest in an unfashionable summer cliff.

S 1978	12 Jul	Pythagoras	A.Fyffe, S.J.Crymble
S 1978	12 Jul	Poison Dwarf	A.Fyffe, S.J.Crymble
S 1978	Jul	Bastille	R.Archbold, T.Syme
W 1979	4 Feb	Eastern Approach Route	A.Fyffe, A.Liddell
W 1978	4 Feb	The Guillotine	A.Fyffe, A.Liddell
W 1979	28 Feb	Siberia	A.Fyffe, T.Walker
W 1980	27 Feb	Pagan Slit	M.Fowler, A.Strapcans
W 1981	13 Jan	Crevasse Route	S.Kennedy, A.Nisbet
W 1981	14 Feb	Equinox	S.Kennedy, A.Nisbet, N.Morrison
W 1981	15 Feb	Boa	A.Nisbet, S.Kennedy, N.Morrison

Slings on axe used once for aid.

W 1981	9 Dec	Python	A.Nisbet, P.Langhorne
W 1982	15 Jan	Bastille	A.Nisbet, S.Allan
W 1982	16 Jan	The Hairpin Loop	A.Nisbet, S.Allan
W 1982	23 Dec	Nom-de-Plume	A.Nisbet, P.Langhorne
W 1986	12 Apr	Pythagoras	A.Cunningham, A.Nisbet
W 1986	2 Nov	The Poison Trail	A.Cunningham, A.Nisbet
W 1986	14 Dec	The Kremlin	G.Taylor, J.McKeever

3 rest points. FFA: I.Dillon, J.Lyall, A.Nisbet, 6 Jan 1995

W 1987	3 Jan	Time Traveller	A.Cunningham, A.Nisbet
W 1987	28 Nov	Inside Edge	I.Barron, S.Kennedy
W 1988	12 Mar	Revelation Arete	A.Nisbet, A.Newton
W 1989	19 Dec	Western Approach Route	A.Nisbet, D.McCutcheon

W 1989	28 Dec	The Silent Approach	A.Nisbet, J.Lyall
W 1990	5 Mar	Snakebite	A.Nisbet, J.Lyall
S 1990	1 Aug	Snakebite	A.Nisbet, D.Gaskell
W 1992	22 Dec	Solstice	A.Nisbet, J.Preston
W 1993	4 Jan	Apogee	G.Ettle, J.Finlay, A.Nisbet
W 1994	20 Dec	The Winter Palace	J.Lyall, A.Nisbet
W 1994	22 Dec	Crystal Maze	G.Ettle, J.Lyall, N.Main, A.Nisbet

SHELTER STONE CRAG

S 1904	Jul	Pinnacle Gully	H.Stewart, A.B.Duncan
S 1907	16 Jun	Castle Wall	H.Raeburn, F.S.Goggs
S 1907	16 Jun	Raeburn's Buttress	H.Raeburn, F.S.Goggs

An amazing days climbing involving cycling from Kingussie, walking in to the cliff, descending Castle Wall, climbing this route and still being finished before lunch. The pioneers were of the opinion that this route was dangerous: it still is in summer. "A long stride onto disintegrating shelflets of grass."

| S 1912 | Jul | Forefinger Pinnacle | H.G.Drummond, J.McCoss |
| | | Clach Dhian Chimney | W.S.Thomson and party |

Route now followed by W.Brooker, J.Morgan, 1950.

| S 1953 | 14 May | Sticil Face | J.M.Taylor, T.W.Patey |
| S 1957 | Jun | Postern | K.A.Grassick, A.G.Nicol |

2 pegs for aid. The lower section by J.Y.L.Hay, G.Adams, Sep 1956. FFA unknown

| W 1957 | 27 Dec | Sticil Face | K.A.Grassick, A.G.Nicol |

One of the most impressive ascents of the step cutting era.

| S 1958 | Aug | The Citadel | R.H.Sellars, G.Annand |

The biggest fifties route in the area although it used 2 pegs for aid at the lower crux and several aid points on the upper crux. FFA unknown.

| S 1962 | 8 Jun | The Needle | R.Smith, D.Agnew |

The first big "modern" route on the crag. A superb achievement and years ahead of its time as far as the Cairngorms were concerned.

| S 1968 | Aug | The Pin | R.Carrington, J.Gardiner |

Another break-through producing a great climb although 1 peg and 1 nut were used for aid. The 1961 guide considered these slabs "manifestly impossible". FFA: B.Campbell-Kelly, M.Kosterlitz, early 1970s. Alternative start: A.Cunningham, A.Fyffe, summer 1990.

| S 1968 | Aug | The Steeple | K.Spence, M.Watson |

2 nuts for aid. The top pitches were climbed in the rain. Pitches 1-6 by J.Porteous, K.Spence. Pitches 7-9 by Spence and Watson. FFA: J.Lamb, P.Whillance, May 1975

| S 1968 | 7 Sept | Thor | M.Rennie, G.S.Strange |

Originally A1 and A2 on pitches 2 and 3. FFA: R.Campbell and N.Craig, 15 July 1989

| S 1969 | Summer | West Ridge Route | W.March and party |
| S 1969 | Aug | Snipers | R.Carrington, G.Shields |

2 pegs for aid in the big overlap. Freed by R.Campbell on the first ascent of Aphrodite.

| S | 1969 | Aug | Postern Direct | J.Cunningham, W.March |
| S | 1969 | Aug | Consolation Groove | J.Cunningham, W.March |

3 pegs for aid on the crux which is often greasy. FFA unknown.

| W | 1970 | 31 Jan | Castle Wall | B.S.Findlay, G.S.Strange |
| S | 1970 | Summer | Threadbare | J.Cunningham, W.March |

Considerable aid used on pitch 3 and 2 pegs for aid below the roof. Some aid eliminated on shared pitches with Rib Tickler.

| W | 1971 | Feb | Raeburn's Buttress | W.March, J.Hart |
| S | 1971 | Summer | Haystack | R.Carrington, I.Nicolson |

1 peg for aid. For a long time the hardest route in the area. FFA unknown.

| W | 1972 | Feb | Clach Dhian Chimney | C.Butterworth, A.Frost |
| W | 1972 | Feb | Quartz Gully | A.Fyffe, E.Fyffe |

Climbed in descent T.W.Patey in Aug 1954.

| W | 1972 | Feb | Garbh Gully | A.Fyffe, E.Fyffe |
| W | 1975 | Winter | The Citadel, Winter Variation | A.Rouse, B.Hall |

In some ways the logical way to do this route in winter.

S	1976	Summer	Blockbuster	J.Jones, M.Burrows-Smith
W	1977	12 Mar	Breach Gully	M.Freeman, G.S.Strange
W	1978	4 Mar	Blunderbuss	J.C.Higham, D.Wright
W	1978	Mar	Western Grooves	A.Fyffe, R.D.Barton
S	1978	27 May	Cupid's Bow	D.Dinwoodie, R.Renshaw

An impressive and much sought after route which eventually fell with a peg for aid in the Thor diedre and 3 pegs for aid on the main pitch. FFA: M.Hamilton, R.Anderson, 4 Jun 1982.

| W | 1979 | Mar | Unknown Gully | A.Fyffe and party |
| W | 1980 | 5/6 Jan | Postern | M.Hamilton, K.Spence, A.Taylor |

The first route in this area to be graded VI. The second pitch climbed direct by R.Anderson.

| W | 1980 | 23 Feb | The Citadel | M.Hamilton, K.Spence |

The "big" route of the times. Subject to many attempts. K.Spence and J.Porteous retreated from above the lower crux in 1969. Cunningham and March had to descend from higher after a benightment in 1971.

S	1981	Summer	The Missing Link	D.Cuthbertson, D.Jamieson
S	1982	5 May	The Spire	M.Hamilton, R.Anderson
S	1982	24 Jul	The Run of the Arrow	P.Whillance, T.Furnis

Had previously repulsed some strong parties. A couple of in situ wires wires left by Dinwoodie on an earlier on-sight attempt attempt gave at least psychological help for a number of years until they were removed.

| S | 1983 | 27 Jul | The Harp | P.Whillance, R.Parker |
| W | 1985 | 13/14 Feb | The Needle, Winter Variations | C.McLean, A.Nisbet |

1 peg for aid. A major undertaking on which Nisbet used "trampons" and MacLean had walking crampons with no front points (unrepeated).

W 1986	19 Jan	The Imposter	M.Charlton, W.Webb, J.McKeever
W 1986	18 Apr	Sticil Face, Direct Finish	G.Cohen, D.Rubens
S 1986	13 Jun	Pointlace	R.Anderson, A.Russell
W 1987	25 Feb	Consolation Groove, Winter Variation	J.McKeever, G.Taylor
W 1987	21 Mar	Citadel, Winter Variation, Independent Finish	R.Anderson, G.Nicoll
W 1988	5 Mar	Postern Direct	A.Cunningham, A.Nisbet
S 1989	15 Jul	Thor	R.Campbell, N.Craig

First free ascent to produce an excellent modern route.

| S 1990 | Summer | Aphrodite | R.Campbell, A.Moses |

The first route in the area to be graded E7. Done over two days because of the length of the pitch and the shortness of the rope. On-sight to above the Run of the Arrow crux, then finished from the belay in Snipers.

W 1991	Feb	Games of Chance	A.Fyffe, R.Mansfield.
S 1991	20 Aug	Rib Tickler	J.Lyall, A.Nisbet
S 1993	29 Aug	Realm of the Senses	R.Campbell, G.Latter

A desperate route, the result of 7 attempts and about 30 falls before success on one of the hardest slab routes in the country.

| S 1994 | 23 Jul | Stone Bastion | R.Anderson, C.Anderson. |

Pitches 1-4 climbed by R. and C.Anderson, 17 May 1992. Pitches 7-9 cleaned on abseil then dogged and redpointed.

| S 1994 | 23 Jul | L'Elisir d'Amore | R.Campbell unseconded. |

Top roped in 1991 and 1993: an impressive lead of a hard and serious route.

HELL'S LUM CRAG

| S 1950 | Sep | Deep Cut Chimney | I.M.Brooker, M.Newbigging |
| S 1952 | 12 Apr | Hell's Lum | I.M.Brooker, M.Newbigging |

A semi-winter ascent as snow masked half of the big gully pitch and also covered several other sections.

| S 1953 | 8 Aug | Kiwi Slab | R.Naylor, M.W.Parkin |

1 peg for aid. The original start was up the green buttress but it is more usual to follow the lower diagonal fault. FFA unknown

S 1955	30 Sep	The Escalator	A.G.Nicol, T.W.Patey, E.M.Davidson
W 1956	Mar	Hell's Lum	G.McLeod and party
S 1956	21 Oct	The Pothole	R.W.P.Barclay, R.H.Sellers
S 1957	4 Aug	Devil's Delight	R.H.Sellers, G.Annand

The move onto the open faces shows the quality of the climbing to be found here.

| W 1958 | 19 Jan | Deep Cut Chimney | T.W.Patey, D.Holroyd |
| S 1958 | 14 Sep | Hellfire Corner | G.Annand, R.H.Sellers |

Slings for aid at the crux bulge. FFA unknown

| S 1958 | Oct | Brimstone Groove | G.Annand, R.H.Sellers, R.Reid |

1 peg for aid. FFA unknown

W 1959	Feb	Kiwi Slab	T.W.Patey, V.N.Stevenson
W 1960	Jan	The Escalator	J.Y.L.Hay, A.Thom
S 1961	Sep	Hell's Lump	J.R.Marshall, J.Stenhouse
S 1961	Sep	The Clean Sweep	R.Smith, G.Tiso

A typical Smith find, perhaps the best route of the crag.

S 1961	Sep	Hellfire Corner Direct Start	R.Smith, G.Tiso

Now the normal start.

S 1961	3 Sep	The Wee Devil	T.W.Patey, J.M.Taylor
S 1963	1 Jun	The Girdle	D.Pyper, M.George
S 1963	27 Jun	Sneer	A.McKeith
S 1963	11 Oct	Auld Nick	G.Brown, I.Houston, I.Small
W 1966	23 Jan	Sneer	D.Haston, B.Robertson, J.Heron
S 1968	31 Aug	The Vacuum	R.A.Croft, J.R.Sutcliffe
S 1969	24 Jun	Sic	G.Boyd, P.Kale

A previously neglected part of the cliff begins to receive some attention, but with route names which hardly ensured interest.

S 1969	28 Jun	Puke	J.Bower, P.Kale
S 1969	29 Jun	Raw Mince	J.Bower, R.Simpson
S 1969	27 Jul	Styx	W.March, D.K.Mardon
S 1969	12 Sep	Drop Out	W.March, M.McArthur

Peg, nut and tension traverse for aid. FFA: A.Fyffe, R.D.Barton

S 1969	12 Sep	Good Intentions	W.March, M.McArthur

An aid nut used which was eliminated soon after.

W 1969	Nov	Sic	J.Bower, H.Pinkerton
W 1969	28 Dec	The Gullet	J.Bower, B.S.Findlay
W 1970	Jan	The Chancer	J.Cunningham, W.March

4 ice screws and tension used but this route was the high point of "dagger" technique developed by Cunningham and March as the forerunner of front pointing.

S 1970	Summer	Hell's Lum Direct	J.Cunningham, W.March

The last of the gullies in the Cairngorms to be climbed!

S 1970	14 Nov	Puke	T.Anderson, J.Bower
W 1970	27 Dec	Brimstone Groove	S.Docherty, K.Spence

The first route on the big ice sheet.

S 1971	18 Sep	Big De'il	G.S.Strange, D.Stuart

1 point of aid. FFA unknown

S 1971	18 Sep	Salamander	D.Dinwoodie, J.Tweddle
W 1971	17 Nov	Wee Devil	D.Dinwoodie, J.Mothersele
W 1971	20 Nov	Auld Nick	M.Freeman, G.S.Strange
W 1972	2 Jan	Kiwi Gully	W.March, I.Nicholson
W 1973	Feb	Salamamder	J.Cunningham, W.March, R.O'Donovan
W 1973	Feb	Devil's Delight	J.Cunningham, W.March, R.O'Donovan

The biggest and best of the pure ice routes.

S	1975	Jun	The Exorcist	A.Liddell, R.Smith
S	1975	13 Aug	Squirk	K.Schwartz, R.Morrow
S	1976	Jul	The Omen	A.Liddell, M.Burrows-Smith
S	1976	4 Jul	The Underworld	A.Fyffe, R.D.Barton
S	1977	4 Jul	Towering Inferno	R.D.Barton, A.Fyffe, E.Fyffe

Barton and Fyffe also climbed the VS variation to pitch 3.

S	1977	5 Jul	Devil Dancer	A. Fyffe, R.D.Barton
W	1978	Winter	The Clean Sweep	G.Smith, A.Slater
W	1979	Winter	Nobody's Fault	G.Smith and party

The name reflects the history of the route as several parties all climbed it at about the same time and Smith did not record his ascents in this area.

W	1980s	Winter	Big De'il	A.Fyffe and party (probably)
S	1981	1 Aug	The Devil's Alternative	A.Fyffe, R.D.Barton
W	1982	24 Jan	Boke	F.Brunton, C.Dale, A.Dytche, A.Horner
S	1982	3 Aug	Second Sight	A.Fyffe, R.D.Barton
S	1984	10 Aug	Prince of Darkness	R.D.Barton, A.Fyffe
S	1984	25 Aug	Damien	A.Liddell, M.Seaton
W	1985	13 Feb	Hellfire Corner	J.Grosset, M.Sclater
W	1986	6 Jan	Hell's Lump	A.Cunningham, I.Fox
S	1986	26 Jun	Evil Spirits	A.Fyffe, R.D.Barton
W	1986	5 Feb	Towering Inferno	A.Fyffe, R.D.Barton
W	1986	14 Dec	Good Intentions	A.Cunningham, A.Nisbet
S	1988	18 Jun	Firewater	A.Fyffe, J.Hepburn
S	1988	18 Jun	The Bengal Lancer	A.Fyffe, J.Hepburn
S	1988	25 Jun	Arc of a Diver	J.Hepburn, A.Fyffe
S	1988	30 Jul	Beelzebub	A.Ross, I.Davidson, P.Stewart
W	1989	Winter	The Pothole	C.Forrest and party
S	1990	25 Jul	Lion of Judah	J.Lyall, J.Pickering
W	1991	Jan	The ice pencil right of Chancer	G.Ettle

A good solo effort.

S	1991	29 Jul	Glasnost	S.G.Elishashvili, J.Lyall, A.Nisbet
S	1991	29 Jul	Peristroika	S.G.Elishashvili, J.Lyall, A.Nisbet
S	1991	29 Jul	Independence	S.G.Elishashvili, J.Lyall, A.Nisbet
S	1991	4 Aug	Chariots of Fire	J.Lyall, A.Nisbet, J.Preston
W	1994	28 Mar	The Underworld	I.Dillon, J.Lyall

STAG ROCKS

S	1930	Jul	Serrated Rib	J.Nimlin and party
S	1949	17 Jul	Pine Tree Route	E.L.Smith, R.Mennie
S	1954	Aug	Triple Towers	T.W.Patey, G.H.Leslie
S	1955	Aug	Relay Climb	T.W.Patey

An inpressive solo at that time. Patey solved the problem of the lower bulge after work by others. Upper section: K.Winram, Aug 1953. Lower section: G.H.Leslie, M.Smith.

S	1955	14 Aug	The Tenements	G.H.Leslie, M.Smith, C.Petrie
S	1956	Sep	Afterthought Arete	R.H.Sellers, M.Smith
S	1956	Nov	Final Selection	R.H.Sellers, M.Smith
S	1957	Jun	Quartz Diggers' Cave Route	R.H.Sellers, G.Adams, F.Henderson
S	1960	May	Deception Inlet	A.Thom, M.Smith, G.Annand
S	1962	29 Jul	Wigwag	J.Stenhouse, G.J.Ritchie
S	1962	Aug	Longbow Direct	D.Pyper, J.McArtney
S	1962	Aug	Groove and Rib	R.Marshall, J.R.Marshall
S	1962	Oct	The Sand-Pyper	D.Pyper, C.A.Sands

1 peg for aid: FFA unknown. Direct finish: M.G.Geddes, J.C.Higham, 1 Jul 1972

W	1969	Jan	Stag Route	J.T.Campbell, B.Findlay, N.D.Keir, G.S.Strange

Direct version: W.March, J.Brailsford, Mar 1971

S	1969	6 Aug	Alb	B.Taplin and party
S	1969	7 Aug	Purge	B.Taplin, D.Taplin
S	1969	6 Sep	Longbow Direct Alternative Start	G.Shields, S.Wikinson
W	1969	Nov	Afterthought Arete	W.March
W	1969	Nov	Triple Towers	W.March
W	1969	Nov	Serrated Rib	W.March
W	1969	Nov	Final Selection	W.March
W	1970	Winter	C M Gully	J.Cunningham, W.March

Never properly recorded.

W	1970	7 Feb	Pine Tree Route	J.Bower, A.Morgan
W	1971	17 Feb	Amphitheatre Gully	W.March, J.Hart

1 point of aid. FFA unknown

W	1971	17 Feb	Apex Gully	W.March, J.Hart
S	1972	Aug	Addenda	A.Fyffe, W.March
S	1972	3 Aug	Rodent	A.Kimber, D.Wearing, T.Calvert

Appears to be the same as Groove and Rib.

W	1977	Feb	Cascade	W.March, D.Alcock

A much eyed ice problem, several axe rests taken but later dispensed with.

S	1977	Jul	Windchill	A.Fyffe, R.D.Barton
S	1977	13 Aug	Amphitheatre Wall	A.Fyffe, E.Fyffe
S	1978	10 Jul	Shotgun	A.Fyffe, E.Fyffe
W	1978	27 Dec	Wigwag	G.Smith, M.Fowler

Rather loosely based on the summer line.

W	1979	Winter	Central Route	G.Smith, G.Ball

One of a series of fine routes by Smith which were never recorded so the exact line of some remains uncertain.

W	1979	Winter	The Tenements	G.Smith
W	1979	Winter	Deception Inlet	G.Smith, K.Gasely

W 1981	Winter	Relay Climb	K.Spence, R.Milne, R.Anderson
W 1985	Jan	Groove and Rib	M.Hamilton, R.Anderson
W 1986	Winter	The Overflow	A.Fyffe, I.Peter
W 1986	12 Dec	Purge	A.Cunningham, A.Nisbet
W 1986	13 Dec	Albino	J.McKeever, G.Taylor
W 1986	15 Dec	Honest Outlet	J.McKeever, G.Taylor
W 1986	16 Dec	Longbow Direct	A.Cunningham, A.Nisbet
W 1986	17 Jan	Flock of Chickens	A.Cunningham, A.Nisbet
W 1986	26 Jan	Quartz Diggers' Cave Route	J.McKeever, N.Green
W 1986	27 Jan	Amphitheatre Gully, Right-hand Finish	A.Cunningham, P.Aubrey
S 1987	18 Aug	Lonesome Pine	C.Forrest, A.Ross
W 1988	21 Jan	Gemstone	S.Aisthorpe, J.Lyall, M.Sclater
W 1988	22 Jan	The Windpiper	A.Cunningham, A.Nisbet
S 1988	18 Aug	Flakes of Fear	C.Forrest, A.Ross
W 1988	Nov	Final Groove	J.Lyall, M.Sclater
S 1988	18 Sep	Barndance	A.Ross, M.Sutherland
S 1989	9 Jul	Blue Serge Variation	I.Davidson, M.Sutherland, R.Cookson
W 1989	25 Nov	Light Entertainment	J.Lyall, D.Bulmer
W 1989	20 Dec	Open Cast	A.Nisbet, D.McCutcheon
W 1989	24 Dec	Maranatha	S.Aisthorpe, J.Lyall
S 1989	9 Jul	Optical Illusion	A.Ross, A.Nisbet
W 1991	12 Jan	Monarch of the Glen	J.Lyall, R.Wild
W 1992	4 Apr	Shotgun	S.Allan, A.Nisbet
S 1992	16 Sep	Monarch of the Glen	J.Lyall, E.Lawther
W 1995	6 Jan	Stagnant Gully	G.Ettle, S.Kitchin
W 1995	10 Jan	Diamond Groove	S.Frost, J.Turner
W 1995	25 Jan	Wee Timorous Beastie	G.Ettle, J.Preston
W 1995	3 Mar	Faintly Amusing	J.Lyall, Z.Webster

Variation Start: A.Fyffe, J.Hepburn 21 Mar 1995

STAC AN FHARAIDH

| S 1952 | 10 Aug | Rectangular Rib | J.Hansbury, W.Rae |
| S 1969 | Summer | Pushover | J.Cunningham and party |

The start of the development of the slabs led by locally based climbers, notably Cunningham and Shields. Variation: W.March and party

S 1969	Summer	Whispers	J.Cunningham, G.Shields
S 1969	10 Jul	Apres Moi	J.Cunningham, G.Shields
S 1969	Jul	Sermon	G.Shields, S.Wilkinson
S 1969	24 Jul	Mack's Dilemma	G.Shields, S.Wilkinson
S 1970	4 Jun	Shielden	W.March, S.Matthewson, L.Rae
S 1970	4 Jun	Linden	W.March, L.Rae, S.Matthewson
S 1970	5 Jun	Jillden	W.March and party

S	1970	14 Jun	Pippet Slab	J.Cunningham, W.March
S	1970	5 Jul	Bellows	R.Carrington, J.Marshall
S	1971	11 Aug	Throwover	K.Schwartz, D.Regan, M.Horsburgh

The name refers to the manner of placement of the aid nut

S	1971	11 Sep	Deja Vu	A.Fyffe, D.S.B.Wright
S	1971	18 Sep	The Deluge	G.Shields, C.Norris, D.S.B.Wright

1 peg for aid. FFA: G.Ettle, M.Hamilton 15 Sep 1991

W	1972	5 Jan	Rectangular Gully	W.March
S	1975	Summer	Cherry	A.Liddell, M.Burrows-Smith
S	1978	17 Jun	Speakeasy	A.Fyffe, D.S.B.Wright
W	1980	7 Dec	Apres Moi	K.Spence, R.Anderson
W	1980	7 Dec	Hoity-Toity	K.Spence, R.Anderson
W	1981	22 Feb	Rectangular Rib	R.Anderson, A.Russell

Originally recorded as Spare Ribs

S	1981	Summer	Nosey Parker	R.Anderson, A.Taylor
W	1985	4 Dec	Shallow Gully	R.Anderson, M.Hamilton
W	1986	28 Jan	Sermon	A.Fyffe, I.Peter
S	1990	Jul	Yin and Yang	A.Liddell, A.MacLean, A.Gerrard
W	1991	12 Jan	Spirit Voices	A.Fyffe, R.Mansfield
W	1992	Dec	Pushover	C.Steer, S.Steer
S	1994	23 Jul	Rockover	R.Kenyon, B.Cosby

COIRE SPUTAN DEARG

S	1948	2 May	Pinnacle Buttress	S.R.Tewnion, J.Tewnion, W.A Russell

Variation start: J.McArtney, D.Pyper, Summer 1964

S	1948	16 May	Anchor Gully	I.M.Brooker, A.E.Anton, G.Mathieson
S	1948	1 Sep	Crystal Ridge	R.Still, E.J.Lawrence

Soon became a classic and changed the poor reputation of Sputan.

W	1949	5 Jan	Crystal Ridge	W.D.Brooker, M.Smith
W	1949	17 Mar	Slab Chimney, Right Branch	A.Parker, J.Young

Left Branch by same party in the same month.

S	1949	29 Mar	Hanging Dyke	A.Parker, J.Young
S	1949	22 May	Flake Buttress	J.Tewnion, E.L.Smith, M.Smith, K.Winram
S	1949	22 May	Janus	K.Winram, M.Smith, E.L.Smith, J.Tewnion
S	1949	25 Jun	Snake Ridge	W.D.Brooker, D.A.Sutherland, C.Hutcheon
S	1949	26 Jun	Anchor Route	W.D.Brooker, C.Hutcheon, D.A.Sutherland
S	1949	3 Jul	Cherub's Buttress	J.Tewnion, A.Alexander, E.L.Smith, M.Smith
S	1949	11 Sep	Terminal Buttress	J.Tewnion, E.L.Smith, M.Smith
S	1949	18 Sep	Pilgrim's Groove	S.R.Tewnion, J.Tewnion, E.L.Smith

Variation finish: R.Kerr, M.Main, early 1960s.

W	1950	5 Jan	Pinnacle Buttress	W.D.Brooker, J.W.Morgan
W	1950	10 Apr	Flake Buttress	W.D.Brooker, S.McPherson
S	1950	20 May	Ardath Chimney	J.Tewnion, M.Smith
S	1950	1 Jul	Janus Chimney	E.L.Smith, T.Shaw, A.Cameron
S	1951	Feb	Glissade Buttress	J.Tewnion, G.Dey
S	1952	21 Apr	The Black Tower	T.W.Patey, G.B.Leslie, J.M.Taylor
S	1952	21 Apr	April Wall	G.B.Leslie, T.W.Patey, J.M.Taylor
S	1952	22 Aug	Slab Chimney	G.B.Leslie, M.Smith, J.Harper, G.Davidson
W	1955	2 Apr	Ardath Chimney	J.Y.L.Hay
W	1955	25 Dec	Anchor Route	G.Adams, R.W.P.Barclay
S	1956	12 Apr	Hackingbush's Horror	J.Y.L.Hay, A.O'F.Will, G.Adams, J.Ross, C.Martin

Approx 4 pegs for aid. FFA: B.Lawrie, J.McArtney, 1966.
Hackingbush was Mac Smith's nickname. A reference to the 1960s guidebook author's disapproval of the aid: he also refused the name and called the route Janus Left Face.

S	1956	10 Jun	Amethyst Wall	R.W.P Barclay, W.D.Brooker

Combined tactics used.

S	1956	10 Jun	The Plumbline	R.W.P Barclay, W.D.Brooker
S	1956	21 Oct	Lucifer Route	M.Scott, D.Macrae, R.Ellis
S	1960	Sep	The Swing	D.Reid, D.Pyper
W	1961	4 Feb	Terminal Buttress	D.Reid, D.Pyper
W	1963	2 Mar	Snake Gully	J.McArtney, T.Mackie, B.T.Lawrie
S	1963	8 Sep	Teminal Wall	B.T.Lawrie, J.McArtney
S	1963	14 Sep	Grey Slab	M.Higgins, J.C.Innes, B.T.Lawrie
S	1964	13 Jul	Girdle Traverse	B.T.Lawrie, D.Mercer
W	1966	4 Jan	Flying Ridge	A.Fyffe, M.D.Y.Mowatt
S	1966	15 May	The Web	M.Rennie, M.C.MacLennan
W	1967	3 Jan	Right-Hand Icefall	A.Fyffe, P.Williams, M.McArthur, I.McLean
S	1970	7 Jun	Umberella	B.T.Lawrie, J.Bower, H.Thain
S	1970	13 Jun	The Chute	J.Ingram, B.S.Findlay, G.S.Strange, D.Stuart
S	1970	20 Jun	Rainmate	B.T.Lawrie, R.Kerr
S	1970	27 Jun	Sundance	G.S.Strange, D.Stuart
W	1970	21 Nov	Cherub's Buttress	G.S.Strange, D.Stuart
W	1971	2 Jan	Hanging Dyke	J.Bower, D.F.Lang

1 peg for aid. FFA: C.Forrest, A.Nisbet, Dec 1988

W	1971	5 Jan	Janus	J.Bower, D.F.Lang, G.R.Simpson

2 pegs for aid (unrepeated?)

W	1971	21 Feb	The Ladders	G.R.Simpson, K.Menmuir
S	1971	22 May	Ferlas Mor	J.Mothersele, G.S.Strange, D.Stuart, B.T.Lawrie, D.Dinwoodie
S	1971	19 Jun	The Fly	D.Dinwoodie, B.T.Lawrie

S	1971	19 Jun	Wee Heavy	B.T.Lawrie, D.Dinwoodie
S	1972	Jul	Ghost Crack	B.T.Lawrie, R.Kerr
S	1975	Mar	Sundance	J.Fyfe, G.Reilly, W.Taylor, G.Skelton
S	1975	28 Jun	The Chebec	G.Skelton, I.Vause
S	1976	20 Jun	The Hin'most	R.J.Archbold, G.S.Strange
W	1977	6 Mar	Left-Hand Icefall	R.J.Archbold, D.M.Nichols
S	1979	10 Jun	Amethyst Pillar	R.J.Archbold, D.M.Nichols

Sometimes known as Topaz. Final crack (crux) by J.McArtney, J.Stenhouse, 13 Jul 1964.

W	1979	10 Nov	The Black Tower	R.A.Smith, G.S.Strange

By the variation.

W	1981	22 Feb	Pilgrim's Groove	S.Kennedy, A.Nisbet, E.Clark, N.Morrison
W	1983	30 Dec	Lucifer Route	G.Livingston, A.Nisbet

1 peg for aid (unrepeated?)

W	1984	12 Jan	Grey Slab	S.Allan, A.Nisbet

1 peg for aid (unrepeated?)

S	1984	26 Jul	The Skater	C.MacLean, A.Nisbet
S	1985	13 Oct	Contra-Flow	A.Nisbet, G.S.Strange
W	1985	17 Nov	Snake Ridge	W.Moir, N.Ritchie
S	1986	13 Sep	Sapphire	S.Richardson, R.Everett
S	1986	1 Nov	Janus Chimney	W.Moir, C.Whittit
W	1987	14 Nov	The Web	R.Clothier, S.Richardson
W	1988	30 Oct	The Black Tower	S.Richardson, G.Hornby

By the summer line.

W	1988	24 Nov	Amethyst Wall	A.Nisbet, A.Black
S	1990	26 Jul	Next to Last	A.Fyffe, K.Geddes, N.Ritchie
W	1990	1 Dec	Ferlas Mor	S.Richardson, C.Cartwright
W	1991	20 Apr	Plumbline	S.Richardson, S.Helmore
W	1991	9 Nov	Aurora	S.Richardson, R.Everett
S	1992	7 Jun	Zircon	S.Richardson, J.Ashbridge
S	1992	7 Jun	Joker's Buttress	S.Richardson, J.Ashbridge
S	1993	13 Jul	Aurora	J.Lyall, R.Revill
S	1993	29 Aug	Dark Horse	R.J.Archbold, R.Ross, G.S.Strange
W	1993	14 Nov	Flake Buttress Direct	S.Richardson, G.Scott
W	1993	4 Dec	April Wall Direct	C.Cartwright, S.Richardson

CREAGAN A'CHOIRE ETCHACHAN

S	1949	26 Mar	Cambridge Route	A.Parker, J.Young
W	1950	2 Jan	Winter Route	W.D.Brooker, J.W.Morgan, D.A.Sutherland
S	1950	26 Mar	Flanking Ribs	W.D.Brooker, D.A.Sutherland
S	1950	1 Apr	Original Route	D.A.Sutherland, K.Winram
S	1950	6 Jul	Juniper Rib	I.M.Brooker, M.Newbigging
S	1952	15 Jun	Quartzvein Edge	K.Winram, G.C.Greig, M.Smith

S 1953   31 May   Bastion Wall   W.Kelly, P.Leys
S 1953   25 Oct   Red Scar Route   T.W.Patey, W.D.Brooker
W 1954   20 Mar   The Corridor   F.R.Malcolm, A.Thom
   The first of the cliff's classic ice routes and a fine achievement in stepcutting.
   The steps froze overnight after a slushy first attempt.
S 1954   9 Jul   Bodkin   T.W.Patey, W.W.Hutchison, A.Watson
   Rib finish: G.Reilly, B.Simpson, M.D.Webster 28 Sep 1975.
S 1954   7 Aug   Pikestaff   T.W.Patey, W.D.Brooker, J.Y.L.Hay
W 1955   27 Feb   Central Chimney   T.W.Patey, G.Adams, M.Smith,
                                               A.O'F.Will
S 1955   21 Jul   The Corridor   J.Y.L.Hay, A.P.Crichton, W.Christie
   Direct version: T.W.Patey, A.Duguid, 15 Aug 1955.
S 1955   Jul   Avalanche Route   J.Gadd, Mrs Gadd
   A considerable achievement on a hard and dangerous route.
S 1955   Jul   The Red Chimney   J.Gadd, Mrs Gadd
   The upper half is unclimbed in summer being very wet and loose.
S 1955   4 Sep   The Dagger   T.W.Patey, J.Y.L.Hay
   4 pegs for aid but still a breakthrough with first route on the Crimson Slabs. FFA
   unknown, early 1960s?
S 1956   24 Jun   The Talisman   W.D.Brooker, K.A.Grassick
   Another summer classic. Direct start: A.Nisbet, S.Kennedy, N.Mollison, 13 Jul
   1981
S 1956   22 Jul   Djibangi   J.Y.L.Hay, R.Wiseman, A.Cowie
   2 pegs for aid and an intriguing name. FFA unknown, early 1960s? Last 2
   pitches: M.Main, M.George, E.Brown, 1963
W 1956   29 Dec   Quartzvein Edge   J.Y.L.Hay, G.Adams, A.Thom
S 1960   Aug   Architrave   C.A.Sands, M.Main
S 1961   Jun   Girdle Traverse   T.W.Patey
S 1961   Jul   The Serpent   T.W.Patey, A.O'F.Will, F.R.Malcolm
S 1961   Aug   The Gangway   M.Main, A.Milne
S 1961   15 Nov   The Sheath   R.Kerr, A.Kane
W 1962   15 Feb   Pikestaff   D.Pyper, W.B.Gault
W 1963   23 Feb   Bastion Wall   J.McArtney, D.Pyper
W 1965   31 Jan   Djibangi   J.McArtney, W.J.Barclay
   An outstanding, modern style route. Unrepeated for 18 years.
W 1965   20 Feb   Juniper Rib   M.D.Y.Mowatt, J.E.Inglis
W 1965   14 Mar   The Talisman   K.A.Grassick, J.J.Light
   Another impressive ascent in the modern buttress style. 1 peg for aid. FFA:
   A.Nisbet, D.Thomson, Jan 1986
W 1966   Winter   Cambridge Route   J.McArtney, D.Halliday
   Taking the left edge of Pioneer Buttress.
W 1966   Mar   Square-Cut Gully   M.Forbes, M.Rennie
   2 ice screws and 1 peg for aid. FFA: D.Rubens, D.Broadhead, 16 Mar 1985
S 1966   17 Aug   Stiletto   M.Forbes, M.Rennie
   3 pegs for aid. A jump in technical difficulty on a line previously tried by strong
   parties. FFA: D.Dinwoodie, A.McIvor, 1976.

S	1966	Sep	Scabbard	M.Forbes, M.Rennie
W	1967	6 Jan	Flanking Ribs	J.McArtney, A.Fyffe
W	1967	Jan	The Red Chimney	I.A.Patterson, S.P.Hepburn

Lower section: J.Y.L.Hay, R.Ibbotson, Feb 1959.

S	1969	19 Sep	The Cutlass	B.T.Lawrie, J.Bower
S	1969	Sep	Enigma	M.Rennie, I.Staples
W	1969	23 Dec	Original Route	J.Bower, G.Boyd
W	1969	29 Dec	Architrave	A.Fyffe, J.McArtney
S	1970	1 Aug	Square-Cut Gully	D.Stuart, G.S.Strange
S	1971	10 Jul	The Hex	M.Forbes, B.T.Lawrie, D.Dinwoodie
S	1971	17 Jul	Carmine Groove	G.S.Strange, D.Stuart, D.Dinwoodie
S	1971	17 Jul	Pioneer Buttress Direct	D.Dinwoodie, D.Riley
S	1972	Sep	Original Route Direct	N.D.Keir, G.S.Strange

Variation: A.Nisbet, B.Clough, Sep 1982.

S	1974	21 Jul	Umslopogaas	D.Dinwoodie, R.A.Smith
W	1974	Nov	Carmine Groove	R.A.Smith, G.Stephen
W	1977	29 Jan	The Dagger	A.Nisbet, A.Robertson
W	1977	30 Jan	Bodkin	R.Renshaw, G.S.Strange

1 peg and 1 nut for aid. FFA: W.Moir, C.Stewart, Dec 1989

S	1977	11 Jul	Scalpel	D.Dinwoodie, G.S.Strange

Direct finish: A.Nisbet, A.Ross, 20 Oct 1985

S	1978	May	Sgian Dubh	A.Nisbet, M.Bridges

First pitch originally a direct start to Djibangi: A.Fyffe, M.D.Y.Mowat, R.Burnett, W.Forbes, Oct 1966.

S	1980	18 May	Stanley	A.B.Lawson, T.Ryan
W	1980	8 Dec	Red Scar Route	S.Kennedy, N.Morrison, A.Nisbet
S	1982	28 Jul	Sabre	S.Kennedy, C.McLeod
S	1983	Jun	Scythe	B.Davison, R.F.Allen, S.Kennedy, G.P.Muhlemann, A.Nisbet
S	1983	Jun	Delicatessen	A.Nisbet, R.F.Allen, B.Davison, S.Kennedy, G.P.Muhlemann
S	1983	Jun	Henchman	M.Hamilton, R.Anderson
S	1984	16 Jun	Crimson Cringe	B.T.Lawrie, N.Morrison
S	1984	25 Aug	King Crimson	A.Ross, G.S.Strange
W	1985	10 Feb	Scabbard	C.MacLean, A.Nisbet
W	1985	17 Feb	Avalanche Gully	D.Hawthorn, D.Dinwoodie
S	1985	13 Oct	The Sharp End	A.Nisbet, G.S.Strange
S	1985	20 Oct	Scarlet Fever	A.Nisbet, A.Ross
S	1985	27 Oct	In the Pink	A.Nisbet, A.Ross
S	1986	4 Jul	Talking Drums	C.MacLean, A.Nisbet
S	1986	13 Jul	Tickler	A.Ross, K.Murphy
S	1986	6 Sep	Blinker	R.J.Archbold, J.C.Higham, G.S.Strange
S	1990	10 Jun	Talismanic	W.Moir, N.Ritchie
W	1991	2 Feb	Switchblade	J.Lyall, A.Nisbet
W	1991	10 Nov	Pioneer Buttress Direct	R.Everett, S.Richardson

W 1992	29 Nov	Original Route Direct	J.Ashbridge, S.Richardson
W 1992	6 Dec	Cambridge Route Direct	S.Richardson, S.Helmore
W 1992	28 Dec	The Red Snake	A.Nisbet, G.Ollerhead
W 1992	28 Dec	Djibooty	A.Nisbet, G.Ollerhead
W 1992	29 Dec	Umslopogaas	A.Nisbet, G.Ollerhead

Lesser crags of Stob Coire Etchachan/Loch Etchachan

S 1952	19 Aug	Bellflower Buttress	K.Winram, G.C.Grieg, M.Smith
S 1953	15 Aug	Stag Buttress	A.Murray, A.Imray, J.McLeod
S 1954	4 Apr	Amphitheatre Edge	G.C.Grieg, G.H.Leslie
S 1955	Sep	Lochside Chimney	M.Scott, R.Ellis
W 1962	28 Jan	Lochside Chimney	H.Spencer, M.Main
W 1971	2 Jan	Bellflower Buttress	D.Stuart, G.S.Strange

1 peg for aid (unrepeated?).
Note: Sunday Crack is now worthless and The Slug does not have first ascensionists recorded.

CORRIE OF THE CHOKESTONE GULLY: CAIRNTOUL

S 1911	25 Sep	Chokestone Gully	J.McCoss and party
S 1958	Jul	Bugaboo Rib	R.W.P.Barclay, C.Annand, M.Smith, D.Steele
W 1964	9 Feb	The Shroud	J.Knight, I.A.MacEacheran
W 1970	13 Apr	Bugaboo Rib	B.S.Findlay, G.S.Strange

3 pegs and 2 nuts for aid. Alternative start: D.Hawthorn, D.Lawrence, Dec 1983.
1 peg for aid. FFA: R.Anderson, G.Nicoll, J.Naismith, Feb 1986.

W 1970	19 Apr	South-East Couloir	J.Campbell, G.R.Simpson
W 1974	31 Mar	Sasquatch	R.J.Archbold, D.King, G.R.Simpson, G.S.Strange
W 1975	1 Mar	The Wanderer	R.A.Smith, G.S.Strange

1 peg for aid. FFA: A.Nisbet, E.Clark

W 1983	3 Apr	Angel's Delight	B.S.Findlay, G.S.Strange
W 1987	Jan	The White Hotel	G.Taylor, J.McKeever
W 1987	Jan	The Waster	A.Cunningham, A.Nisbet
W 1992	15 Feb	Flying Fox	S.Richardson, R.Everett

GARBH CHOIRE MOR: BRAERIACH

S 1924	20 Jul	Pinnacle Gully	J.A.Parker, H.Alexander

First winter ascent unknown.

S 1940	Jul	Great Gullly	A.Tewnion, S.R.Tewnion
S 1941	Jul	Solo Gully	A.Tewnion
S 1941	Sep	Pinnacles Buttress	A.Tewnion, S.Tewnion, A.McArthur
S 1950	13 Aug	Crown Buttress	K.Winram, C.Petrie, M.Smith, J.Tewnion

S 1952	25 May	Sphinx Ridge	K.Winram, G.Dey, M.Smith, W.Kelly

Originally graded 'V.Diff up to July' because of the snow cover on the lower nose.

S 1952	22 Jul	Bunting's Gully, Right Fork	G.Dey, M.Smith W.Winram, G.C.Greig,
S 1953	24 May	She-Devil's Buttress	K.Winram, M.Smith
S 1953	14 Jun	Egyptian Fantasy	K.Winram, C.Petrie, G.C.Greig, M.Smith
S 1953	Aug	Bunting's Gully, Left Branch	K.Winram, M.Smith
S 1954	29 Sep	Michaelmas Fare	J.M.Taylor, G.B.Leslie
W 1954	31 Oct	Sphinx Gully	A.Watson, P.D.Baird
S 1957	Summer	West Buttress (Lower Corrie)	R.H.Sellers, G.Annand, M.Smith
S 1959	Jun	Tiara	A.Thom, G.Annand, R.Wiseman
W 1964	8 Jan	Solo Gully	J.J.Light, O.J.Ludlow
W 1964	9 Jan	Bunting's Gully, Left Fork	J.J.Light, O.J.Ludlow
W 1966	14 Mar	Sphinx Ridge Right	J.J.Light, J.Vigrow
W 1966	15 Mar	Bunting's Gully, Fork (Snowbunting)	J.J.Light, J.Vigrow
S 1966	18 Jun	Phoenix Gully	J.J.Light
W 1967	26 Jan	Crown Buttress	J.Bower, P.Kale

The party were forced to bivouac on the plateau in a blizzard and descend into Glen Geusachan the next day.

W 1967	19 Mar	Phoenix Gully	J.J.Light, G.McGregor, M.McArthur, D.Halliday
W 1967	17 Sep	Phoenix Buttress	J.J.Light, A.W.Manwell, A.G.Nicol, R.A.North
W 1968	12 Apr	Pinnacles Buttress	J.Bower, G.R.Simpson, G.S.Strange
S 1968	4 Jul	Vulcan	J.J.Light, J.Vigrow

1 peg for aid. FFA: G.Cohen, G.Macnair, Jul 1979

W 1969	19 Apr	She-Devil's Buttress, Corner Line	G.Boyd, B.S.Findlay, G.R.Simpson, G.S.Strange.

Late season start: S.Aisthorpe, J.Lyall, 9 Apr 1988

W 1969	20 Apr	West Buttress, Lower Corrie	P.C.D.Kale, C.A.McIntyre
S 1969	6 Jul	Tower of Babel	J.J.Light, A.G.McGregor

2 pegs for aid. FFA: G.Cohen, G.McNair, Jul 1979

W 1971	10 Apr	Pinnacles Couloir	J.Bower, B.S.Findlay, G.S.Strange, D.Stuart
W 1971	10 Apr	Gaunt Gully	D.B.Redway
W 1971	21 Dec	Phoenix Buttress	M.G.Geddes, J.S.Robinson
S 1973	Aug	Hot Lips	G.Cohen, G.Hardy
W 1974	30 Mar	Forked Lightning Route	R.J.Archbold, D.King, G.R.Simpson, G.S.Strange

W 1975	1 Mar	Vulcan	J.Bower, J.Ingram, K.Turnbull
W 1977	12 Mar	White Nile	R.J.Archbold, M.Hillman
		Finale for step cutting.	
S 1979	Jul	Phoenix Edge	R.J.Archbold, G.S.Strange
W 1982	5 Dec	Michaelmas Fare	A.Nisbet, C.Bruce
W 1984	22 Feb	Tiara	A.Nisbet, E.Clark
W 1987	16 Dec	The Tower of Babel	C.Forrest, A.Nisbet
W 1988	30 Oct	Sidetracked	A.Black, J.Cuthbert
W 1990	21 Jan	Phoenix Edge	A.Cunningham, A.Nisbet
W 1993	21 Nov	Virago	R.Everett, S.Richardson
W 1993	28 Nov	She Devil's Buttress, Original Route	R.Everett, S.Richardson
W 1993	22 Dec	Hot Lips	B.Davison, A.Nisbet, J.Preston

GARBH CHOIRE DHAIDH: BRAERIACH

S 1810	17 Jul	Dee Waterfall	Dr George Skene Keith, Mr Warren
S 1942	Aug	The Chimney Pot	W.T.Hendry, G.Lumsden
S 1942	Aug	Monolith Gully	W.T.Hendry, G.Lumsden
S 1942	Aug	Slab and Groove	W.T.Hendry, G.Lumsden
S 1949	16 Apr	Helicon Rib	K.Windram, R.Porter, J.W.Morgan
S 1951	5 Aug	Pisa	J.Tewnion, M.Smith
W 1954	Mar	Monolith Gully	M.Scott, G.Sievewright
S 1954	5 Sep	The Great Rift	F.R.Malcolm, A.Thom, M.Smith
S 1955	12 Jun	Boomerang	R.H.Sellars, G.Annand
S 1955	3 Jul	The Culvert	R.H.Sellers, G.Annand
S 1957	31 Mar	St Andrews Climb	L.J.Morris, W.S.Yeaman
		4 pegs for aid. Possible FFA: G.R.Simpson, G.S.Strange, 23 Sep 1967	
W 1959	Feb	The Chimney Pot	R.H.Sellers, K.A.Grassick
W 1962	23 Feb	Boomerang	D.Pyper, D.Reid
S 1963	Jun	Kangeroo	J.McArtney, B.T.Lawrie
S 1963	Jun	Kookaburra	J.McArtney, B.T.Lawrie
W 1964	7 Jan	Slab and Groove	O.J.Ludlow, J.J.Light, D.K.Marden
W 1964	Mar	Helicon Rib	D.W.Duncan, A.J.D.Smith
S 1964	Summer	Billabong	J.C.Innes, M.Higgins, A.J.D.Smith, D.W.Duncan
W 1964	21 Feb	The Great Rift	A.G.Nicol, J.J.Light
W 1967	Apr	Pisa	D.W.Duncan, S.P.Hepburn
S 1967	23 Sep	Koala	D.W.Duncan, A.Fyffe, J.McArtney
W 1969	18 Apr	Billabong	G.Boyd, B.S.Findlay, G.R.Simpson, G.S.Strange
W 1971	11 Apr	Twighlight Gully	J.Bower, B.S.Findlay, G.S.Strange, D.Stuart
W 1981	17 Dec	The Culvert	A.Nisbet, P.Barass
W 1985	26 Jul	Digeridoo	A.Nisbet, J.Hepburn
W 1986	6 Nov	Kangaroo	M.Duff, A.Black

W 1986	19 Nov	St Andrews Climb	A.Cunningham, C.MacLean, A.Nisbet, J.Lyall, S.Aisthorpe
W 1987	Jan	Koala	J.McKeever, G.Taylor
W 1991	28 Feb	Digeridoo	B.Davison, A.Nisbet

COIRE BHROCHAIN: BRAERIACH

| S 1898 | 10 Sep | West Gully | A.Fraser, A.W.Russell |

First winter ascent unknown.

W 1901	5 Apr	East Gully	J.Drummond, T.Gibson, A.W.Russell
W 1908	20 Apr	Central Buttress Gully	W.N.Ling, H.Raeburn
S 1911	Oct	Black Pinnacle, Ordinary Route	J.A.Parker, H.Alexander, J.B.Millar, W.A.Reid
S 1925	22 Aug	Pioneer's Recess Route	A.Harrison, L.St.C.Bartholomew
S 1931	27 Mar	Braeriach Pinnacle, Original Route	P.D.Baird, R.N.Traquai
S 1931	22 Jun	Braeriach Pinnacle, South Face	J.Sutherland, P.D.Ritchie
S 1933	Jul	Braeriach Pinnacle, Eastern Route	C.G.Cowie, S.R.Tough, G.L.Ritchie
S 1938	19 Jun	Black Pinnacle, Direct Route	J.H.B.Bell
S 1940	Jul	East Gully	W.T.Hendry, L.Durno, G.Morrison, W.L.Walker
S 1942	Aug	Campion Gully	W.T.Hendry, A.Tewnion, G,Lumsden
S 1942	Aug	Black Pinnacle, Slab Route	W.T.Hendry, A.Tewnion, G.Lumsden
S 1942	Aug	Central Chimney	W.T.Hendry, A.Tewnion, G.Lumsden
S 1942	Aug	West Wall Route	A.Tewnion, W.T.Hendry, G.Lumsden
S 1942	Aug	Pyramus	W.T.Hendry, G.Lumsden
S 1942	Aug	Thisbe	W.T.Hendry, G.Lumsden
S 1944	Aug	Bhrochain Slabs	G.W.Ross, G.O.Clark

Direct start: D.Pyper, D.Reid, May 1961. Direct finish: B.T.Hill, D.J.Pullin, I.T.W.Sloan, J.Thomson, 8 Jul 1967

S 1948	27 Mar	Near East Buttress	I.M.Brooker, A.D.Lyall, D.McConnach
S 1948	18 Sep	North-West Chimney	G.W.Ross, J.Fleming
W 1949	Mar	Black Pinnacle	A.Parker, J.Young
S 1949	17 Apr	The Lion	K.Winram, R.Porter, J.W.Morgan
W 1950	12 Apr	Pyramus	W.D.Brooker, S.McPherson
S 1952	29 Jun	Ninus	G.C.Grieg, J.Tewnion, K.Winram, G.Dey, M.Smith
S 1953	1 Mar	Babylon Rib	G.C.Grieg, M.Smith, K.Winram
S 1953	28 Jun	Azalea Rib	K.Winram, C.Petrie, M.Smith
W 1954	5 Apr	Campion Gully	K.A.Grassick, A.G.Nicol
W 1955	3 Jan	Thisbe	G.H.Leslie, M.Smith

W 1955	9 Apr	Domed Ridge	A.G.Mitchell, W.P.L.Thomson
S 1955	19 Jun	Vanishing Shelf	G.H.Leslie, M.Smith
S 1955	17 Jul	Direct Route, West Buttress	A.Stevenson, J.Y.L.Hay
S 1955	7 Sep	The Great Couloir	J.Y.L.Hay
S 1956	24 Sep	Braeriach Direct	R.H.Sellers, M.Smith, R.W.P.Barclay
S 1957	28 Dec	The Great Couloir	J.Y.L.Hay, H.Ross
W 1959	Feb	Vanishing Shelf	R.H.Sellers, K.A.Grassick
W 1960	Feb	Bhrochain Slabs	W.Gault, D.Bruce, A.Milne
W 1965	4 Apr	The Lion	W.Luke, M.D.Y.Mowatt, R.Robertson
S 1967	10 Sep	Ebony Chimney	P.Macdonald, D.K.Stephen
W 1968	13 Apr	Direct Route, West Buttress	J.Bower, G.R.Simpson, G.S.Strange
W 1969	3 Feb	Near East Buttress	P.C.D.Kale, C.A.MacIntyre
W 1969	16 Feb	Eastern Route. Braeriach Pinnacle	J.Bower, J.Buchanan, A.Sproul
W 1969	19 Apr	Tigris Chimney	P.C.D.Kale, C.A.MacIntyre
W 1969	20 Apr	Pioneer's Recess Route	G.R.Simpson, G.S.Strange
S 1969	17 Jul	The Fang	B.S.Findlay, G.S.Strange
W 1970	12 Apr	Ninus	B.S.Findlay, G.S.Strange
W 1970	14 Apr	Western Couloir	B.S.Findlay, G.S.Strange
W 1970	18 Apr	South Face, Braeriach Pinnacle	J.Campbell, G.R.Simpson
W 1978	25 Mar	The Lampie	J.C.Higham, J.H.Moreland
W 1981	18 Dec	Babylon Rib	P.Barrass, A.Nisbet
W 1982	Feb	Ebony Chimney	A.Nisbet, C.McLeod
W 1983	30 Jan	Braeriach Direct	E.Clark, A.Nisbet
S 1984	12 Aug	Ivory Tower	R.J.Archbold, G.S.Strange
W 1984	16 Dec	West Wall Route	G.Livingston, D.Lawrence, A.Nisbet
W 1987	Jan	Midwinter	G.Taylor, J.McKeever
W 1988	3 Apr	Vanishing Point	B.S.Findlay, G.S.Strange
W 1992	16 Jan	Fang Face	G.Ettle, J.Lyall

COIRE AN LOCHAIN: BRAERIACH

S 1945	Jun	Derelict Ridge	R.B.Frere, P.A.Densham
W 1980	26 Oct	Derelict Ridge	I.Dalley, R.J.Archbold, G.S.Strange
W 1984	4 Dec	The Icefall	D.McCutcheon, A.Nisbet

LAIRIG GHRU, NORTHERN SECTION

S 1950	7 July	Lairig Ridge	W.D.Brooker, T.Shaw
W 1965	23 Dec	North Gully	R.Campbell, F.Harper, M.A.Thompson

W	1970	4 Mar	Central Gully	B.Taplin, O.Ludlow
W	1972	9 Mar	Window Gully	W.March, J.Cleare, J.Bradshaw
W	1982		'Gormless	K.Geddes, R.D.Barton
W	1985	8 Dec	Lairig Ridge	G.Strange, B.Ross
W	1992	15 Mar	Sinclair's Last Stand	B.Findlay, G.Strange
W	1994	27 Dec	Deerhound Ridge	I.Dillon, J.Lyall
W	1994	27 Dec	Irish Wolfhound	I.Dillon, J.Lyall

DEVIL'S POINT

S	1908	Apr	South-East Corner	S.H.Cowan, E.B.Robertson
W	1926	Winter	Geusachan Gully	unknown
	1929		First visit to Devil's Cave.	
S	1940	Mar	Corrour Slabs	Dr.Hobson, W.L.Walker, W.T.Hendry
S	1949	Mar	South-West Arete	A.Parker, J.Young
W	1966	3 Apr	Corrour Slabs	G.R.Simpson, J.Elrick, G.S.Strange

Other routes not recorded.

DEE FACE, BEINN BHROTAIN

S	1949	Sep	Green Gully	M.Smith, C.Petrie
W	1952	Apr	Green Gully	B.Furmiston, D.Hilton, J.Kershaw, G.Whitham
S	1970's		Very Difficult slabs	B.T.Lawrie, D.Mercer
S	1983	11 Jul	Brodan's Dyke	B.S.Findlay, G.S.Strange
S	1984	31 May	Clonedyke	S.Allan, A.Nisbet

COIRE CATH NAN FIONN, BEINN BHROTAIN

W	1931	29 Mar	B Gully	P.D.Baird, R.N.Traquair
S	1950	Sep	A Gully	C.Petrie, M.Smith
S	1950	Sep	B Gully	C.Petrie, M.Smith
S	1952	8 Jun	Tiered Cracks	K.Winram, G.C.Grieg, M.Smith
W	1969	20 Apr	A Gully	G.Boyd
W	1986	14 Dec	Tiered Cracks	I.Barron, S.Kennedy

THE PALETTE, CARN A'MHAIM

S	1955	Jul	Gadd's Route	J.Gadd, Mrs Gadd
			Combined tactics, 1 peg for aid. FFA: D.Dinwoodie, G.S.Strange, 22 Aug 1981	
S	1981	22 Aug	Tickled Pink	D.Dinwoodie, G.S.Strange
S	1981	22 Aug	Pink Dwarf	C.Miller, A.Paul
S	1984	30 May	Medium-Rare	A.Nisbet, S.Allan

LUIBEG SLABS, CARN A'MHAIM

| S | 1940 | Jul | The Diagonal Route | W.L.Walker, W.T.Hendry |
| S | 1943 | Apr | The Direct Route | J.D.Auld, G.Lumsden, W.T.Hendry |

GLEANN EINICH

| S | 1902 | 8 Mar | Pinnacle Ridge | H.G.S.Lawson, H.Raeburn |
| W | 1902 | 28 Mar | The Willow Spout | G.T.Glover, Leathart |

First summer ascent: A.L.Cram, R.W.Wordsell

S	1902	28 Mar	Original Route, No.3 Buttress	H.C.Boyd, S.A.Gillon, A.M.Mackay, H.Raeburn
S	1902	30 Mar	Original Route, No.1 Buttress	H.Kynaston, W.A.Mounsey, H.Raeburn
S	1902	30 Mar	Batchelors' Chimney	W.W.Naismith, A.M.Mackay, F.G.Squance, H.Raeburn
S	1902	31 Mar	Married Men's Buttress	W.W.King, A.E.Maylard, G.A.Solly
S	1902	21 Jun	Original Route, No.4 Buttress	A.Mackay and party
S	1904	29 Apr	Rose Ridge	W.A.Morrison, W.C.Newbigging, A.E.Robertson
S	1929	8 Jul	No.5 Gully Buttress	G.R.Symmers, N.Bruce
S	1932	14 May	Bell's Route	J.H.B.Bell, C.M.Allen, D.Myles
S	1932	14 May	Diamond Buttress	J.H.B.Bell, C.M.Allen, D.Myles
S	1935	21 Jul	Cram's Route	A.L.Cram, E.C.Bailey
S	1938	24 Apr	Roberts' Ridge	J.H.B.Bell, E.E.Roberts, D.W.Howe
S	1940	7 Apr	Central Route	G.S.Ritchie, H.I.Oglivy
S	1940	Aug	Ogilvy's Route	H.I.Oglivy, L.S.Robson
S	1940	6 Oct	Fan Rib	J.F.Scott, K.McLaren
S	1945	28 Mar	Cripple's Cleft	R.B.Frere, P.A.Densham
S	1947	5 Oct	Far South Route	G.S.Ritchie, J.Pilnacek
S	1947	10 Oct	Crowberry Rib and Slab	J.H.B.Bell, Mrs Bell
S	1948	15 May	Pinnacle Rib	G.S.Ritchie, J.G.Ferguson
S	1952		Solus	R.B.Frere
S	1953	4 Apr	Einich Rib	J.Bruce, A.Brebner, G.McPherson
S	1953	5 Oct	No.1 Buttress Rib	J.B.Hyne, F.L.Swinton, R.Harper
S	1953	4 Oct	Nig	J.B.Hyne, F.L.Swinton, R.Harper
S	1953	4 Oct	Nog	J.B.Hyne, F.L.Swinton, R.Harper
S	1954	30 Aug	The Minaret	T.W.Patey, D.Scott
W	1956	2 Jan	No.5 Buttress Gully	T.W.Patey, A.Beanland, L.S.Lovat, J.Y.L.Hay, E.M.Davidson
W	1959	15 Feb	The Slash	T.W.Patey, V.N.Stephenson

Graded VS for semi-winter condition but probably a winter ascent by today's standards. Direct ascent: J.Lyall, J.Grosset, 14 Mar 1987.

S 1981	13 Sep	Resurrection	R.Archbold, W.McKerow, G.S.Strange, H.Towler
W 1986	Jan	Decoy Ridge	R.Jones, G.Rowbotham

First summer ascent unknown.

W 1986	23 Dec	Diamond Buttress	R.Ross, G.S.Strange
W 1986	26 Dec	Sporran	J.Lyall, E.Pirie
W 1986	26 Dec	Pick-pocket	J.Lyall, E.Pirie
W 1986	30 Dec	Tristar Chimney	J.Lyall, P.Cliff
W 1987	14 Feb	The Auld Wifie	J.Grosset, J.Lyall
W 1987	14 Mar	Cripple's Cleft	R.J.Archbold, J.C.Higham
W 1987	27 Nov	Roberts' Ridge	S.Aisthorpe, J.Lyall, A.Nisbet, M.Sclater, R.Wild
W 1988	23 Jan	Einich Rib	J.Grosset, J.Lyall, S.Lampard, G.Scott
W 1990	24 Nov	Batchelor's Chimney	S.Kennedy, D.Ritchie
W 1989	25 Feb	Cram's Route B	J.Lyall, H.Talbot

GLEN FESHIE

S 1932	5 Oct	Hermit's Ridge	D.Myles, J.H.B.Bell
W 1968	2 Nov	Hermit's Ridge	B.S.Findlay, G.S.Strange
W 1977	Dec	Waterfall Gully	E.Henderson, A.Douglas
W 1977	Dec	Coylum Crack	E.Henderson, A.Douglas
W 1977	Jan	Cascade Cave	E.Henderson, A.Douglas
W 1979	27 Jan	The Chasm	I.Dalley, G.S.Strange
W 1986	19 Jan	Eastenders	S.Kennedy, I.Barron, G.Rowbotham, A.Scace
W 1989	16 Dec	Garbh Ridge	J.Lyall, A.Nisbet